Katy Geissert
Civic Center Library
3301 Torrance Blvd.
Torrance, CA 90503

SHERWOOD ANDERSON

TAR: A MIDWEST CHILDHOOD

THE MAJOR FICTION OF SHERWOOD ANDERSON

Ray Lewis White, GENERAL EDITOR

A STORY TELLER'S STORY (1968)
TAR: A MIDWEST CHILDHOOD (1969)
MARCHING MEN (forthcoming)

SHERWOOD ANDERSON

TAR: A MIDWEST CHILDHOOD

A CRITICAL TEXT

Edited with an Introduction by
RAY LEWIS WHITE

CLEVELAND AND LONDON
THE PRESS OF CASE WESTERN RESERVE UNIVERSITY
1969

In honor of Malcolm Cowley

ACKNOWLEDGMENTS

For help with the preparation of this work I am grateful to the director and staff of The Press of Case Western Reserve University and to the following individuals: Henry Adams, Illinois State University; James Ray Blackwelder, Western Illinois University; Richard Bond, Illinois State University; Charles Chappell, Virginia Polytechnic Institute; Lambert Davis, Director, University of North Carolina Press; David B. Kesterson, North Texas State University; James V. Miller, Ball State University.

Amy Nyholm, The Newberry Library; Patricia Powell, Harold Ober Associates, Incorporated; H. B. Rouse, University of Arkansas; Stanley Shuman, Illinois State University; William A. Sutton, Ball State University; Lawrence W. Towner, Director and Librarian, The Newberry Library; Ivan von Auw, Harold Ober Associates, Incorporated; Maude N. White, Abingdon, Virginia; and James M. Wells, The Newberry Library.

Again I am grateful to Mrs. Sherwood Anderson for her help and encouragement.

Illinois State University   RLW

CONTENTS

INTRODUCTION

Two of Sherwood Anderson's autobiographies are "formal," if invaluable and delightful, re-creations of the writer's life. One, *A Story Teller's Story* (1924), is Anderson's subjective investigation into the experiences that led him, at thirty-seven, to forsake a constricting, unsatisfying life in business for the literary milieu of the Chicago Renaissance that produced *Winesburg, Ohio* (1919). The other, *Sherwood Anderson's Memoirs* (1942), begun in 1933 and almost completed at the author's unexpected death in 1941, was to be Anderson's final study of the meaning of his life—perhaps mythically the most important life of any recent American writer. These two works have become and will remain major documents for students of contemporary American letters.

But Sherwood Anderson wrote a third, less famous autobiography. *A Story Teller's Story* had brought Anderson's life history up to 1923, perhaps the date of the author's greatest popularity and literary influence. *Winesburg, Ohio* and the early short stories were by then being recognized as American classics. Anderson, knowing intuitively that his childhood years in small Ohio towns, from 1876 to 1895, were the inspiration for his best writing, decided in 1925 to re-create that childhood imaginatively. The resulting semi-fictional memoir, *Tar: A Midwest Childhood* (1926), is a very special document in the Anderson canon: in *Tar* young Sherwood Anderson becomes a younger George Willard, and Clyde, Ohio, becomes another Winesburg, Ohio—"a background on which to paint the dreams of . . . manhood."[1]

I.

THE earliest expression of Sherwood Anderson's interest in

---

1. *Winesburg, Ohio*, edited by Malcolm Cowley (New York: Viking Press, 1960), p. 247. Other data in this Introduction are taken from documents in The Newberry Library's Sherwood Anderson Papers, the central resource for students of Anderson's life and works.

using semi-fictionally his childhood in late nineteenth-century Ohio occurred in July, 1919, when Anderson asked his publisher, Ben W. Huebsch: "Do you publish any juvenile books? Most of the children's books are such asinine sentimental nonsense that I have been thinking of writing out a series of tales of country life at the edge of a middle-western small town— little pictures of the actual life of the boy, the farm hand, the dog, the cow, etc. I want to do these primarily for my own children but would like to make a book of them for other children." As with many of Anderson's tentative projects, nothing immediately came from this suggested series of tales; but the planned approach of realistic treatment of midwestern childhood experience would later recur to Sherwood Anderson.

Although the exact genesis for *Tar* is lost, Anderson's inspiration to write the book apparently came from an expression of interest in such a work by *The Woman's Home Companion*. On February 15, 1925, Anderson wrote from New Orleans that "for the fall I hope to have ready the 'Childhood' book, most of the work on which is already done." Probably very little, if any, of the work really was completed; but, on March 6, Anderson promised his agent, Otto Liveright, that within a week or two he would have "something really good" to show the editors of *Companion*.

On March 20, 1925, Anderson wrote his agent: "I have made the first draft of the Mid-American Childhood—first installment—but want to be very careful with it and have it right before I send it to you. When I send it I will also send an outline of several chapters." The first tale and the outline were mailed on March 25, when Anderson projected a dozen or more tales, "each having its own flavor and dramatic interest," with *The Woman's Home Companion* editors to select for their use approximately forty thousand words. Future tales (never written) were to relate such events as the boy's seeing a great fire, his first days at school, and his having and spreading measles. The tales were to be "gentle and whimsical and yet with plenty of dramatic force to carry the reader forward." The whole book was to be finished in the coming summer and placed for publication with the house of Boni and Liveright.

In April, Anderson delivered between fifty thousand and

fifty-five thousand words to *Companion,* knowing the editors would trim the work but stating, "it has that indefinable thing we call charm. . . . Think it one of the best colts I have ever sent to the races." On April 18, Anderson's faith was proved justified, for the magazine bought six installments for one thousand dollars each.

Renewed inspiration for quickly completing the work came to Anderson as he arranged to spend the summer of 1925 as boarder with a mountain family in southwest Virginia, an area so appealing that it became the writer's permanent home from 1927 to his death.[2] In the mountains, Anderson recalled in his *Memoirs,* he lived near Troutdale, a logging town, with the Greear family: "It was a strange, a new sort of country to me. On all sides were the magnificent hills, in the Greear family a troop of boys. They all bore Biblical names, John, Joshua, David, Philip, Solomon. There was a corn field beyond a hillside apple orchard in a little hollow in the hills, and in the corn field a small one-room cabin that had not been occupied for years."

Anderson worked on *Tar* in his cabin in the corn field: "The corn had begun to wither in the long drought. When there was a breeze blowing there was a sharp rustling sound. My feet, as I sat writing, were on the warm earth of the little floorless cabin. The corn seemed talking to me. . . . I even tried what I had often thought of doing. When I had written a chapter of my book I went outside my cabin and read it aloud to the corn. It was all a little ridiculous but I thought, 'No one knows.' And the corn did seem to talk back to me."

Actually, the writer's progress with *Tar* was not so fortunate as the *Memoirs* passage indicates, for he had become engrossed in a new work on the Mississippi River and was trying to write at once of his childhood and of the Mississippi. So frustrated did this method of writing make Anderson that he confessed to Otto Liveright on July 10: "I have had an odd experience in regard to the childhood articles. I suppose I have written a

2. For Anderson's life in the Virginia highlands, especially his fascinating career as a country newspaper editor, see *Return to Winesburg,* edited by Ray Lewis White (Chapel Hill: University of North Carolina Press, 1967).

dozen of them and thrown them away, because they did not satisfy me. I know I can get them right but I got worried and nervous about them, because I thought they ought to be done. As a matter of fact, I worked myself into a regular state of mind over the whole matter that has quite upset me. Now I am going to put the whole matter aside for a time, so I can come back to them with a fresh point of view."

Sherwood Anderson returned to New Orleans in mid-August and, on September 1, recorded: "A good deal of the matter that I wrote so fluently at Troutdale I have had to throw away as not being quite up to the standard but I still have a good deal left that I think will pass." Of perhaps fifty thousand words of *Tar* written in Virginia, Anderson kept one-half. Yet, on September 15, Anderson informed his agent that he had thirty-five thousand words in fair copy and twenty thousand unrevised; he estimated that *Tar* was then two-thirds finished.

In November, Anderson revised his original title, "A Mid-American Childhood," to "Tar: The Story of a Mid-American Childhood" (later changed to *Tar: A Midwest Childhood*); but he abandoned further work on the book until February 23, 1926. The installments for *The Woman's Home Companion* finished and to be published in the coming summer, Anderson determined to complete expansion and revision for book publication in the fall of 1926, a year behind the original deadline that he had set for himself.[3]

Sherwood Anderson apparently worked steadily, if not constantly, on *Tar*, for he told his agent on June 23 that the finished manuscript would reach the Boni and Liveright offices that week. Whenever *Tar* was actually mailed, Horace Liveright had the work by July 27 and promised soon to read it. Then Boni and Liveright had the work rapidly copyread and printed, because on August 23 the galley proofs, already office-read and marked, were mailed to Anderson, who returned

3. *The Woman's Home Companion* published six installments of *Tar:* "Tar Moorehead's Father," LIII (June, 1926), 19–20, 154–55; "A Small Boy Looks at His World," LIII (July, 1926), 19–20, 42, 45; "Worlds of Fancy and of Facts," LIII (September, 1926), 27–28, 79; "Tar's Day of Bravery," LIII (October, 1926), 25–26, 184–85; "Tar's Wonderful Sunday," LIII (November, 1926), 29–30, 50; "What Makes a Boy Afraid," LIV (January, 1927), 19–20, 96.

them to New York by September 16, along with a telegraphed list of corrections to be incorporated. Page proofs were mailed to the author on September 24; and bound copies of *Tar* were posted to Anderson on November 5, 1926, the official publication date being November 20.

Unfortunately, all meaningful printing size and sales figures for *Tar* have been lost. One surmises, however, that the work did not sell well enough to please either Anderson or Boni and Liveright, for the only reissue (except for a British issue by Martin Secker of London in 1927) came from Boni and Liveright in 1931.

Thus, *Tar: A Midwest Childhood* has remained out of print since 1931; and the present volume is the first attempt to establish an accurate text and to annotate the work as autobiography.

II.

PREPARATION of the corrected text of *A Story Teller's Story* [4] was facilitated by the existence of the actual printer's typescript for that work, while the project was made difficult by the original publisher's unsympathetic and actually careless over-editing of Sherwood Anderson's text. With *Tar*, however, the editor faces the obverse situation; the actual printing typescript is lost, but the printed text shows fairly careful handling by the original publisher. The house of Boni and Liveright apparently treated its authors' typescripts as material to be "corrected" as little as possible. But Sherwood Anderson, having been told for a decade that his spelling, grammar, diction, and punctuation were unacceptable, encouraged his publishers to standardize his submitted texts. It is, therefore, necessary, in the interest of accuracy, to consult the latest available typescript of *Tar: A Midwest Childhood*.

There are two versions of most of the twenty-two chapters of *Tar*. Both versions are typescripts with copious authorial corrections in ink. The earlier versions are written in deleted first-person narration, showing that Anderson began *Tar* as a second direct autobiography but soon changed to third-person

4. *A Story Teller's Story: A Critical Text*, edited by Ray Lewis White (Cleveland: Press of Case Western Reserve University, 1968).

style. The later set of typescripts, probably made for the author early in 1926, served as his final revision sheets for the making of a printer's copy in the spring of 1926.

In order to arrive at the most useful critical text of *Tar*, it is necessary to consult the earlier typescripts only for evidence of substantive deletions of biographical importance (such deleted passages are printed in the third appendix of this volume) and for occasional copyist errors, made in re-typing the first revised fair copy. The later typescripts, however, are the closest extant guides to Sherwood Anderson's final textual intentions. Collation of these typescripts with the 1926 printed text reveals the existence of several hundred undesirable, but not reprehensible, changes in the author's words and punctuation, as exemplified in the following table:

Original	Corrupt Printings
can't	cannot
and of course I	and, of course, I
telling	tellings
tonight	to-night
again, but	again. But
theatre	theater
to talk	of talk
a half dozen	half a dozen
then.	then
hands	hand
property	prosperity
Welliver	Wellwer
this	his
women	woman
grey	gray
not as	not so
Tar only	Only Tar
farm house	farmhouse
nowdays	nowadays
talk with	talk to
babe	baby
the	a
upon	up on

Original	Corrupt Printings
nothing at all	anything at all
practise	practice
alone	along
stacks . . . were	stack . . . was
should	would
on the jaw	in the jaw
for it	at it
any	a
cuff	clip
onto	to
woods	wood
tree's trunk	tree trunk
to his buggy	of his buggy
their	the
there	near
birch	beech
mouldy	moldy
difs	diff
hands of a mother that touches	hands of a mother that touch
ponchoon	poncho
different from	different than
good	well
dast	"dast"
looked up at	looked at
awhile	a while
into	up into

Futhermore, Anderson's loose punctuation, meant to reproduce for the reader a flowing, simple style, was standardized and "stiffened" by the Boni and Liveright editors, who also ignored the author's clearly marked episode spacings and paragraphing.

The present critical text, therefore, makes over fifteen hundred corrections, restoring Anderson's words, personal spellings, punctuation, and spacing. Words and passages that occur undeleted in the late typescripts but not in the 1926 book are restored within brackets. Words and passages added by the author in the printer's copy or in the galleys are indicated herein with brackets and asterisks. Whenever revision prohibits inclusion of original substantive material, such passages are included in the third appendix.

Because *Tar* is an autobiographical work, the present annotations are intended to present two kinds of information: (1) biographical data for identification and explanation of Anderson's fictionalized characters and events and (2) bibliographical data as guides to (a) discussions of Anderson's life and works and (b) parallel autobiographical discussions in *A Story Teller's Story* and *Sherwood Anderson's Memoirs*.

Finally, appended articles contributed by William Alfred Sutton and William V. Miller present for the first time material essential to Anderson scholars. First, Mr. Sutton, the foremost biographer of Sherwood Anderson's youth, discusses the newly re-discovered diaries of the writer's parents, revealing the great dichotomy between Anderson's literary memories and reality. Second, Mr. Miller presents, through the courtesy of Mrs. Sherwood Anderson and Mr. Ivan von Auw of Harold Ober Associates, Incorporated, his transcription of an early draft of "Death in the Woods," Anderson's masterful short story first published as Chapter XII of *Tar*.

The Bibliography contains lists of books by and about Sherwood Anderson, translations and reviews of *Tar*, and selected comparable American autobiographies by other writers. The Index provides a brief but convenient person-and-subject guide to *Tar: A Midwest Childhood,* treating the work strictly as autobiography.

III.

IN *Winesburg, Ohio*, Sherwood Anderson beautifully describes the moment of maturity for George Willard: "There is a time in the life of every boy when he for the first time takes the backward view of life. Perhaps that is the moment when he crosses the line into manhood. The boy is walking through the street of his town. He is thinking of the future and of the figure he will cut in the world. Ambitions and regrets awake within him. Suddenly something happens; he stops under a tree and waits as for a voice calling his name. Ghosts of old things creep into his consciousness; the voices outside of himself whisper a message concerning the limitations of life." [5]

As Sherwood Anderson was fifty when *Tar: A Midwest Childhood* was published, it is proper to consider this second autobiography the writer's backward view into the circumstances of early youth that created his sensibility—his bittersweet, tenderly melancholy attitude toward life. Anderson's parents were dead. His sisters were dead. His youngest brother had disappeared for ten years. Two younger brothers were indifferent toward him. Only with his older brother, Karl Anderson the painter, did the writer have a close relationship. The pain of loss, the inevitable "walls" between people, the need for aesthetic distance—these factors prompted Anderson to recreate his childhood fictionally as the story of "Tar Moorehead":

The Anderson Family	The Moorehead Family
Irwin, father	Dick, father
Emma, mother	Mary, mother
Karl	John
Stella	Margaret
Sherwood	Edgar ("Tar")
Irwin	Robert
Ray	Will
Earl	Joe
Fern	Fern

(In *Tar*, Anderson's closest boyhood friend, Herman Hurd, appears as Hal Brown. Noteworthy also is the fact that the fictional names for the two brothers and the sister nearest in age to Sherwood Anderson—"John," "Margaret," and "Robert" —are the real names of the author's own children, with whom he had not been closely associated since 1913.)

The structure of *Tar: A Midwest Childhood* is loosely based on the growth of a child's consciousness.[6] Because Anderson remembered little of his birthplace, Camden, Ohio, he presents

---

5. *Winesburg, Ohio*, p. 234.
6. See David D. Anderson, "Emerging Awareness in Sherwood Anderson's 'Tar,'" *Ohioana*, IV (Summer, 1961), 40–42, 51.

that town as his adult dream of the ideal small town. The child's father is romantically pictured as a transplanted southerner, one of the fancies that Irwin Anderson actually cultivated about himself. The mother is drawn as a sensitive, strong, hard-working, but almost brutalized woman, similar in *Tar* to the author's other descriptions of Emma Anderson. The child, Tar Moorehead, moves from family protection into an awareness of his town, Clyde, Ohio, and the surrounding farms. He fathoms the true condition of his family as he incorporates into knowledge the well-to-do friend, the mystery of birth, the motiveless antipathy of a schoolmate, the beauty of horses and country threshing, the first strivings at sexual expression, and the need to work at easing the family's poverty.

But it is knowledge of the essential sadness of human existence that gives deepest significance to the boy's growth. The vagaries of wealth and justice, the discovery of the buried life of the grotesque town reprobate, and especially the deaths of an infant sister, a hideously defeated yet wonderful old country woman, and finally of Tar's own mother—these help to explain the mysterious beauty later created in *Winesburg, Ohio*.

At the end of *Tar*, the boy grieves for and then accepts the loss of his mother as he enters adolescence. (Emma Anderson actually lived until her son Sherwood was eighteen.) In *Winesburg, Ohio*, George Willard, after the death of his mother as he nears twenty, leaves his town to enter the worldly struggle of life. In *A Story Teller's Story*, Sherwood Anderson rejects that struggle for fulfillment in literary achievement. Finally, in *Sherwood Anderson's Memoirs*, after thirty years of writing, the author concludes: "And I say that when I die I should like this inscription put upon my grave . . . LIFE, NOT DEATH, IS THE GREAT ADVENTURE."

In *Tar: A Midwest Childhood*, we have the beginning of Sherwood Anderson's adventure, his life.

SHERWOOD ANDERSON

TAR: A MIDWEST CHILDHOOD

To
ELIZABETH ANDERSON

FOREWORD

I HAVE a confession to make. I am a story teller starting to tell a story and cannot be expected to tell the truth. Truth is impossible to me. It is like goodness, something aimed at but never hit. A year or two ago I determined to try to tell the story of my own childhood.[1] Very well, I set to work. What a job! I went at the task bravely but presently came to a dead halt. Like every other man and woman in the world I had always thought the story of my own childhood would be an absorbing[*ly interesting] one.

I began to write. For a day or two all went well. I sat at my desk scribbling away. I, Sherwood Anderson, an American man, in my youth did so and so. Well, I played ball, stole apples out of orchards, began presently, being male, to think of the female, was sometimes afraid in the dark at night. What nonsense to speak of it all. I grew ashamed.

And yet there was something I had wanted of which I need not be ashamed. Childhood is something wonderful. Manhood, sophistication, is something worth striving for but innocence is somewhat sweeter.[2] It may be the greater wisdom to remain innocent but it can't be done. I wish it could.

In a New Orleans restaurant I heard a man explaining the fate of crabs.[3] "There are two good kinds," he said. "Busters

1. Sherwood Anderson is referring either to *Tar* or to his first autobiography, *A Story Teller's Story* (New York: B. W. Huebsch, 1924). Notes herein apply to *A Story Teller's Story: A Critical Text*, edited by Ray Lewis White (Cleveland: Press of Case Western Reserve University, 1968).

2. In Anderson's classic *Winesburg, Ohio* (New York: B. W. Huebsch, 1919), George Willard, the central figure, wavers between "sophistication" and adolescence. See "Sophistication" in the corrected text of *Winesburg, Ohio*, edited by Malcolm Cowley (New York: Viking Press, 1960), pp. 233–43. References herein are to the Cowley edition.

3. Sherwood Anderson was in New Orleans in the winter of 1922 and from the spring of 1924 to the building of "Ripshin" in Southwest Virginia in 1926. On New Orleans, see Anderson, "New Orleans," *Double Dealer*, III (March, 1922), 119–26; "A Meeting South," *Dial*, LXXVIII (April, 1925), 269–79; and "New Orleans: A Prose Poem in the Expressionist Manner," *Vanity Fair*, XXVI (August, 1926), 36, 97.

are so young they are sweet. Soft shell crabs have the sweetness of age and weakness."

It is my weakness to want to speak of my youth, a sign perhaps I am getting old, but I am ashamed. There is a reason for my shame. All writing of self is egotistical. There is however another reason.

I am a man who has brothers living and they are strong, and I daresay hard-hitting, fellows. Suppose it please my fancy to have a certain kind of father or mother. That is the [one] great privilege of being a writer—that life may be constantly recreated in the field of fancy. But my brothers, respectable men, may have quite different notions of how these worthy people, my parents and theirs, should be presented to the world. We modern writers have got a reputation for boldness, for too much boldness most people think, but none of us like to be knocked down or cut on the street by former friends or by our relatives. We are not prize-fighters or [*horse wranglers, most] of us. A poor enough lot, if the truth be told. Cæsar was quite right in detesting scribblers.

Now it happens that my friends and relatives have already stood much from me. I am forever writing of myself and dragging them in, re-creating them to suit my fancy, and they have been a forbearing lot. It is dreadful really having a scribbler in the family. Avoid it if you can. If you have a son who has a leaning that way hurry him into industrial life. If he become a writer he may give you away.

You see, if I began writing of my childhood, I had to ask myself how much more these people would stand. Heavens knows what I might do to them when I got going.

I kept writing and tearing up. Oh, pshaw! My progress was too lamentably slow. I could not very well create a lot of little Lord Fauntleroys growing up in a Middle-western American town.[4] If I made myself too good I knew it would not work and if I made myself really bad—which was a temptation—no one would believe. Bad people, when you come close to them, are such simpletons.

4. The flawless child hero of the novel *Little Lord Fauntleroy* (1866) by Frances Hodgson Burnett, made into a movie starring Mary Pickford in 1921.

"Where is the Truth?" I asked myself, "Oh, Truth, where are you? Where have you hidden yourself?" I looked under my desk, under the bed, went out and looked up and down the road. I have always been looking for the rascal but have never been able to find him. Where does he keep himself?

"Where is Truth?" What an unsatisfactory question to be compelled to keep asking, if you are a teller of tales.

Let me explain—if I can.

The teller of tales, as you must all know, lives in a world of his own. He is one thing, as you see him walking in the street, going to church, into a friend's house, [or] into a restaurant, and quite another fellow when he sits down to write. While he is a writer nothing happens but that it is changed by his fancy and his fancy is always at work. Really, you should never trust such a man. Do not put him on the witness stand during a trial for your life—or for money—and be very careful never to believe what he says under any circumstances.

Take myself for example. I am, let us say, walking on a country road and there is a man running in a nearby field. Such a thing happened once and what a tale I made of it.[5]

I see the man running. Nothing else actually happens. He runs across the field and disappears over a hill but now look out for me. Later I may tell you a tale of the man. Leave it to me to make up a tale of why the man ran and to believe my own tale after it is made.

The man lived in a house just beyond the hill. Sure there was a house there. I created it. I ought to know. Why, I could draw you a picture of the house, although I never actually saw it. He lived in a house behind the hill and something absorbingly interesting and exciting just now happened in the house.

I tell you the tale of what happened with the straightest face in the world, believe the tale myself, at least while I am telling it.

You see how it is. When I was a child this faculty I have was a nuisance. It kept getting me into hot water. Everyone thought me a little liar and of course I was. I went ten yards beyond the house and stood behind an apple tree. There was a gentle

5. Anderson refers to "The Untold Lie," *Winesburg, Ohio*, pp. 202–9; the experience is recounted in *A Story Teller's Story*, pp. 243–48.

rising hill and near the top of the hill a clump of bushes. A cow came out of the bushes, nibbled grass no doubt, and then went back into the bushes. It was fly time and I daresay the bushes were a comfort to her.

I made up a tale concerning the cow. She became for me a bear. There had been a circus in a nearby town and a bear had escaped. I had heard father speak of reading an account of the escape in the newspapers. I gave my story a certain air of probability and the strange part of all this is that, having thought out the tale, I believed it myself. All children, I think, do tricks like that. It worked so well that I had the men of the neighborhood, with guns on their shoulders, scouring the woods for two or three days and all the neighborhood children shared in my fright and excitement.

[*A literary triumph—and I so young.] [6]

All tale telling is, in a strict sense, nothing but lying. That is what people cannot understand. To tell the truth is too difficult. I long since gave up the effort.[7]

However, when it came to the telling of the tale of my own childhood—well, for once, I said to myself, I will hew to the line. An old pit I had often fallen in before I fell in again. Bravely I set myself to my task. I pursued Truth back through my own memory like a dog chasing a rabbit through dense bushes. What toil, what sweat dropped upon the sheets of paper before me. "To be honest," I said to myself, "is to be good, and for once I will be good. I will prove how essentially sterling is my character. People who have always known me and who have perhaps, in the past, had too much reason for doubting my word will now be surprised and delighted."

I had dreams of people giving me a new name. As I went along the street people would whisper to each other. "There

6. For Anderson's first childhood tales, see A Story Teller's Story, pp. 71–78, 81–90, and 92–96.

7. On Anderson's theories of fancy and fact, see A Story Teller's Story, pp. 59–60, 76–77, 81, 90–94, 103–4, 107–8, 150, 156–60; "Man and His Imagination," The Intent of the Artist, edited by Augusto Centeno (Princeton: Princeton University Press, 1941), pp. 39–79; Sherwood Anderson's Memoirs (New York: Harcourt, Brace and Company, 1942), pp. 3–9; and Robert Charles Hart, "Writers on Writing: The Opinion of Six Modern American Novelists on the Craft of Fiction," Ph.D. Thesis, Northwestern University, 1954.

goes Honest Sherwood." Perhaps they would insist on electing me to Congress or sending me as an ambassador to some foreign country. How happy all of my relatives would be.

"At last he is giving all of us a good character. He has made us out respectable folk."

As for the people of my native town, or towns, they also would be happy. Telegrams would be received, meetings held. There might be an organization formed for raising the standard of citizenship of which I would be elected president.

I have always so wanted to be president of something. What a splendid dream.

Alas—it would not work. I wrote one sentence, ten, a hundred pages. They had to be torn up. Truth had disappeared into a thicket so dense that it could not be penetrated.

Like everyone else in the world I had so thoroughly recreated my childhood, in my own fancy, that Truth was utterly lost.

And now for a confession. I have a love of confessions. I do not remember the face of my [own mother, of my] own father. My wife is in the next room as I sit writing, but I do not remember what she looks like.

My wife is to me an idea, my mother, my sons, my friends are ideas.

My fancy is a wall between myself and Truth. There is a world of the fancy into which I constantly plunge and out of which I seldom completely emerge. I want every day to be absorbingly interesting and exciting to me and if it will not, I, with my fancy, try to make it so. If you, a stranger, come into my presence there is a chance that for a moment I shall see you as you are but in another moment you will be lost. You say something that starts my fancy working and I am off. Tonight perhaps I shall dream of you. We will have fancied conversations. My fancy will throw you into strange, noble—or perhaps even mean situations. Now I have no scruples. You are my rabbit and I am a hound pursuing you. Even your physical being changes under the driving lash of my fancy.

And here let me say something regarding a writer's responsibility for the characters he creates. We writers are always getting out of it by disclaiming responsibility[. We deny responsibility] for our dreams. How absurd. How often, for example, have I dreamed of making love to some woman who actually wouldn't have me. Why deny responsibility for such a dream? I do it because I like it [*—although I do not do it consciously. We writers must take the responsibility of the unconscious, too—it seems].

Am I to blame? I am made that way. I am like all people. You are yourself more like me than you would care to admit. After all the fault was partly your own. Why did you interest my fancy? Dear reader, I am sure that, if you came into my presence, my fancy would at once be caught.

Judges and lawyers who have had to handle witnesses during trials in court know how common is the disease I have, know how little people are to be depended upon for the truth.

As I have suggested, when it came to writing of myself, I, the teller of tales, would be all right if there were no living witnesses to check up on me. They, of course, will also have changed the actual happenings of our common lives to suit their own fancies.

I am doing it.

You are doing it.

Everybody's doing it.

Much better to meet the situation as I have done here—create a Tar Moorehead to stand for myself.

At least that lets my friends and relatives out. It is, I admit, a writer's trick.

And anyway, it was only after I had created Tar Moorehead, had brought him into life in my own fancy, that I could sit down before my sheets and feel at ease. It was only then I faced myself, accepted myself. "If you are a born liar, a man of the fancy, why not be what you are?" I said to myself, and having said it I at once began writing with a new feeling of comfort.

PART I

CHAPTER I

POOR people have children without much feeling of exaltation. Alas, the children just come. It is another child and children come easily. On such an occasion a man is for some obscure reason a little ashamed. The woman escapes because she is ill. Let's see, now there were two boys and one girl. This makes only three so far. It is well this last one is another boy. He won't cost much for a long time. He can wear the cast off clothing of his older brother and then, when he gets older and demands things of his own, he can work. It is the common fate of man to work. That was provided for in the beginning. Cain killed Abel with a club. It happened at the edge of a field. There is a picture of the scene in the Sunday school leaflet. Abel lies dead on the ground and Cain stands over him with the club in his hand.

In the background is one of God's angels pronouncing the dreadful sentence. "By the sweat of your brow shall you eat your bread." That sentence to go reverberating down through the ages to catch a small Ohio boy among all the others. Well, boys find places more readily than girls. They earn more.

The boy, named Edgar Moorehead, was called Edgar only while he was very young. He lived in Ohio but his father was a North Carolina man and North Carolina men are [*in derision] called "Tar-heels." [1] A neighbor spoke of him as another little "Tar-heel" and after that he was called, first, "Tar-heel" and then simply "Tar." What a black sticky name!

Tar Moorehead was born in the town of Camden, Ohio, but when he left there he went in his mother's arms.[2] As a conscious

1. Sherwood Anderson's father was not from North Carolina. Irwin McLain Anderson was born August 7, 1845, in West Union, Ohio, the son of James Anderson (1796–1886) and Isabella Bryan Higgins. Irwin Anderson died at a soldiers' home in Dayton, Ohio, May 23, 1919, after seeing little of his children from 1895 to his death. In *A Story Teller's Story*, p. 5, Anderson writes of "My father, a ruined dandy from the South. . . ."

2. Records indicate that "Lawrence Anderson" was born September 13, 1876, in Camden, Ohio. The reference is an unexplained error for Sher-

human being he never saw the town, never walked in its streets
and later when he grew to manhood he was careful never to
go back.

Being an imaginative child and not fond of disillusions he
preferred having one place all his own, the product of his own
fancy.

Tar Moorehead became a writer and wrote tales of people
in small towns, how they live, what they think, what things
happen to them, but he never wrote of Camden.[3] As a matter
of fact there is such a place. It is on a railroad. Tourists go
through there, stopping to have their gas tanks filled. There
are stores that sell chewing gum, electric fixtures, automobile
tires, canned fruits and vegetables.

Tar discarded all these things when he thought of Camden.
He thought of it as his own town, the product of his own fancy.
Sometimes it sat at the edge of a long plain and the people
of the town could see from the windows of their houses a vast
expanse of earth and sky. Such a place to walk in the evening,
out on the [wide] grassy plain, such a place to count the stars,
feel the evening wind on the cheek, hear, coming from [*a]
distance, the little sounds of the nights.

As a man Tar awoke, let us say, in a city hotel. All of his
life he had been trying to put life into the tales he wrote but
his job was difficult. Modern life is complex. What are you
going to say about it? How are you going to get things straight?

There is [*a] woman, for example. How are you, being a

---

wood Berton Anderson. See *A Story Teller's Story*, pp. 5, 78–81, and 87;
and *Memoirs*, p. 16.

    The standard biography of Sherwood Anderson's youth is William Alfred
Sutton, "Sherwood Anderson's Formative Years (1876–1913)," Ph.D.
Thesis, Ohio State University, 1943. See Sutton, "Sherwood Anderson:
The Clyde Years, 1884–1896," *Northwest Ohio Quarterly*, XIX (July,
1947), 99–114.

    3. Besides *Winesburg, Ohio*, Anderson published three books of tales:
The Triumph of The Egg (New York: B. W. Huebsch, 1921), *Horses and
Men* (New York: B. W. Huebsch, 1923), and *Death in the Woods* (New
York: Liveright, Inc., 1933). Several tales appeared posthumously in *The
Sherwood Anderson Reader*, edited by Paul Rosenfeld (Boston: Houghton
Mifflin Company, 1947). For a generous sampling, see *Sherwood Ander-
son: Short Stories*, edited by Maxwell Geismar (New York: Hill and
Wang, 1962).

man, going to understand women? Some men writers pretend
they have solved the problem. They write with great confidence
and when you read the printed tale you are quite swept off
your feet but later, when you think things over, it appears all
false.

How are you going to understand women when you can't
understand yourself? How are you ever going to understand
anyone or anything? [4]

As a man Tar sometimes lay in his bed in a city and thought
of Camden, the town in which he was born and which he never
saw and never intended to see, the town filled with people he
could understand and who always understood him. [*There
was a reason for his love of the place.] He owed no one money
there, had never cheated anyone, had never made love to a
Camden woman, he found out later he didn't want.

Now Camden had become, for him, a place among hills. It
was a little white town in a valley with high hills on each side.
You reached it by a stage coach, going up from a railroad town
twenty miles away. Being a realist, in his writing and thinking, Tar did not make the houses of his town very comfortable
or the people particularly good or in any way exceptional.[5]

They were what they were, plain people, leading rather hard
lives, digging a living out of small fields in the valleys and on
the hillsides. Because the land was rather poor and the fields
steep, modern agricultural implements could not be introduced
and anyway the people had no money to buy.

The town of Tar's birth, this purely fanciful place, which has
nothing to do with real Camden, had no electric lights, there
was no waterworks, no one there owned an automobile. By
day men and women went into the fields to plant corn by hand,
they harvested wheat with a cradle. At night, after ten o'clock,

4. For Anderson's later, almost mystic, attitude toward women, see
Perhaps Women (New York: Horace Liveright, 1932); and Edward
Francis Carr, "Sherwood Anderson, Champion of Women," M.A. Thesis,
University of Pittsburgh, 1946.

5. Anderson's description of Camden resembles Marion, Virginia. See
*Return to Winesburg: Selections from Four Years of Writing for a Country
Newspaper*, edited by Ray Lewis White (Chapel Hill: University of North
Carolina Press, 1967), pp. 3–23, 207–11. For a comparable fantasy from
Anderson's country newspapers, see "Going to Nebo," *Return to Wines-
burg*, pp. 115–16.

the little streets, with the poor little houses scattered about, were unlighted. Even the houses were dark, except an occasional one where there was sickness or where company had come. It was, in short, such a place as might have been found in Judea in Old Testament days. Christ on his mission, and followed by John, Matthew, that queer neurotic Judas and the rest, might well have visited just such a place.

A place of mystery—the home of romance.[6] How thoroughly the citizens of the real Camden, Ohio, might have disliked Tar's conception of their town.

To tell the truth Tar was trying, through the creation of a town of his own fancy, to get at something it was almost impossible to get at in the reality of life. In real life people never stood still. Nothing in America stands still very long. You are a boy in a town and go away to live for a mere twenty years. Then one day you come back and walk through the streets of your town. Nothing is as it should be. The shy little girl who lived on your street and whom you thought so wonderful has now become a woman. She has protruding teeth and her hair is already getting thin. What a shame! When you knew her as a boy she seemed the most wonderful creature in the world. You used to go far out of your way, coming home from school, just to go past her house. There she was in the front yard and when she saw you coming she ran to the door and stood just within the house in the half light. You stole one glance and then did not dare look again, but in fancy how lovely she had been.

A sorry day for you when you go back to the real place of your childhood. Better go to China or the South Seas. Sit on the deck of a ship and dream. The little girl is married now and the mother of two children. The boy who played shortstop on the baseball team and whom you envied until it hurt has be-

6. For Sherwood Anderson's feeling for the small town, see the last book he lived to publish: *Home Town* (New York: Alliance Book Corporation, 1940), text complete in *The Sherwood Anderson Reader*, pp. 740–810. The subject is discussed by Evelyn Kintner, "Sherwood Anderson: Small Town Man . . . ," M.A. Thesis, Bowling Green State University, 1942; and by Maxwell Geismar, "Sherwood Anderson: Last of the Townsmen," *The Last of the Provincials* (Cambridge: Houghton Mifflin Company, 1947), pp. 223–84.

come a barber. Everything has gone wrong. Much better to adopt Tar Moorehead's plan, move away from your town early, so early that you can remember nothing very definitely, and then never go back.

Tar kept the town of Camden as something special in his life. Even when he had become a grown man and was called successful he clung to his dreams of the place. He had been spending the evening with some men at a big city hotel and did not go to his room until late. Well, his head was tired, his spirit tired. There had been talk and more talk, perhaps some kind of disagreement. He had quarreled with a fat man who wanted him to do something he did not want to do.

Then he went up into his room and closed his eyes and at once he was back in the town of his fancy, his birthplace, the town he had never consciously seen, in Camden, Ohio.

It was night and he walked in the hills above the town. The stars shone out. A little wind was making the leaves of the trees rustle.

When he had walked in the hills until he was tired he could come down through meadows where cows were being pastured and get among the houses.

He knew the people in every house along the little streets, knew all about them. They were what he had dreamed people were like when he was a small boy. The man he had thought brave and kind was really brave and kind; the little girl he had thought lovely had grown into a beautiful woman.

It is coming close to people that hurts. We find out people are like ourselves. Better [,* if you want peace,] keep far off, dream about people. The men who make a romance of life are [*perhaps] right after all. The reality is too terrible. "By the sweat of your brow shall you earn your bread."

By cheating too, by all kinds of dodges.

Cain made things [*hard] for all of us that time he killed Abel at the edge of the field. He did it with a club. What a mistake [*it was to be] carrying clubs about. If Cain hadn't had the club with him that day long ago the Camden of fact, where Tar Moorehead was born, might have been more like the Camden of his dreams.

But then perhaps it wouldn't have wanted to be that. Camden wasn't a very progressive town as Tar saw it, in dreams.

After Camden how many other towns?[7] Tar Moorehead's father was a drifter as he was himself [to be]. There are certain people who settle down in one place in life, hang on and finally make their mark but Dick Moorehead, Tar's father, wasn't that sort. If he finally settled in one place it was because he was too tired and worn out to make another move.

Tar became a story teller but, if you will notice, it is the shiftless roving fellows who tell tales. Few tellers of tales are good citizens. They only pretend to be.

Dick Moorehead, Tar's father, came from the South, from North Carolina. He must have just drifted down the mountain sides, looking about, smelling out the land as did the two men Joshua, the son of Nun, send out of Shittim to look at Jericho. He crossed a corner of the old state of Virginia, the Ohio River, finally alighting upon a town where he thought he might do well.

What he did on the way, where he slept, what women he saw, what he thought he was up to, no one will ever know.

As a young man he was rather handsome and he then had a little money in a community where money was scarce. When he set up a harness shop in the Ohio town people flocked to him.[8]

For a time it was easy sailing. The other shop in the town was owned by an old crusty fellow who was a good enough workman but not very entertaining. In these earlier days in the Ohio communities people had no theatres, no movies, no radio, no busy brightly-lighted streets. Newspapers were rare. There were no magazines.

What a god-send to have a fellow like Dick Moorehead coming into [a] town. Coming from a distance he had of course tales to tell and people were eager to listen.[9]

And what an opportunity for him. Having a little money and being Southern, he of course hired a man to do most of his work and prepared to spend his own time doing the enter-

7. In 1877, the Andersons left Camden for Mansfield, Ohio. They lived in Caledonia from 1880 to 1884, when they moved to Clyde. See *Memoirs*, pp. 16, 18.

8. On Irwin Anderson's harness shop, see *A Story Teller's Story*, p. 79; and *Memoirs*, p. 17.

9. The father's tales are remembered in *Memoirs*, pp. 20, 45–46.

taining, a kind of work more in his line. He bought himself a suit of black clothes and a heavy silver watch with a heavy silver chain. Tar Moorehead, the son, saw the watch and the chain long afterwards. When bad times came to Dick they were the last things he let go.

Being a young man and for the time prosperous the seller of harness was a public favorite. The land was still new, forests were still being cut away and the fields under cultivation were filled with stumps. At night there was nothing to do. During the long winter days there was nothing to do.

Dick was a favorite with the unmarried women but for a time confined his attentions to the men. There was a certain craftiness in him. "If you pay too much attention to the women the first thing you know you get married and then look where you are."

Being a dark hairy man Dick let his mustache grow and this, with his thick black hair, gave him a certain foreign air. How impressive it was to see him making his way along the street before the little stores in the neat black suit with the heavy silver watch chain dangled across his then slender waist.

He strutted. "Well, well, ladies and gentlemen, do look at me. Here I am, come to live among you." In the backwoods Ohio of that time the man who wore, on week days, a tailor-made suit and who shaved every morning when he got up was bound to make a deep impression. At the little hotel he got the best place at the table and the best room. Awkward country girls, who had come to town to take places as servants at the hotel, went into his room to make the bed and change the sheets trembling with excitement. Dreams for them too. In the Ohio town Dick was, for the time, a kind of [a] king.

He stroked his mustache, he spoke kindly to the landlady and to the waitresses and chambermaids but for the time he courted no woman. "You wait. Let them court me. I am a man of affairs. I must attend to business."

Farmers came to Dick's shop bringing harnesses to be repaired, came wanting to buy new harnesses. Town people came in. There was a doctor, two or three lawyers, a county judge. In the town there was an undercurrent of excitement. It was a time when there was plenty to talk about.

Dick had come into Ohio in the year eighteen hundred and fifty-eight and the story of his coming is not Tar's story. However the tale aims to concern itself, somewhat vaguely to be sure, with the childhood of the Middle-west too.

The background is really a poor badly-lighted village some twenty-five miles back from the Ohio River in Southern Ohio. There was a rather rich valley among the rolling Ohio hills and the people were just such people as could be found nowdays in the hills of North Carolina, Virginia and Tennessee. They had come into the country and taken up land, the more fortunate ones in the valley itself, the less fortunate ones on the hillsides. For a long time they lived largely by hunting and then the timber was cut off, hauled over the hills to the river and rafted South to be sold. The game gradually disappeared. Good farming land began to be worth something, railroads were being built and there were the canals with their canal boats and the steamers on the river. Cincinnati and Pittsburgh were not so far away. Daily newspapers began to circulate and there was presently a telegraph line.

In this community and against this awakening background Dick Moorehead strutted away his few years of prosperity. Then the Civil War came and upset things for him. They were days he always remembered and magnified later. Well, he was prosperous then, was popular, he attended to business.

He lived then at the town hotel, run by a short fat man who let his wife attend to the affairs of the hotel while he tended bar, [and] talked of race horses and politics, and it was in the bar Dick spent much of his time. It was a time when women worked. They milked the cows, did the washing, cooked the food, had children and made clothes for them. After they married they stayed pretty much out of sight.

It was such a town as, being located in Illinois, might well have been visited on court days by an Abraham Lincoln, a Douglas, a Davis.[10] In the bar, the harness shop, the hotel

10. Anderson discusses Lincoln in *A Story Teller's Story*, pp. 24, 31–32, 61, 148, 159, 176, 179, 202; "Betrayed," *Golden Book*, I (May, 1925), 743–44; and "Father Abraham," *The Sherwood Anderson Reader*, pp. 530–602. The subject is discussed by David D. Anderson, "Sherwood Anderson's Use of the Lincoln Theme," *Lincoln Herald*, LXIV (Spring, 1962), 28–32.
Stephen A. Douglas (1813–61), Vermont senator who debated Lincoln

office, the livery stable, men gathered of an evening. There was talk. Men drank whiskey, told stories, chewed tobacco and talked of horses religion and politics and Dick was there among them, setting 'em up at the bar, expressing his opinions, telling stories, getting off jokes. At night, when nine o'clock came and if the men of the town had not drifted to his shop, he closed up and made his way to the livery stable where he knew they could be found. Well it was time for talk now and there was something special to talk about.

For one thing Dick was a Southerner in a Northern community. That set him apart. Was he loyal? You bet. He was a Southerner and knew niggers and niggers were now to the fore. The Pittsburgh paper had come. Samuel Chase of Ohio had made a speech, Lincoln of Illinois was holding a debate with Stephen Douglas, Seward of New York spoke of war.[11] Dick held to Douglas. All this nonsense about the niggers. Well, well! What an idea! The Southerners in Congress, Davis, Stevens, Floyd, were so in earnest, Lincoln, Chase, Seward, Sumner and the other Northerners were so in earnest.[12] "If war comes we'll catch it hot here in Southern Ohio. Kentucky will go in and Tennessee and Virginia. The city of Cincinnati is none too loyal."

Some of the little towns nearby were Southern in their feeling but Dick had got into a place that was hotly Northern. A lot of mountain men had happened to settle in there in the early days. It was just his luck.

At first he kept quiet and listened. Then people began to want him to speak out. Very well, he would. He was a Southerner, fresh from the South. "What have you got to say?" It was a perplexing question.

"What have I got to say, eh?" Dick had to think fast. "There

in 1858 and who was defeated by Lincoln for the Presidency in 1860. Jefferson Davis (1808–89), President of the Confederate States of America.

11. Anderson meant to refer to Salmon P. Chase (1808–73), American statesman; William H. Seward (1801–72), New York senator who in 1855 joined the Republican Party and later became Lincoln's Secretary of State.

12. Alexander Hamilton Stephens (1812–83), Vice-President of the Confederacy; John Buchanan Floyd (1806–63), Secretary of War to President Buchanan and a major-general of Virginia troops; Charles Sumner (1811–74), Massachusetts senator and leader of Reconstruction.

won't be any war—about niggers." At home in North Carolina
Dick's people had owned niggers, a few of them. They weren't
cotton raisers but lived in another hill country and raised corn
and tobacco. "Well, you see." Dick hesitated and then plunged.
What did he care about slavery? It meant nothing to him. A
few niggers hanging around. They weren't very good workers.
At home you had to have a few to be respectable, to avoid
being called a "poor white." [13]

While he was hesitating and keeping quiet, before he took
the plunge and became a thorough-going abolitionist and a
Northerner, Dick did a good deal of thinking.

His father had been prosperous once, had inherited lands,
but he was a shiftless man and before Dick had left things at
home had not gone too well. The Mooreheads weren't broke
or really hard up but from owning two thousand acres of land
they had been reduced to four or five hundred.

Things had happened. Dick's father went to a nearby city
and bought some niggers, a pair of them, both over sixty. The
old nigger woman had no teeth and her old nigger man had
a bad leg. He just could hobble about.

Why had Thad Moorehead bought the pair? Well, the man
who owned them was broke and wanted them to have a home.
Thad Moorehead had bought them because he was a Moorehead. He got the two of them for a hundred dollars. It was a
Moorehead kind of thing to do, buying such niggers.

The old nigger man was really a rascal. No *Uncle Tom's
Cabin* monkey business about him.[14] He had been owned far
South, in a half dozen places, and had always managed to keep
himself attached to some negro woman who stole for him, had
children by him, took care of him. In the Far South, when he
was owned down there on a sugar plantation, he had made
himself a set of reed pipes and could play. It was the playing
of the pipes that had attracted Thad Moorehead.

Too many of that kind of niggers about.

13. See Anderson's third novel, *Poor White* (New York: B. W.
Huebsch, 1920). On Negroes, see *Dark Laughter* (New York: Boni and
Liveright, 1925); and Robert Crist, "Sherwood Anderson's *Dark Laughter*:
Sources, Composition, and Reputation," Ph.D. Thesis, University of
Chicago, 1966.

14. *Uncle Tom's Cabin, or, Life Among the Lowly* (1852), by Harriet
B. Stowe (1811–96), the most famous novel of the slavery controversy.

When Dick's father got the old couple home they could do little enough work. The woman helped some in the kitchen and the man made a pretense of working with the Moorehead boys in the fields.

The old black man told stories, he played his pipes and Thad Moorehead listened. Finding himself a shady place under a tree at the edge of a field the old rascally black got out his pipes and played or he sang songs. One of the Moorehead boys was superintending the work in the field and a Moorehead is a Moorehead. The work went to pieces. All gathered about.

The old black could keep it up all day and all night. Tales of strange places, of the Far South, of the sugar plantations, the big cotton fields, of the time when he was leased out by his owner to be a hand on a river steamer on the Mississippi.[15] After the talk a turn on the pipes. Sweet strange music making echoes in the woods at the edge of the field, creeping up the nearby hillside. It fairly made the birds stop singing in envy sometimes. Strange that an old man could be so wicked and make such sweet heavenly sounds. It made you doubt the value of goodness, that sort of thing. Not strange though that an old black woman liked her nigger man, stuck to him. The trouble was [*that] all the Mooreheads listened, letting the work go. Always too many of that kind of niggers around. Thanks be, a horse can't tell tales, a cow can't play pipes when she should be giving milk.

You pay less for a cow or a good horse and a cow or a horse can't tell strange tales of far places, can't tell stories to young men when they should be plowing corn or chopping tobacco, can't make music on reed pipes that will make you forget any kind of work should ever be done.

When Dick Moorehead had made up his mind he wanted to strike out for himself old Thad had simply sold a few [more] acres of land to give him his start. Dick had put in a few years as an apprentice in a harness shop in a nearby town and then the old man had produced the money. "I think you had better go up North, it's a more enterprising place," he said.

Enterprising indeed. Dick had tried to be enterprising. Up

15. For Anderson's ideas of the Mississippi River, see *Poor White; Dark Laughter;* "In Washington," *Return to Winesburg,* pp. 60–68; and "Old Mississippi River Men," *Return to Winesburg,* pp. 173–78.

North, specially where [*abolitionists] have come in, they would never put up with wasteful niggers. Suppose an old nigger man can play the pipes until it makes you sad and glad and careless about getting work done. Better let music alone. [You can get the same thing on a talking machine nowdays.] [*It's the devil's business.] Enterprise is enterprise.

Dick was the sort who turn out to believe what the people about him believe. In the Ohio town *Uncle Tom's Cabin* was being read. Sometimes he thought of the blacks at home and smiled in secret.

"I've got into a place where people are against shiftlessness. The niggers are responsible." He began to hate slavery now. "This is a new century, new times. The South is too pigheaded."

Being enterprising, in business, the retail kind anyway, was simply standing in with [*the] people. You had to stand in with [*the] people to get them into your shop. If you are a Southerner in a Northern community and go over to their point of view you are stronger with them than you would be if you were born a Northerner. There is more joy in Heaven over one sinner, etc.

How could Dick tell he was himself a player of the pipes?

Blow your reed pipes, get a woman to take care of your children—if you are unfortunate enough to have any—tell tales, go with the crowd.

Dick went over bang. His popularity in the Ohio community went up to boiling point. Everyone wanted to buy him drinks at the bar, in the evening his shop was full of men. Now Jeff Davis, Stevenson of Georgia [16] and others were making fiery speeches in Congress, making threats. Abraham Lincoln of Illinois was running for president. The Democrats were all split up, had put three tickets in the field. The fools!

Dick even joined the crowd who were running off niggers at night. If you go in for a thing you might as well go the whole hog and anyway running off niggers was half the fun of the game. It was against the law for one thing—against the law

16. Apparently an error for Alexander H. Stephens, Note 12, above. Stephens led the Confederate peace delegation in 1865 and was governor of Georgia, 1882–83.

and all the good law-abiding citizens, the very best in fact, going into it.

Fun, eh? Plenty of excitement. They slipped the niggers across the Ohio River at night in a row boat. A lot of them not of much account to their owners if they had stayed South, Dick thought. Well, he was no special judge of good niggers. The kind his father had at home weren't of much account. "If you want to make niggers pay you got to own land down in Alabama or Mississippi. Then you put a good overseer in charge and pretty much keep out of the fields yourself." A lot of the best overseers were Northern men, nigger drivers. "Small owners got all the worst of it in the slavery business. You owned four or five or even a dozen niggers and got acquainted with them. The worst [thing] was that they got acquainted with you, knew your weaknesses, knew how to work you." More niggers like that old reed-blower all through the South in slavery days than the North ever dreamed of. They got through life pretty easy, flattered their masters, flattered the women and the children. "A shrewd canny lot, the niggers of the South," Dick thought.

Dick kept smiling to himself, helping run niggers off at night, Northern Methodist and Baptist preachers in the party, superintendents of Sunday schools, earnest men. When they got their niggers across the river wagons were waiting. Sometimes the niggers were made to lie on the wagon beds and straw was piled on them. There was a husky young wench with two children, worth about eighteen hundred dollars in Alabama— the three of them—and a negro preacher who wanted to begin shouting until Dick made him shut up. "Shut up, nigger," he growled and the tone of his voice shocked some of the members of the party.

Dick did not do much thinking. They took the runaway niggers to some farm house, usually on a side road, and after feeding hid them in a barn. The next night they would be shoved on their way, toward Zanesville, Ohio, toward a distant place called Oberlin, Ohio, places where the abolitionists were thick. "Damn an abolitionist anyway." They were bound to raise hell for Dick.

Sometimes the parties running the escaped niggers off had

to hide in the woods. The next town to the west was as strong
in its Southern feeling as Dick's town was for abolition. The
citizens of the two towns hated each other and the neighboring
town got up parties to catch the nigger runners. Dick would
have been among them had he happened to settle in that town.
It was a game for them too. None of the crowd owned any
slaves. Sometimes shots were fired but no one in either of the
towns ever got hit.

For Dick it was, for the time, fun, excitement. His getting
to the front in the abolitionists ranks made him a marked man,
an outstanding figure. He never wrote letters home and his
father of course knew nothing of what he was doing. Like everyone else he did not think war would really come and if it did
what of it? The North thought it could lick the South in sixty
days. The South thought it would take them thirty days to
whip the North. "The Union must and will be preserved," said
Lincoln, who had been elected president. That seemed good
sense anyway. He was a backwoods fellow, that Lincoln. People in the know said he was tall and gawky, a regular country
man. The smart fellows down East would handle him all right.
When it came to a showdown the South would give in or the
North would.

Dick went sometimes to see the runaway niggers hidden in
the barns at night. The other white men were in the farm
house and he was alone with two or three blacks. He stood over
them, looking down. It's the South's way. There were a few
words passed. The niggers knew he was [*a] Southern[*er]
all right. Something in his tone told them. He thought of what
he had heard his father say. "For the smaller whites, the common white farmers in the South, it would have been better had
there never been any slavery, never any blacks." What happened, when you had them around, was that you got the notion
into your head you didn't have to work. Dick's father had seven
strong sons before his wife died. They were a shiftless lot,
really. Dick himself was the only one who had any enterprise,
had ever wanted to get out. Had there never been any niggers
he and all of his brothers might have been taught to work, the
Moorehead place in North Carolina might have amounted to
something.

Abolition, eh? If abolition could only abolish. A war wouldn't make any deep essential difference in the attitude of the whites toward the blacks. Any black man or woman would lie to a white man or woman. He made the niggers in the barn tell him why they had run away. They lied of course. He laughed and went back to the house. If the war came his father and his brothers would get in on the Southern side [*as casually as he would get in on the Northern side]. What did they care about slavery? They really cared about the way the Northerners talked. The North cared about the way the South talked. Both sides sent talkers to Congress. That was natural. Dick was a talker himself, an adventurer.

And then the war came and Dick Moorehead, Tar's father, got in. He was made a captain and wore a sword. Could he resist that? Not Dick.[17]

He went south, to Middle Tennessee, was in Rosecrans' army and then later in Grant's.[18] His harness shop had been sold. When he paid his debts there wasn't much left. He had set 'em up too often at the tavern, during the exciting days when enlistment was going on.

What fun, during enlistment, what excitement. Women scurrying about, men and boys scurrying about. They were grand days for Dick. He was the town's hero. You don't get many such chances in life if you are not born a money-maker and can't pay to get yourself into a prominent position. In times of peace you just go along, telling stories, drinking with other men at the bar, spending your money for a good suit of clothes and a heavy silver watch, letting your mustache grow, stroking it, talking when some other man wants to talk as much as you do. He may be a better talker, at that.

At night sometimes, during the excitement, Dick thought of his brothers, going into the Southern army, much in the spirit

17. Sherwood Anderson's father was in the Ohio infantry from August 25, 1863, to July 1, 1865, serving in Georgia, Alabama, and Tennessee. See *A Story Teller's Story*, pp. 6–7, 28–37, 45–56; and *Memoirs*, pp. 45–46.
18. William Starke Rosecrans (1819–98), Union general. See *A Story Teller's Story*, pp. 139–60; and "Tim and General Grant," *The Sherwood Anderson Reader*, pp. 846–50.

in which he had gone in with the North. They would hear speeches, the women of the neighborhood would be holding meetings. How could they stay out? They would go in to hold on to such fellows as that shiftless old black, playing his reed pipes, singing his songs, lying about his past, entertaining the whites so he wouldn't have to work. Dick and his brothers might be shooting at each other someday. He refused to think of that side of the matter. The thought came only at night. He had been made a captain and wore a sword.[19]

One day a chance came to distinguish himself. The Northerners, among whom he lived, who were his fellows now, were great rifle shooters. They called themselves "the squirrel shooters of Ohio," bragged a lot of what they would do when they drew a bead on a Reb. During the time when the companies were being formed they held shooting matches.

It was all the go. The men went to the edge of a field near town and fastened a small target to a tree. They stood off an unbelievable distance and nearly every man hit the target. If they did not hit the center of the target they at least made the bullets do what they called "biting paper." Everyone had the illusion that wars are won by good shots.

Dick yearned to shoot but did not dare. He had been elected captain of a company. "You be careful," he told himself. One day when all the men had gone to the shooting ground he picked up a rifle. He had hunted some as a boy but not much, was never a good shot.

Now he stood with the rifle in his hands. A small bird flew far up in the sky over the field. Quite casually he raised the rifle, took aim and fired, and the bird came down, almost at his feet. It had been shot cleanly, through the head. One of those strange accidents that get into stories but never happen in fact—when you want them to.

Dick strutted out of the field and never went back. Things were on the wing for him, he was a hero already, before the war started.

19. Sherwood Anderson may be recalling his own enlistment in the Spanish-American War. See *A Story Teller's Story*, pp. 167, 199–208; *Memoirs*, pp. 120–35. The definitive discussion is William Alfred Sutton, "Sherwood Anderson: The Spanish-American War Year," *Northwest Ohio Quarterly*, XX (January, 1948), 20–36.

A marvelous shot, a captain. Already he had got his sword and had spurs fastened on his bootheels. When he walked through the streets of his town young women looked at him from behind window curtains. Almost every night there was a party at which he was the central figure.

How was he to know that after the war he was to marry and have many children, that he would never be a hero again, that all the rest of his life he would have to build on these days, creating in fancy a thousand adventures that never happened.[20]

The race of the tale tellers is always an unhappy race but luckily they never find out how unhappy they are. They are always hoping somewhere they will find believers, living in that hope. It is in the blood.

20. Anderson's very sympathetic understanding of his father appears in *A Story Teller's Story*, pp. 14–15, 43–44; and "Discovery of a Father," *Reader's Digest*, XXXV (November, 1939), 21–25, reprinted in *Memoirs*, pp. 45–49.

CHAPTER II

For Tar Moorehead life began with a procession of houses. They were at first very dim in his mind. They marched. Even when he grew to be a man the houses went across the walls of his fancy like soldiers in a dusty road. As when soldiers marched some few were sharply remembered.

Houses were like people. An empty house was like an empty man or woman. There were houses cheaply built, thrown together. Others were carefully built and carefully lived in, having careful loving attention.[21]

When you went into an empty house the experience was sometimes terrifying. Voices kept calling. They must have been the voices of people who had lived there. Once, when Tar was a boy and had gone out of town alone to pick wild berries in the fields, he saw a small empty house, standing in a field of corn.

Something induced him to go in. The doors were open and many panes had been broken in the windows. There was grey dust on the floor.

A small bird, a swallow, had flown into the house and could not get out. In its terror it flew directly at Tar, at the doors, at the windows. Its body struck the window sash and its terror began to get into Tar's blood. The terror had something to do with empty houses. Why should houses be empty? He ran away and at the edge of the field looked back and saw the swallow make its escape. It flew gladly, joyously, circling about over the field. Tar was half beside himself with desire to leave the ground and fly away through the air.

To a mind like Tar's—the truth always washed by the colors being brushed on by his fancy—houses in which he lived as a child could not be definitely placed. There was one house [he was quite sure] he had never lived in that was very clearly

21. Anderson's philosophy of houses and rooms appears in *A Story Teller's Story*, pp. 289–96; and *Memoirs*, p. 16.

remembered. The house was low and long and a grocer with a large family lived in it. Back of the house, its roof almost touching the kitchen door, was a long low barn. Tar's own family must have lived near this house and no doubt he wanted to live under its roof. A child is always wanting to try the experiment of living in some house other than his own.

There was always laughter in the grocer's house. In the evening songs were being sung. One of the grocer's daughters thumped on a piano and the others danced. Also there was an abundance of food. Tar's sharp little nose could smell it being cooked and served. Did not a grocer deal in foods? Why not an abundance of food in such a house? At night he lay in bed in his own house dreaming he had become the son of the grocer. The grocer was a strong-looking man with red cheeks and a white beard and when he laughed the sides of his house seemed to shake. In desperation Tar told himself that he did live in the house, that he was the grocer's son. What he dreamed became, in fancy at least, a fact. It had happened that all of the grocer's children were daughters. Why not a trade that would make everyone happy? Tar selected the grocer's daughter who was to come and live in his house while he went to her house as a son. She was small and rather quiet. Perhaps she would not protest so much as the others. She did not look like a protester.[22]

What a glorious dream! As the only son of the grocer Tar would be given the first choice of the food on the table, he would ride the grocer's horse, sing songs, dance, be treated as a kind of prince. Already he had read or heard fairy tales in which such a prince as he wanted to be lived in such a place. The grocer's house was his castle. So much laughter, so much song and food. What more could a boy want?

Tar was the third child of a family of seven, five of whom were boys. From the beginning the family of Dick Moorehead, the ex-soldier, was on the march and no two were born in the same house.[23]

22. Compare this home with that of the Hurd family, in Chapter XVII, below. See *A Story Teller's Story*, p. 97; *Memoirs*, pp. 53–54.

23. The Anderson children, all now dead, were: Karl (born January 13, 1874), Stella (b. April 13, 1875), Sherwood (b. September 13, 1876), Irwin (b. June 18, 1878), Ray (b. May 21, 1883), Earl (b. June 18, 1885), and Fern (b. December 11, 1890).

And what does not the house mean to the child? There should be a garden with flowers, vegetables and trees. Also there should be a barn with horses standing in stalls and back of the barn a vacant lot in which tall rank weeds grow. For older children in the house it is all very well, no doubt, to have an automobile but for the small child nothing will take the place of an old gentle black or grey horse. If the later and grown Tar Moorehead were to be born again surely he would have selected as parent a grocer with a fat jolly wife and he would not have wanted him to own a delivery truck. He would have wanted him to make his grocery deliveries with horses and in the morning Tar would have wanted older boys to come to the house and drive them away.

Then Tar could run out of the house and touch each horse on the nose. The boys would give him presents, apples or bananas, things they had got at the store, and after that he would breakfast in state and go through the empty barn to play in the tall weeds. The weeds would grow high above his head and he could hide among them. There he could be a robber, a man making his fearless way through dark forests— anything he pleased.[24]

Other houses than the ones in which Tar's family lived during his early childhood, houses often on the same street, had all of these things while his house always seemed to sit on a small grassless lot. In the barn back of the neighbor's house there was a horse, often two horses, and a cow.

In the morning sounds from the neighboring houses and from the barns. Some of the neighbors kept pigs and chickens that lived in pens in the back yard and were fed from the table scraps.

In the mornings the pigs grunted, the cocks crowed, the hens made soft clucking sounds, the horses neighed, the cows bawled. Calves were born—strange fascinating creatures with long ungainly legs on which they, at once and in a funny uncertain manner, began to walk, following the mother cow about the barn yard.

In Tar's mind later a dim memory of early mornings in bed,

24. See "Godliness," *Winesburg, Ohio,* pp. 82–83.

his older brother and sister at a window. Already, in the Moorehead house of the moment, another baby had been born, perhaps two babies since Tar's turn. Babies did not get up and
walk about like calves and colts. They lay on their backs in
bed sleeping like puppies or kittens and then they awoke to
make dreadful noises.

Children, just coming into consciousness of life, as Tar was
at that time, do not fancy younger children about. Kittens are
something and puppies something else. They lie in a basket
back of the kitchen stove. It is nice to put the hand into the
warm nest in which they lie sleeping but other babies of one's
own family about the house are a nuisance.

How much better a dog or a kitten. Cows and horses are for
rich people but a dog or a cat the Mooreheads might have had.
How gladly would Tar have traded a baby for a dog and as
for a horse—it was well he was not tempted. If the horse were
gentle and would let him ride on its back or if he could sit
alone in a cart and hold the reins over a horse's back, as did
an older neighbor boy in one of the towns in which he lived,
he might have traded off the whole Moorehead family.

In the Moorehead house they had a saying. "The baby has
put your nose out of joint." What a terrible saying! The new
baby cried and Tar's mother went to take it into her arms.
There was some strange connection between the mother and the
baby that Tar, who had begun walking about the floor, had
already lost.

He was four, his older sister seven and the first born son of
the household nine. Now, in some odd way that was not understandable, he belonged to the world of his older brother and
sister, to the world of neighbor children, to the front and back
yard into which other children came to play with his brother
and sister, to a tiny section of the great world in which he
would presently have to try to live, not really to his mother at
all. His mother was already a dark strange being, a little far
off. He might still cry and she would call to him and he might
run and put his head in her lap while she stroked his hair but
there was always that later child, the baby, far up there in her
arms. His nose was indeed out of joint. What would set it
straight?

To cry and win favor that way was already a shameful trick in the eyes of his older brother and sister.

Surely Tar did not want to remain always a baby. What did he want?

How huge the world. How strange and terrible it was. His older brother and sister, out in the yard at play, were so impossibly old. If they would only stand still, stop growing, stop getting older for two or three years. They wouldn't. Something told him that would not happen.

And now his tears had stopped, already he had forgotten what made him cry as though he were still a babe. "Run now and play with the others," his mother said.

But how difficult the others! If they would only stand still until he caught up.

A spring morning in the house on a street in a Mid-American town. The Moorehead family changed towns as they did houses, slipping them on and off as one slips on and off a night dress. Between them and the others in the town a kind of separateness. The ex-soldier, Dick Moorehead, had never got himself settled [again] after the war. Marriage had perhaps upset him.[25] Now was the time to become a solid citizen and he was not made to be a solid citizen. Towns and the years slipped away together. A procession of little houses in grassless lots that had no barns, a procession of streets, of towns too. Tar's mother was always busy. There were so many children and they came so fast.

Dick Moorehead had not married a rich woman, as perhaps he might have done. He married the daughter of an Italian working woman but she had beauty.[26] It was a strange kind of dark beauty to be found in the Ohio town where he had met her after the war and it [had] fascinated him. It always fascinated Dick and his children.

---

25. Irwin Anderson married Emma Smith in Morning Sun, Ohio, March 11, 1873. Emma was born October 1, 1852, near Oxford, Ohio. See *Memoirs*, p. 16.

26. Sherwood Anderson's maternal grandmother, Margaret Austry, was not Italian. Born September 10, 1830, in Germany, she came to the United States as a child; she married William H. Smith in Butler County, Ohio, December 22, 1851, and then Lewis Maer, March 29, 1858. See *A Story Teller's Story*, pp. 8–9, 10, 77–78, 187; *Memoirs*, pp. 93–96.

Now, however, while children were coming so fast, no one had time to breathe, to look out. Tenderness between people grows slowly.

A spring morning in a house on a street in a Mid-American town. Tar now a grown man and a writer was staying at the house of a friend. His friend's life had been utterly unlike his own. The house was surrounded by a low garden wall and Tar's friend was born in it and had lived in it all his life. He, like Tar, was a writer but what a difference in the two lives. Tar's friend has written many books—all histories of men who lived in another age—books of men at war, great generals, politicians, explorers.[27]

All the man's life had been lived in books while Tar's life had been lived in the world of men.

Now the friend had a wife, a gentle soft-voiced woman Tar could hear moving about in a room upstairs in the house.

Tar's friend was in his workroom reading. He was always reading, while Tar seldom read. His children played in the garden. There were two boys and a girl and an old negro woman looked out for them.

Tar sat in a corner of the porch at the back of the house under rosebushes thinking.

On the day before he and his friend had a talk. The friend spoke of some of Tar's books, raising his eyebrows. "I like you," he said, "but some of the people you write about. I never saw any [*of the] people. Where are they? Such thoughts, such terrible people."

What Tar's friend had said of his books others had said.[28] He thought of the years his friend had spent over books, of the life the man had lived behind the garden wall while Tar had knocked about. Even then, as a grown man, he had no

27. This man cannot now be identified. For information on Anderson's wide circle of important friends, see *Letters of Sherwood Anderson,* edited by Howard Mumford Jones and Walter B. Rideout (Boston: Little, Brown and Company, 1953).

28. The only reputation studies of Sherwood Anderson are William Robert Moses, "Sherwood Anderson: His Life, His Philosophy, His Books, and What Has Been Said About Him," M.A. Thesis, Vanderbilt University, 1933; and the Introduction to *The Achievement of Sherwood Anderson: Essays in Criticism,* edited by Ray Lewis White (Chapel Hill: University of North Carolina Press, 1966), pp. 3–15.

house of his own. He was an American, had always lived in America and America was vast, but not a square foot of it had ever belonged to him.[29] His father had never owned a square foot of it.

Gypsies, eh? Worthless kind of people in an age of property. If you want to be something in this world own lands, own goods.

When he had written books about people the books had often been condemned, as they were condemned by his friend, because the people in the books were of the common sort, because they often did mean commonplace things.

"But I am myself a commonplace man," Tar said to himself. "It is true my father wanted to be a man of distinction and he was also a teller of tales, but the tales he told would never hold water.

"Dick Moorehead's tales went well enough with the farmers and the farm hands who used to come into his harness shops when he was a young man but suppose he had been compelled to write them out for people—like the man in whose house I am now visiting," Tar thought.

And then his mind leaped back to his own childhood. "Surely childhood is always distinguished," he said to himself. "It is only when we grow up that we become common and vulgar. Has there ever been such a thing as a vulgar child? Could there be such a thing?"

As a grown man Tar thought much on the subject of childhood and houses. He sat in one of the little rented rooms in which he as a man was always living and his pen slipped over the paper. It was early spring and he thought the room nice enough. There was a fire.

He had begun again, as he was always beginning, on the theme of houses, places in which people live, into which they come at night and when it is cold and stormy outside the house—houses with rooms in which people sleep, in which children sleep and dream.

The later Tar was a little cracked on the subject. The room

29. "Ripshin," in Southwest Virginia, was indeed Anderson's only property. See "Why I Live Where I Live," *Golden Book*, XVI (November, 1932), 389–400; *Memoirs*, pp. 356–75.

in which he sat, he told himself, contained his body but it contained also his thoughts. Thoughts were as important as bodies. How many people tried to make their thoughts color the rooms in which they slept or ate, how many tried to make the rooms a part of themselves. At night when Tar was in bed and when there was a moon, shadows played on the walls and his fancies also played. "Do not befoul the house in which the child must live and remember that you are also a child, will always be a child," he whispered to himself.

In the East when a guest came to a house his feet were washed. "Before I invite the reader into the house of my fancy I should see that the floors are cleaned, that the doorsills have been washed."

Houses were like people standing silently and at attention, along a street.

"If you honor and respect me and come into my house come softly. For the moment think gentle thoughts, leave quarrels and the ugliness of your life outside my house."

There is the house and to the child the world outside the house. What is the world like? What are people like? Older people, neighbor men and women, men and women who walked along the sidewalk before the Moorehead house when Tar was a small child went straight on about their affairs.

A woman named Mrs. Welliver was going toward that mysteriously exciting place known as "uptown" with a market basket on her arm. Tar, the child, had never been beyond the nearest corner.

A day came. What an event! A neighbor woman, who must have been rich as she had two horses in the barn back of her house, had come to take Tar and his sister—[*three] years older—for a ride in a buggy. They were to go into the country.

They were to go far out into a strange world, through Main Street. In the early morning they were told and Tar's older brother, who was not to go, was angry, while Tar was made happy by his brother's misfortune.[30] There were so many things

---

30. Karl Anderson became a magazine cover artist and illustrator. He writes of Sherwood in "My Brother, Sherwood Anderson," *Saturday Review of Literature*, XXXI (September 4, 1948), 6–7, 26–27; and in an un-

the older brother already had. He wore pants while Tar still wore skirts. There was something to be gained then by being small and helpless. How Tar had wanted to come to the time of pants. Willingly enough, he thought, would he have traded the trip into the country for his brother's additional five years and the pants but why should the brother expect all of the good things of this life? The older brother wanted to cry because he was not going but how many times had Tar wanted to cry because of things the brother had that Tar could not have.

They set out and Tar was excited and happy. What a huge strange world. The little Ohio town was to Tar's eyes a vast city.[31] Now they had come into Main Street and there was an engine attached to a train, a great terrifying thing. The horse half ran across the tracks in front of the nose of the engine, a bell clanged. Tar had heard that sound before—at night in the room where he slept—the clanging of an engine bell in the distance, the scream of a whistle, the crashing rumble sound of a train rushing through town, out in the darkness and silence, outside the house, outside the windows and the wall of the room where he lay.

In what way was the sound different from the sounds that came from horses, from cows, sheep, pigs and chickens? Warm friendly sounds the others. Tar himself cried, he screamed when he was angry. Cows, horses and pigs also made sounds. The animal sounds belonged to a world of warmth, of nearness, while the other sound was strange romantic and terrible. When Tar heard the sound of the engine at night he crept closer to his sister and said nothing. If she awoke, if his older brother awoke, they would laugh at him. "It's only a train,"

---

published novel, "Knots in the Weaver's Loom," Newberry Library Manuscript. For Sherwood Anderson's comments on his older brother, see *A Story Teller's Story*, pp. 5, 10, 63, 189, 226; *Memoirs*, pp. 28–29, 51, 76. The correspondence is represented in *Letters of Sherwood Anderson.*

31. For descriptions of Clyde, Ohio, see "Winesburg, Ohio: A *Life* Artist Visits Sherwood Anderson's Town," *Life*, XX (June 10, 1946), 74–79; John H. Sullivan, "Winesburg Revisited," *Antioch Review*, XX (Summer, 1960), 213–21. For Anderson's later serious view of his native state, see "Ohio: I'll Say We've Done Well," *These United States: A Symposium*, edited by Ernest Gruening (New York: Boni and Liveright, 1923), pp. 109–17. *Letters*, pp. 461–62, describes one of Sherwood Anderson's last visits to Clyde.

they said, their voices filled with contempt. It had seemed to Tar that something [*gigantic] and terrible was about to crash through walls into the room.

On the day of his first great voyage out into the world and when the horse, a creature of flesh and blood like himself, frightened by the breathing of the great iron horse, had carried the buggy rushing past, he turned to stare. There was smoke issuing from the engine's long up-thrust nose and the dreadful metallic clang of a bell rang in his ears. A man put his head out of the cab window and waved his hand. He spoke to another man standing on the ground beside the engine.

The neighbor woman was pulling at the lines and striving to quiet the excited horse who had infected Tar with his fright, and his sister, filled with her three additional years of worldly knowledge and a little contemptuous of him, put her arms about his shoulders.

And now the horse was trotting sedately along and they all turned to look back. The engine had begun to move slowly, majestically pulling its train of cars. How fortunate that it did not choose to follow along the road they had taken. It had crossed the road and was going away, past a row of small houses toward distant fields. Tar's fright passed. In the future and when he was awakened by the sound of a passing train at night he would not be afraid. When his brother, two years younger, grew a year or two older and became frightened at night he could speak to him with contempt in his voice. "It's only a train," he could say, scorning his younger brother's childishness.

They drove on, over a hill and across a bridge. At the top of a hill they stopped and Tar's sister pointed to the train moving across a valley below. Far off there in the distance, going away, the train seemed beautiful and Tar clapped his hands with delight.

As it was to the child so it was to be to the man. Trains moving across distant valleys, the rivers of automobiles that flowed through modern city streets, squadrons of æroplanes in the sky, all of the wonders of the modern mechanical age, when seen from a distance, filled the later Tar with wonder and awe but when he drew near to them he was afraid. Power, hidden away, deep down in the belly of an engine, made him tremble.[32] Where did it come from? The words "fire," "water," "oil" were old words signifying old things but the combining of these things within iron walls from which, at the touch of a button or a lever, power sprang seemed the work of a devil— or a god. He did not pretend to understand devils or gods. Men and women were difficult enough.

Was he an old man in a new world? Words and colors might be combined.[33] In the world his imagination could sometimes penetrate blue did something strange when combined with red. Words might be thrown together and sentences made and the sentences had uncanny power. With a sentence one might destroy a friendship, win a woman, make a war. The later Tar walked unafraid among words but what happened within the narrow walls of steel was never understandable to him.

But now he was still a child and was being driven out into the vast world and was already a little frightened and homesick. His mother, who was already too much separated from him by [*an]other [and later child up there in her arms], was nevertheless the rock on which he was trying to build the house of his life. Now he was on shifting sands. The neighbor woman looked strange and forbidding. She was occupied in driving the horse. The houses along the road were far apart. There were wide open spaces, fields, great red barns, orchards. What a [huge] world!

The woman who had taken Tar and his sister for the ride must have been very rich. She had a house in town, with two horses in the barn, and also owned a farm in the country where there were a house, two large barns, and horses, sheep, cows and pigs without number. They turned into a driveway with an apple orchard on one side and a corn field on the other and went into a farm yard. Home seemed to Tar thou-

32. Anderson's idea of the machine is discussed in *Poor White, Perhaps Women*, and *Puzzled America* (New York: Charles Scribner's Sons, 1935). See Thomas Reed West, *Flesh of Steel: Literature and the Machine in American Culture* (Nashville: Vanderbilt University Press, 1967), pp. 21–34.

33. Sherwood Anderson enjoyed two expositions of his paintings, one at the Radical Bookshop in 1920, and a later one at the Arts Club. See *Letters*, p. 64.

sands of miles away. Would he know his mother when he returned? Could they ever find their way back? His sister was laughing and clapping her hands. A wobbly-legged calf was tied to a rope on the lawn before the house and she pointed at it. "Look, Tar," she cried, and he did look with serious thoughtful eyes. Already he was beginning to realize something of the utter frivolity of women.

They were in a barn yard, facing a large red barn, and a woman came out at the back door of the house and two men emerged from the barn. The farm woman looked not unlike Tar's mother. She was tall and her fingers were long and roughened by toil like his mother's fingers.[34] Two children clung to her skirt as she stood by the door.

There was talk. Women were always talking. What a little chatterbox his sister already was. One of the men from the barn, no doubt the husband of the farm woman and the father of the strange children, came forward but had little to say. The people from town had got out of the buggy and the man, after mumbling some few words, went away again to the barn accompanied by one of the two children and while the women continued talking he emerged from the barn door, a child, a boy like Tar but two or three years older, astride a great farm horse the father was leading.

Tar was left with the women, his sister and the other farm child, also a girl.

What a come-down for him! The two women having gone into the farm house he was left with the two girls. In this new world it was as at home in his own yard. At home his father was gone all day at his shop and his older brother had little use for him. The older brother thought of him as a babe but Tar was no longer a babe. Was there not another child in his mother's arms? His sister took care of him. Women ran everything. "You take him and the little girl to play with you," the farm woman said to her daughter, pointing to Tar. The woman touched his hair with her fingers and [the two women] smiled. How far [away] everything seemed. At the door one of the

34. Anderson uses his mother's hands in *A Story Teller's Story*, pp. 11–12, 17–18, 20–21. "Hands" are a recurrent image in *Winesburg, Ohio*, dedicated to Emma Anderson.

women stopped to give other instructions. "Remember he is only a babe. Do not let him get hurt." What an idea!

The boy of the farm sat astride the farm horse and a second man, no doubt a hired man, came out at the barn door leading another horse but did not offer to take Tar aboard. The men and the farm boy went off along a lane beside the barn and toward distant fields, the boy on the horse turning to look back, not however at Tar but at the two girls.

The girls with whom Tar had been left looked at each other and laughed. Then they led the way to the barn. Well, Tar's sister was up to her tricks. Did he not know her? She wanted to hold his hand, pretend she was his mother, but he would not let her. It was a thing girls did. They pretended they were taking care of you when they were only showing off. Tar marched sturdily along wanting to cry because he had been dropped suddenly in a [huge] strange place but not wanting to give his sister, but three years older than himself, the satisfaction of showing off before the strange girl by mothering him. If women would but do their mothering in secret how much better it would be.

Tar was now so altogether alone in the midst of such vast strange beautiful and at the same time [*terrifying surroundings]. How warmly the sun shone. Long, long afterward, oh [how many] many times afterward, he was to dream over the scene, use it as a background for tales, use it all his life as a background for some great dream he was always having of someday owning his own farm, a place of great barns with unpainted timber beams, grown steely grey with age, of the rich smell of hay and animals, of sun-washed and snow-covered hills and fields and smoke going up out of the chimney of a farm house into wintry skies.

These for Tar the dreams of another and much later time. The child going toward the great [*yawning] doors of the barn, his sister clinging to his hand, the while she joined in a stream of talk she and the farm girl were to keep up until they drove Tar half mad with loneliness, had no such thoughts. In him there is no conciousness of barns and their smell, of tall corn growing in fields, of wheat shocks standing like sentinels on distant hills. There was just a little animal in short skirts and with bare legs and feet, the son of a harness maker in an Ohio village who felt himself neglected and alone in the world.

The two girls went into the barn through wide swinging doors and Tar's sister pointed to a box near the door. It was a small box and an idea had come to her. She would get rid of [*him for a time]. Pointing to the box and assuming, as nearly as she could, his mother's tone when she gave a command, the sister told him to sit down. "You stay right there until I come back and don't you dare go away," she said, shaking her finger at him. Huh! Indeed! What a little woman she thought herself! She had black curls and wore shoes and Tar's mother had let her wear her Sunday dress while the farm girl and Tar were both bare-footed. She was being a grand lady now. If she only knew how much Tar resented her tone. If he had been a bit older he might have told her but, had he tried to speak just at that moment, tears would surely have come.

The two girls began climbing a ladder to a hay loft above, the farm girl leading the way. Tar's sister was afraid and trembled as she climbed and would have liked being a town girl and timid but having assumed the role of grown woman [*with the child] had to play it out. They disappeared through a dark hole above and for a time rolled and tumbled about on the hay in the loft, laughing and screaming as girls do at such times. Then silence settled down over the barn. Now the girls had hidden themselves away in the loft and were no doubt talking of women's affairs. What do women talk of when they are alone together? Tar always wanted to know. Grown women in the farm house talking, girls in the loft talking. Occasionally he could hear them laughing. Why all the laughing and talking?

Women were always coming to the door of the house in town to talk to his mother. Left alone she might have remained always sensibly silent but they would not let her alone. Women could not let each other alone as men did. They are not as sensible and brave. If women and younger babes had but stayed away from his mother Tar might have had more of her for himself.

He sat on the box near the door of the barn. Was he glad to be alone? One of those odd things happened that were always happening later when he was grown. A particular scene, a country road climbing over a hill, the yard of a railroad seen from a bridge in a city at night, a grass-grown road leading into a wood, the garden of a deserted tumbled-down house— some scene that, outwardly at least, had no more meaning than a thousand other scenes swept by his eye perhaps on the same day printed itself with the most minutely worked out details on the walls of his mind. The house of his mind had many rooms and each room was a mood. On the walls pictures were hung. He had hung them there. Why? Some inner sense of selection had perhaps been at work.

There was the open barn doors making a frame for his picture. Back of him, in the shed-like entrance to the barn, was, on the one side, the blank barn wall up which the ladder climbed to the loft above and up which the girls had gone. On the wall were wooden pegs on which hung work harnesses, horse collars, a row of iron horse shoes and a saddle and on the opposite walls were openings through which horses, standing in their stalls, could thrust their heads.

A rat came from some unknown place and ran quickly across the earthen floor to disappear under a farm wagon at the back of the shed and an old grey horse, her head thrust through one of the openings, looked at Tar with sad impersonal eyes.

And so there he was, for the first time thrust out alone into the world. How isolated he felt! His sister, in the face of all her grown-up mother-manner, had reneged on her job. She had been told to remember he was a babe and had not remembered.

Well, he was no longer a babe and was resolved he would not cry. He sat stoically staring out through the open barn doors at the scene before him.

What a strange scene. It was thus that later hero of Tar's, Robinson Crusoe, must have felt when he found himself alone on his isle.[35] What a vast world this into which he had been thrust. So many trees, hills, fields. Suppose he were to arise from his box and begin to walk. At one corner of the frame opening through which he looked was a small section of the white

35. On Anderson's early reading, see "A Businessman's Reading," *Reader*, II (October, 1903), 503–4; *A Story Teller's Story*, pp. 115–18, 121, 164–68, 172, 184–85, 220; *Memoirs*, pp. 57–59.

farm house into which the women had gone. Tar could not hear
their voices. Now he could not hear the voices of the two girls
in the loft. They had disappeared through a dark hole over
his head. Occasionally there was a buzzing whisper and then
girlish laughter. It was really giggling. Perhaps every one in the
world had gone away into some strange dark hole leaving him
sitting there in the midst of a vast empty space. Terror had
begun to take hold of him. In the far distance, as he looked
out through the barn doors, were hills and as he sat gazing a
tiny black dot appeared in the sky. The dot grew slowly larger
and larger. What seemed to him a long time passed and the
dot grew into a great bird, a hawk wheeling and circling in
the vast sky over his head.

Tar sat staring at the hawk moving slowly, in great circles,
up in the sky. In the barn at his back the head of the old horse
was withdrawn and then appeared again. Now the horse had
taken a mouthful of hay and was eating. The rat, that had
run into some dark hole under the wagon at the back of the
shed, came forth and began creeping toward him. What shining little eyes! Tar was about to cry out but now the rat had
found what he wanted. An ear of corn lay on the barn floor and
he began gnawing at it. His sharp little teeth made a soft grind-
ing sound.

Time passed slowly, oh so slowly. What a trick Tar's sister
has played on him. Why were she and the farm girl, named
Elsa, so silent now? Had they gone away? In another part of
the barn, somewhere in the darkness back of the horse, something began to stir about making a rustling sound in the straw
on the barn floor. The old barn was full of rats.

Tar got off his box and went softly out through the barn
doors into the warm sunlight and toward the house. In a
meadow near the house some sheep were pastured and one of
them raised its head to look at him.

Now all of the sheep were looking, were staring. In an orchard beyond the barns and the house there was a red cow
that also raised her head to stare. What strange impersonal
eyes.

Tar hurried across the farm yard and to the door through
which the two women had gone but it was closed. Inside the

house also there was silence. He had been left alone for perhaps five minutes. It seemed to him hours.

He pounded at the back door with his fists but there was no answer. The women had only gone upstairs in the house but it seemed to him they must have gone far away—that his sister and the farm girl had gone far away.

Everything had gone far away. Looking up into the sky he could see the hawk circling now far above. The circles grew larger and larger and then suddenly the hawk flew straight away into the blue. When Tar had seen him first he was a tiny dot, no larger than a fly, and now he was becoming like that again. As he looked the black dot grew smaller and smaller. It wavered and danced before his eyes and then disappeared.

He was alone in the farm yard. Now the sheep and the cow were no longer looking at him but were eating grass. He went to the fence and stood looking at the sheep. How contented and happy they seemed. The grass they ate must be delicious to the taste. For each sheep plenty of other sheep, for the cow the warm barn at night and the company of other cows. The two women in the house had each other, his sister Margaret had the farm girl Elsa, the boy of the farm had his father, a hired man, the work horses and the dog he had seen trotting at the horses' heels.

Tar only was alone in the world. Why was he not born a sheep to be with other sheep and eat grass? Now he was not afraid, only lonely and sad.

He went slowly across the barn yard and along the green lane the men, the boys and the horses had followed. He cried a little, softly, as he went. The grass in the lane was soft and cool under his bare feet and in the distance he could see blue hills and beyond the hills a blue cloudless sky.

The lane which seemed so long to him that day was very short. There was a small woodlot through which it passed to the fields beyond—fields lying in a long flat valley through which a creek ran—and in the woods the trees threw blue shadows on the grass-covered roadway.

How cool and quiet in the woods. A passion Tar had in him all his life may have begun on that day. In the woods he stopped and for what seemed to him a long time sat on the ground beneath a tree. Ants were running here and there and then disappearing into holes in the ground, birds flew about in the branches of the trees and two spiders, who at his approach had hidden themselves away, came out again and worked at the business of spinning webs.

If Tar had been crying when he came into the woods he had stopped now. His mother was very very far away. He might never find her again but if he did not it was her own fault. She had put him out of her arms to take up another and younger member of the family. The neighbor woman, who was she? She had shoved him off on his sister who had, after issuing an absurd command about sitting on a box, promptly forgotten him. There was the world of boys but at the moment boys meant his older brother John, who more than once had shown his scorn of Tar's society, and such people as the farm boy who had ridden away on a horse without bothering to speak to him or even to give him a parting look.

"Very well," Tar thought, filled with bitter resentment, "if I am shut out from one world there is another."

The ants at his feet were happy enough. What a fascinating world that in which they lived. The ants were darting up into the light out of a hole in the ground and were building a little mountain of grains of sand. Other ants went on voyages out into the world and returned bearing burdens. An ant was dragging a dead fly along the ground. There was a stick in his way and now the wings of the fly had caught against the stick and he could not move it. He ran crazily about, pulling now at the stick, now at the fly. A bird flew down off a nearby tree and lighting on a fallen log looked at Tar and far off in the woods, through an opening between trees, a squirrel came down the trunk of a tree and began running on the ground.

The bird was looking at Tar, the squirrel stopped running and sat up straight to look and the ant that could not move the fly made frantic signs with his tiny hair-like feelers.

Had Tar been received into the world of nature? Vast plans had begun to form in his head. He had noticed that the sheep in the field by the farm house ate grass eagerly. Why should he not eat grass? Ants lived warm and snug in a hole in the ground. There were many ants, all apparently of one age and size, in one family, and, after Tar had found his own hole and had eaten much grass so that he had become big like a sheep —or even like a horse or cow—he would find others of his kind.

There was, he had no doubt, a language of sheep, of squirrels, of ants. Now the squirrel had begun to chatter and the bird on the log called and was answered by another bird away somewhere in the woods.

The bird flew away. The squirrel disappeared. They had gone to join their comrades. Tar alone had no comrade.

Leaning over he lifted the stick so that his tiny brother the ant could go on about his affairs and then, getting down on all fours, he put his ear near the ant hill to see if he could hear the talk.

He could hear nothing. Well, he was too large. Far away from others of his own kind he seemed to himself big and strong. Along the lane he went, walking now on all fours like a sheep, and got to the log where but a moment before the bird had been sitting.

The log was hollow at one end and it was obvious that with a little effort he could crawl into it. He would have a place into which to go at night. Of a sudden it seemed to him that he had got into a world in which he could move freely about, in which he could live freely and happily.

[*He] decided it was time for him to go and eat grass. Walking along the roadway through the wood he came to a lane that led down into a valley. In a distant field the two men, driving the two horses, each hitched to a cultivator, were plowing corn. The corn came up to the horses' knees. The farm boy was riding one of the horses. At the heels of the other horse the farm dog trotted. From the distance, it seemed to Tar [*that] the horses looked no larger than the sheep he had seen in the field by the house.

He stood by a fence looking at the men and horses in the field and at the boy on the horse. Well, the farm boy was grown up—he moved in a world of men while Tar was left to the women. But he had renounced the woman's world, he would go at once into a warm comfortable world—the world of animal life.

Getting down on all fours again he began crawling on the

soft grass that grew near the fence beside the lane. White clover grew among the grass and first of all he bit off one of the clover blossoms. It did not taste badly and he ate another and another. How many would he have to eat, how much grass would he have to consume before he grew big like a horse or even like a sheep? He kept crawling about, biting at the grass, but the edges of the grass blades were sharp and hurt his lips. When he had [*chewed] a mouthful of the grass it was strange and bitter to the taste.

He persisted but something within kept warning him that what he was doing was ridiculous and that if his sister or his brother John knew he would be laughed at and so from time to time he arose and looked back along the road through the woods to be sure no one was coming. Then getting again to his hands and knees he crawled over the grass. As it was difficult to tear the grass with his teeth he used his hands. The grass had to be chewed until it was soft before it could be swallowed and how nasty it tasted.

How hard to grow up! Tar's dream of growing suddenly big by eating grass was fading and he closed his eyes. With his eyes closed he could do a trick he sometimes did in his bed at night. He could in fancy re-create his own body, make his legs and arms long, his shoulders broad. With his eyes closed he could be anything he pleased, be a horse trotting through the streets, a tall man walking in a road. He could be a bear in the dense forest, a prince living in a castle with slaves to bring his food, could be the son of a grocer and rule over a household of women.[36]

He sat on the grass with his eyes closed pulling grass and trying to eat it. The green juice of the grass had discolored his lips and chin. Now surely he had begun growing larger. Already he had eaten two, three, half a dozen mouthfuls of the grass. After two or three more he would open his eyes and see what he had accomplished. Perhaps he would already have the legs of a horse. The thought frightened him a little but he put out his hand and tearing loose more of the grass put it in his mouth.

36. Compare this episode with "White Spot," *The Sherwood Anderson Reader*, pp. 708–12.

Something dreadful happened. Jumping quickly to his feet Tar ran two or three steps and then sat quickly down. In reaching for the last handful of grass he had captured a bee, sucking honey out of one of the clover blossoms, and had carried it to his lips. The bee [had] stung him on the lip and then a convulsive moment of his hand had half crushed the insect and it had been thrown aside. He could see it lying on the grass struggling to arise and fly away. Its broken wings beat the air madly and it made a loud buzzing sound.

The most terrible pain had come to Tar. He put his hand to his lip and rolling over on his back closed his eyes and screamed. As the pain grew in intensity his screams grew louder and louder.

Why had he come away from his mother? The sky into which he now looked, when he dared open his eyes, was empty and he had wandered away from all things human into an empty world. The world of crawling and flying things, the world of animals that went on all fours, he had thought so warm and safe, had now become dark and threatening. The little struggling winged beast on the grass nearby was but one of a vast army of winged things surrounding him on all sides. He wanted to get to his feet and run back through the wood and toward the women in the farm house but did not dare move.

There was nothing to do but this humiliating business of screaming and so, lying on his back in the lane and keeping his eyes closed, Tar continued screaming for what seemed to him hours. Now his lip was burning and was becoming large. He could feel it throbbing and pulsating with growth under his fingers. Growth then was a thing of terror and pain. What a fearful world, this into which he had been born.

Tar did not want to grow big like a horse or a man. He wanted someone to come. The world of growth was too empty and lonely. Now his screams were broken by sobs. Would no one ever come?

There was the sound of running feet in the lane. Two men, accompanied by the dog and the boy, had come from the field, the women had come from the house and the girls from the barn. All were running and calling to Tar but he did not dare look. When the farm woman reached him and had taken him into her arms he still kept his eyes closed and presently stopped screaming although his sobs came harder than ever.

There was a hurried consultation, many voices talking at once, and then one of the men stepped forward and lifting his head from the woman's shoulder forced Tar's hand away from his face.

"Why, look," he said, "the little rabbit has been eating grass and has been stung by a bee."

The farmer laughed, the hired man and the farm boy laughed and Tar's sister and the farm girl shrieked with delight.

Tar kept his eyes closed and it seemed to him that the sobs that now shook his body went deeper and deeper. There was a place, far down inside, where the sobs started and it hurt more than his swollen lip. If the grass he had so painfully swallowed were now making something inside him grow and burn as his lip had grown how terrible that would be.

He buried his face on the farm woman's shoulder and refused to look at the world. The farm boy had found the injured bee and was showing it to the girls. "He tried to eat it. He was eating grass," he whispered and the girls shrieked again.

These terrible women!

Now his sister would go back to town and tell John. She would tell neighbor children who came to play in the Moorehead yard. The place inside Tar was hurting harder than ever.[37]

The little party went along the lane through the woods and to the house. The great voyage alone that was to have utterly separated Tar from mankind, from the world that had no understanding, was retraced in but a few minutes. The two farm men and the boy had gone back to the field and the horse that had brought Tar out from town was hitched to the buggy and was standing tied to a post at the side of the house.

Tar would have his face washed and would be put into the buggy and taken back to town. The farm men and the boy he would not have to see again. The farm woman who had him in her arms had made his sister and the farm girl stop laughing but would his sister stop when she had got back to town and to his brother?

37. Sherwood Anderson remembers this scene in *Memoirs,* p. 17.

Alas, she was a woman and Tar had no faith. If women could only be more like men. The farm woman had taken him into the house, had washed the grass stains from his face and had applied a soothing lotion to his swollen lip but the thing inside kept on swelling and swelling.

In fancy he could hear his sister, his brother and the neighbor children whispering and giggling in the yard at home. Shut out from his mother by the presence of the younger babe in her arms and from the yard by malicious voices saying over and over, "The little rabbit tried to eat grass; he was stung by a bee," where could he turn?

Tar did not know and could not think. He kept his face buried in the farm woman's bosom and continued sobbing broken-heartedly.

Growing up, in any way he could conceive of at the moment, seemed a terrible, if not impossible, task. For the moment he was glad enough to be a babe in the arms of the strange woman and in a place where there was no other babe [*waiting to push him aside].

CHAPTER III

MEN live in one world, women in another. People kept coming to the kitchen door to talk to Mary Moorehead when Tar was a small child. There was an old carpenter whose back had been hurt by a fall from a building and who was sometimes [a little] drunk. He did not enter the house but sat on the steps by the kitchen door and talked with the woman while she worked at her ironing board.[38] A doctor also came. He was a tall thin man with strange looking hands. The hands were like old grape vines that cling to the trunks of trees. People's hands, rooms in houses, the faces of fields were things the child did not forget. The old carpenter had short stumpy-looking fingers. The nails were black and broken. The fingers on the doctor['s hands] were like his mother's, rather long. Afterward Tar used the doctor in several of his printed tales.[39] When the boy grew up he did not remember exactly how the old doctor looked but his imagination had by that time invented a figure to take his place. What he got from the doctor, the old carpenter and from several of the women visitors was a sense of gentleness. They were all people defeated by life. Something had gone wrong with them as something had gone wrong with Tar's mother.[40]

Could it have been her marriage? He did not ask himself that question until long afterward. When he grew to be a man Tar found in an old trunk a diary kept by his father during his time in the war and immediately afterwards.[41] The notes were

38. This old carpenter appears in *Winesburg, Ohio*, pp. 21–22.
39. Dr. Reefy appears in two *Winesburg* stories: "Paper Pills," pp. 35–38; and "Death," pp. 220–32.
40. The idea of the "grotesque" in human character forms the basis for the *Winesburg* stories, according to the prefatory "The Book of the Grotesque," pp. 21–25. See David D. Anderson, "Sherwood Anderson's Idea of the Grotesque," *Ohioana*, VI (Spring, 1963), 12–13; and the interpretative essays in *The Achievement of Sherwood Anderson*.
41. In the first appendix to this volume, William Alfred Sutton discusses Irwin Anderson's diary, along with that of Emma Smith Anderson.

short. For several days there would be nothing written and then the soldier had written page after page. He also had an inclination to be a scribbler.

All during the war there was something eating at the soldier's conscience. Knowing his brothers would be enlisted on the Southern side he was beset by the notion that someday he might meet one of them in battle. Then, if nothing worse happened, he would be found out. How could he explain, "Well, the women were cheering, the flags flying, the bands playing." When he fired a shot in a battle the bullet, flying across the space between the Northern and Southern men, might lodge in the breast of a brother or even in his father's breast. Perhaps his father had also enlisted, on the Southern side. He had himself gone into the war without convictions, almost casually, because the men about him were going, for the sake of a captain's uniform and a sword to hang at his side. If a man thought much about any war he wouldn't go in—of course. As for the niggers—their being free men or slaves. . . . He had still the Southern[er's] attitude. If, walking in the street with Dick Moorehead, you had seen a negro woman who was in her own way beautiful, who walked with an easy care-free carriage, whose skin was in color a lovely golden brown, and had mentioned the fact of her beauty, Dick Moorehead would have looked at you with amazement in his eyes. "Beautiful! I say! My dear fellow! She is a nigger." Looking at negroes Dick saw nothing. If a negro served his purpose, if he was amusing— very well. "I am a white man and a Southerner. I belong to the ruling race. We had an old black at home. You should have heard him play the pipes. Niggers are what they are. Only we Southerners understand them."

The book kept by the soldier, during the war and later, was full of notes concerning women. Sometimes Dick Moorehead was a religious man, going regularly to church, and sometimes he was not. In one town, where he had lived immediately after the war, he was superintendent of a Sunday school and at another place taught the Bible class.

When he had become a grown man Tar looked at the [note] book filled with delight. He had quite forgotten his father was so naïve, so charmingly human and understandable. "I was at

the Baptist Church and succeeded in taking Gertrude home.[42]
We went the long way by the bridge and stopped almost an
hour. I tried to kiss her and at first she would not let me but
later she did. Now I am in love with her." "On Wednesday
evening Mable went past the shop. I closed up at once and
followed her to the end of Main Street. Harry Thompson was
after her and had got his boss to let him off, on some trumped
up excuse. We were both sailing down the street but I got there
first. I went home with her but her father and mother were still
awake. They sat up until I had to go so I gained nothing. Her
father is a fearful talker. He has got a new driving horse and
talked and bragged about the horse all evening. For me the
evening was a failure."

Note after note of that sort in the diary kept by the young
soldier after he had got home from the war and when he had
begun his restless march from town to town. At last he had
found, in one of the towns, the woman Mary and had married
her. Life took on for him a new flavor. Having a wife and
children he now sought the company of men.

In some of the towns into which Dick went after the war
life went well enough but in others he was unhappy. For one
thing, and although he had gone into the war on the Northern
side, he would not forget the fact that he was a Southerner and
therefore a Democrat. In one of the towns there was a half
insane man the small boys used to tease. There he was, Dick
Moorehead, the young merchant, the ex-officer in the army
who, whatever his inner feeling may have been, had nevertheless fought for the preservation of the Union, who had helped
hold together these United States, and there on the same street
was that crazy man. The crazy man walked with his mouth
hanging open and with a queer vacant look in his eyes. Winter
or summer he wore no coat but went about in his shirt sleeves.
He lived with a sister in a little house at the edge of the town
and when let alone was harmless enough but when small boys,
concealed behind trees or in the doorways of stores, shouted,
calling him a "Democrat," he became furiously angry. Running
into the roadway he picked up stones and threw them reck-

42. The custom of meeting girls after church services appears in
Memoirs, p. 97.

lessly. Once he broke a window in a store-front and his sister had to pay for it.

Was it not an insult to Dick? A Democrat indeed! When he wrote about it in his notebook his hand trembled. Being the only real Democrat in the town the cries of the small boys made him want to run and beat them. He kept his dignity, did not betray himself, but as soon as he could he sold his shop and moved on.

Well, the crazy man in his shirt sleeves was not really a Democrat, he wasn't like Dick, a born Southerner. The word, picked up by the boys and repeated over and over, merely touched off his half-hidden insanity but for Dick the effect was something special. It made him feel that, although he had fought in a long and bitter war, he had fought in vain. "Such people," he muttered to himself as he hurried away. When he had sold his shop he had to buy, in the next town, a somewhat smaller one.[43] After the end of the war and his marriage Dick was constantly sliding down the financial hill.

For the child the man of the home, the father, is one thing and the mother quite another. The mother is something warm and safe toward which the child may go while the father is the one who goes out into the world. Now the house in which Tar lived was something he began to understand a little. Even though you live in many houses in many towns a house is a house. There are walls and rooms. You go through doors into a yard. There is a street with other houses and other children. You can see a long way along the street. On Saturday evenings, sometimes, a neighbor woman, who had been engaged for the purpose, came to care for the other children and Tar was permitted to go uptown with his mother.

Now Tar was five and his older brother John was ten. There was Robert, now three, and a new babe, always lying in a crib.[44] Although the babe could do nothing but cry it already had a name. It was called Will and when she was at home was always in the mother's arms. What a little pest! And to have a

43. Irwin Anderson's loss of his harness shop is mentioned in *A Story Teller's Story*, p. 5; and *Memoirs*, pp. 19–20.

44. "Robert" is Sherwood Anderson's brother Irwin, almost two years younger. "Will" is Ray Anderson.

name too, a boy's name! There was another Will in the street,
a tall freckle-faced boy who sometimes came to the house to
play with John. He called John "Jack" and John called him
"Bill." He could throw a ball like a shot. There was a trapeze
John had hung from a tree and the boy named Will could hang
by his toes. He went to school, as John and Margaret did, and
had been in a fight with a boy two years older than himself. Tar
had heard John speak of it. When John was not about he himself spoke of it to Robert, pretending he had seen the fight.
Well, Bill had punched the boy, had knocked him down. He
had given the boy a bloody nose. "You should have seen it."

It was something right and proper that such a one should be
named Will and be called Bill but a babe in a crib, a little
thing always in its mother's arms. What nonsense!

On Saturday nights, sometimes, Tar was permitted to go with
his mother down into town. They could not start until the
lights were lit. First of all the dishes had to be washed, Margaret helping, and then the baby had to be put to sleep.

What a fuss he made, the little wretch. Now, when he might
so well have ingratiated himself with his brother [Tar] by
being reasonable, he cried and cried. First Margaret had to
hold him and then Tar's mother had to take her turn. It was
fun for Margaret. She could pretend she was a woman and
girls like that. When there are no babies around they make
them out of rags. They talk and scold and coo and hold the
things in their arms. Tar was already dressed and so was his
mother. The best part of going to town was the feeling of being
alone with her. Nowdays that so seldom happened. The baby
was spoiling everything. Pretty soon it would be too late to go,
the stores would be closed. Tar moved restlessly about the
front yard wanting to cry. If he did he would [*have to stay
at home]. He had to appear at ease, say nothing.

The neighbor woman came and the baby went to sleep.
Now his mother had stopped to talk with the woman. They
talked and talked. Tar had hold of his mother's hand and
kept pulling but she paid no attention. At last however they got
into the street and into darkness.

Tar walked along holding his mother's hand and took ten
steps, twenty, a hundred. He and his mother had got through

the gate and were walking on a sidewalk. They passed the Musgrave house, the Wellivers' place. When they had got to the Rogers' house and had turned a corner they would be safe. Then, if the baby cried, Tar's mother could not hear.

He began to feel at ease. What a time for him. Now he was going out into the world, not with his sister—who had her own ways and thought too much of herself and her own desires—or with a neighbor woman in a buggy, a woman who could understand nothing, but with his mother. Mary Moorehead had put on her black Sunday dress. That was fine. When she wore the black dress she wore also a bit of white lace about the neck and other bits about the wrists. The black dress made her look young and slender. The lace was fine and white. It was like cobweb. Tar wanted to touch it with his fingers but did not dare. He might tear it.

They walked past one street lamp and then another. Electric lights had not yet come and the streets of the Ohio town were lighted by kerosene lamps set on posts. They were far apart, at the street corners mostly, and between the lamps was darkness.

What fun to walk in darkness feeling safe. Going anywhere with his mother was to Tar like being at home and at the same time [being] abroad.

When he and his mother had got out of their own street the adventure began. The Mooreheads lived nowdays always in small houses in streets far out at the edges of towns but when they went to Main Street they went through streets lined with tall houses. The houses were set far back in lawns and great trees were growing along the sidewalks. There was a large white house with women and children sitting on a wide front porch and as Tar and his mother passed a carriage with a negro driver came out at a driveway. The woman and child had to stand aside to let it pass.

What a princely place. The white house had at least ten rooms and lamps of its own hanging from the ceiling on the front porch. There was a girl of about Margaret's age dressed all in white. The carriage, Tar saw the negro driving, could go right into the house. There was a porte-cochère. His mother told him. What splendor!

[What a world this into which Tar had come.] The Mooreheads were poor and were getting every year poorer but that

Tar did not know. He did not ask himself why his mother, he thought so beautiful, had but one good dress and walked while another woman rode in a carriage, why the Mooreheads lived in a small house through the cracks of which the snow sifted during the winter while others were in warm brightly-lighted houses.[45]

The world was the world and he was seeing it, his mother's hand in his. They passed other street lamps, went through other dark places and now they had turned a corner and there was Main Street.

Now life had indeed begun. How many lights, how many people! To the town droves of country people had come for the Saturday night and the street was filled with horses, wagons and buggies. [What a lot to see.]

Young fellows with red faces, who all week had been at work in corn fields, had come into town dressed in their best clothes and wearing white collars. Some of them rode alone while others, more fortunate, had girls with them. They hitched their horses to posts along the street and walked on the sidewalk. Grown men went clattering through the street on horseback and women stood talking at the doors of stores.

The Mooreheads were living for the moment in quite a large town. It was a county seat and there was a square and a court house past which the main street ran. Well, there were stores on the side streets too.

A patent medicine seller had come to town and had set up his stand at a corner. He bawled in a loud voice, inviting [the] people to stop and hear him and for a few minutes Mary Moorehead and Tar stood at the edge of the crowd. There was a sputtering torchlight at the end of a pole and two negro men who sang the songs. Tar remembered one of the verses. What did it mean?

> The white man he lives in a big brick house,
> The yellow man wants to do the same,
> The old black man lives in the county jail,
> But he's got a brick house just the same.

45. Other statements of the family's poverty occur in *A Story Teller's Story*, pp. 5, 7, 38–43, *passim*; and *Memoirs*, pp. 20–21, 26–27, 52–53, 59, 77.

When the black men sang the verses the crowd whooped with delight and Tar also laughed. Well, he laughed because he was so excited. His eyes shone with excitement [now]. When he grew to be a man he would spend all his time in the midst of crowds. He and his mother moved off along the street, the child clinging to the woman's hand. He did not dare wink for fear of missing something. [*Again] the Moorehead house seemed miles away, in another world. Now even the baby could not come between him and his mother. The little wretch might cry [and cry] but [*he need not care].

John Moorehead, his brother, was almost grown [up]. On Saturday evenings he sold newspapers on Main Street. He sold a paper called the *Cincinnati Enquirer* and another called the *Chicago Blade*. The *Blade* had brightly colored pictures and sold for five cents.

There was a man leaning over a pile of money on a table and another fierce-looking man was creeping up on him with an open knife in his hand.

A wild-looking woman was about to throw a baby off a [high] bridge to [*the] rocks [far] below but a boy rushed forward and saved the babe.

Now a train rushed around a curve in the mountains and four men on horseback and with guns in their hands were waiting. They had piled rocks and trees on the tracks.

Well, they intended to force the train to stop and then rob it. It was Jesse James and his band.[46] Tar had heard his brother John explain the pictures to the boy Bill. Later when no one was about he had looked long and long. Looking at the pictures made him dream bad dreams at night but during the day [time] they were wonderfully exciting.

It was fun, during the daytime, to imagine yourself a part of the adventures that went on in life, in the world of men. The people who bought John's papers sure got a lot for five cents. Why, you could take such a scene and change it all about.

What you did was to sit on the porch of your house and close your eyes. John and Margaret had gone to school, the

46. Jesse Woodson James (1847–82), Midwestern outlaw gang leader, appears in *A Story Teller's Story*, p. 61.

baby and Robert were both asleep. The baby slept well enough
when Tar did not want to go somewhere with his mother.

You sat on the porch of the house and closed your eyes.
Your mother was ironing. Damp clean clothes being ironed
made a nice smell. That old crippled carpenter, who could not
work any more, who had been a soldier and drew what was
called a "pension," was on the back porch of the house talking.
He was telling [*Tar's] mother of buildings on which he had
worked when he was young.

He told of how log cabins were built in the forest when the
country was new and of how men went out to shoot wild turkey
and deer.

It was fun enough to hear the old carpenter talk but more
fun to make up your own talk, build your own world.

The colored pictures in the papers John sold on Saturdays
had become indeed alive. In fancy Tar had grown to be a man
and what a brave one. He took part in all of the desperate
scenes, changed them about, thrust himself into the very midst
of the swirl and hurly-burly of life.

A world of grown people moving about and Tar Moorehead
among them. Somewhere in the crowd on the street John was
now running about selling his papers. He [*pushed] them
under people's noses, showed the colored pictures. Like a grown
man John went into saloons, into the stores, into the court
house.

Soon now, Tar himself would be grown. It could not possibly
take very long. How long though the days sometimes seemed.

With his mother he threaded his way through the crowd.
Men and women spoke to his mother. A tall man did not see
Tar and knocked against him. Then another very tall man with
a pipe in his mouth gave him a regular bang.

The man wasn't so nice. He apologized and gave Tar a nickel
but that did not do any good. It was the way he did it that
hurt more than the bang. Some men think a child is only a
child.

And now they had got off Main Street and into the one where
Dick had his shop. There were plenty of people on Saturday
nights. Across the street was a two-storied building in which
a dance was being held. It was a square dance and a man's

voice was calling off. "Do-se-do. Gentlemen all lead to the right. Balance all." The whining voices of fiddles, laughter, many voices talking.

[Into the shop they went.] Dick Moorehead was as yet able to put on some style. He had still the watch with the heavy silver chain and for the Saturday evening's rush had been shaved and had waxed his mustache. A silent old man, much like the carpenter who came to visit Tar's mother, was employed in the shop and was there now at work, seated on his wooden horse. He was sewing a strap.[47]

It seemed to Tar that the life led by his father was something magnificent. When the woman and the child came into the shop Dick ran at once to a drawer and taking out a handful of money offered it to his wife. It may have been all the money he had but that Tar did not know. Money was something with which you bought things. You had it or you did not have it.

As for Tar he had money of his own. He had the nickel the man on the street had given him. When the man had banged him and had given him the nickel his mother had asked sharply, "Well, Edgar, what do you say?" and he had replied by looking at the man and saying rudely, "Give me some more." It had made the man laugh but Tar had not seen the sense of his laughing. The man had been rude and he had been rude too. His mother was hurt. It was [*very] easy to hurt his mother.

In the shop Tar was seated on a chair at the back and his mother was on another chair. She had taken but a few of the coins offered by Dick.

Again there was talk. Grown people are always indulging in talk. A half dozen farmers were in the shop and when Dick had offered the money to his wife he did it with a flourish. Dick did everything with a flourish. That was his nature. He said something about the cost of women and children. He was being rude like the man on the street but Dick's being rude never [*mattered]. He [*did not] mean what he said.

[And] anyway Dick was a man of affairs.

How he bustled about. Men kept coming into the shop bring-

47. Other trips of Sherwood Anderson to his father's shop appear in *A Story Teller's Story*, p. 79; and *Memoirs*, p. 17.

ing harnesses and throwing them down with a bang on the
floor. The men talked and Dick [also] talked. He talked more
than all the others. At the back of the shop there was only
Tar, his mother and the old man on the horse sewing the strap.
The man was like the carpenter and the doctor who came to
the house when Tar was at home. He was small and shy and
spoke timidly, asking Mary Moorehead about the other children
and the baby. Presently he got off the bench and coming to
Tar gave him another nickel. How rich Tar was getting. This
time he did not wait for his mother to ask but said at once
what he knew he should say.

Tar's mother had gone away and left him in the shop. Men
came and went. They talked. With some of the men Dick went
out into the street. A business man who has taken an order
for a new harness is expected to set-em-up. Each time when
he came back from such a trip Dick's eyes shone more brightly
and the mustache stood out straighter. He came and stroked
Tar's hair.

"He's a bright one," he said. Well, Dick was bragging
[*again].

It was better when he talked to the others. He told jokes
and the men laughed. When the men were doubled up with
laughter Tar and the old harness maker on the horse looked
at each other and also laughed. It was as though the old man
had said, "We're out of it, my boy. You are too young and I
am too old." As a matter of fact the old man said nothing
[at all]. It was all imagined. All the best things for a boy are
always imagined. You sit in a chair at the back of your father's
shop on a Saturday night while your mother goes to the stores
and such thoughts you have. There is the sound of the fiddle
in the dance hall outside in the street and the nice sound of
men's voices far away. At the front of the shop there is a hanging lamp and harnesses are hanging on the walls. All is neat
and in order. Harnesses have silver buckles, they have buckles
of brass. Solomon had a temple and in the temple were shields
of brass. There were vessels of silver and gold. Solomon was
the wisest man in the world.

CHAPTER IV

For the boy as for the man there is the world of fancy and the world of facts. Sometimes the world of facts is very grim.

Solomon had vessels of silver, he had vessels of gold, but Tar Moorehead's father was not a Solomon. Within a year after the Saturday evening when Tar sat in his father's shop seeing the bright glitter of the buckles in the swaying lights the shop had been sold to pay Dick's debts and the Mooreheads were living in another town.

All summer Dick had been working as a house painter but now cold weather had come and he had got a job.[48] He was now but a workman in a harness shop and sat on the harness maker's horse sewing straps. The silver watch and the watch chain were gone.

The Mooreheads lived in a mean little house and all through the fall Tar had been ill. As the fall advanced there was a time of bitter cold days and then there came a period of soft [warm] days.

Tar sat on the porch wrapped in a blanket. Now the corn in distant fields was in shocks and the other crops had been hauled away. In a small field near at hand where the corn crop had not been good a farmer had gone into the field to pick the corn and then had turned cows into the field to nibble at the stalks. In the woods the red and yellow leaves were falling fast. With every gust of wind they flew like brightly colored birds across the field of Tar's vision. In the corn field the cows making their way among the dry standing corn stalks made a low crashing sound.

Dick Moorehead had names Tar had never heard before. One day when he sat on the porch of the house a man with a board balanced across his shoulder came along the road past

48. The father as a house painter is described in A Story Teller's Story, pp. 5–7, 72–75, 93–94; and Memoirs, p. 26.

the house and seeing Dick Moorehead coming out at the front door stopped and spoke to him. He called Dick Moorehead "Major." "Hello, Major," he shouted.

The man's hat was tilted jauntily on the side of his head and he smoked a pipe. After he and Dick had gone off along the road together Tar got up out of his chair. It was one of the days when he felt quite strong. The sun was shining.

Going around the house he found a board fallen out of a fence and tried to carry it as had the man in the road, balancing it on his shoulder as he walked up and down a path in the back yard, but it fell and an end of it hit him on the side of the head raising a large bump.

Tar went back to sit alone on the front porch. There was to be a new baby in the house. He had heard his father and mother speak of it at night. With three children in the house younger than himself it was time he grew up.

His father was called "Captain" and "Major." Tar's mother sometimes called her husband "Richard." How grand to be a man and have so many names.

Tar had begun to wonder if he would ever be a man. How long to wait! How annoying to be sick and not [to be] able to go to school.

Nowdays, immediately after he had bolted his food, Dick Moorehead hurried away from the house. At night he did not come home until all had gone to bed. In the new town he had joined a brass band and belonged to several lodges.[49] When he did not have to work in the shop at night there was always a lodge to attend. Although his clothes had grown shabby Dick wore two or three brightly colored badges in the lapel of his coat and on special days gayly colored ribbons.

One Saturday evening when Dick came home from the shop something had happened.

All the house felt it. It was dark in the street outside and the evening meal had been waiting for a long time. When at last the children of the house heard their father's footsteps on

49. Irwin Anderson's career as showman and band member is covered in A Story Teller's Story, pp. 23–26, 56–58; Memoirs, p. 18; and "Discovery of a Father."

the sidewalk that led from the gate to the front door all became silent.

How very strange. The footsteps came along the hard road outside and then stopped before the house. Now the front gate had opened and Dick was going around the house to the kitchen door where all the rest of the Moorehead family were sitting and waiting. It was one of the days when Tar felt strong and [he] had come to the table. When the footsteps were still in the road outside his mother stood silently in the middle of the room but as they moved about the house she hurried to the stove. When Dick came to the kitchen door she did not look at him and all through the evening meal, eaten in a strange new kind of silence, she did not speak to her husband or to the children.

Dick had been drinking. Many times when he came home during that fall he had been drinking but the children had never before seen him when he was really off balance. When he had come along the road and the path that led around the house all of the children had recognized his footsteps that were at the same time not his footsteps. There was something wrong. All in the house felt it. Each step was taken uncertainly. The man had, quite deliberately perhaps, surrendered something of himself to some power outside himself. He had surrendered control over his faculties, his mind, his fancy, his tongue, the muscles of his own body. He was for the time quite helpless in the hands of something his children could not understand. There was a kind of assault upon the spirit of the house. At the kitchen door he a little lost control over himself and had to catch himself quickly, his hand on the door frame.

When he got into the room and had put aside his hat he went at once to where Tar sat. "Well, well, how are you little monkey?" he cried, standing before Tar's chair and laughing, a little foolishly. No doubt he felt the eyes of all the others upon him, felt the frightened silence of the room.

To pass it off he took Tar up in his arms and tried to go toward his place at the head of the table, to sit at the table. He almost fell. "How big you are getting," he said to Tar. He did not look at his wife.

Being in his father's arms was like being in the top of a tree pitched and tossed by a wind. When Dick had managed to get his balance again he got to the chair and sitting down put his cheek against Tar's. For several days he had not shaved and there was a half grown beard that hurt Tar's face and his father's long mustache was wet. His breath smelled of something strange and pungent. The smell made Tar a little ill but he did not cry. He was too frightened to cry.

The fright of the child, of all the children in the room, was something special. The feeling of discouragement that had for months brooded over the house had come to a head. Dick's drunkenness was a kind of assertion. "Well life has proven to be too much of a job. I shall let things go. There is a man in me and there is something else. I have tried being a man but I cannot make it. Look at me. Now I have become what I am. How do you like it?"

Watching his chance Tar crept out of his father's arms and went to sit near his mother. All of the children of the household had instinctively edged their chairs along the floor so that the father was left quite alone, with a wide open space on either side. Tar felt feverishly strong. His brain was making strange pictures, one after the other.

He kept thinking of trees. Now his father was like a tree in the middle of a great open meadow, a tree tossed by a wind, a wind all the others, standing at the edge of the meadow, could not feel.

The strange man who had suddenly come into the house was Tar's father and was at the same time not his father. The man's hands kept making uncertain movements. There were baked potatoes for supper and he tried to begin serving the children by sticking a fork into a potato but missed and the fork struck on the side of the dish. It made a sharp metallic sound. He tried two or three times and then Mary Moorehead, getting up from her place, walked around the table and took the dish away. Having been served all began eating in silence.

The silence was unbearable to Dick. There was a kind of accusation in it. All of life, now that he was married and the father of children, was a kind of accusation. "There is too much accusation. A man is what he is. You are expected to grow up, be a man, but what if you are not made that way?"

It was true Dick drank, that he did not save money, but other men were that way. "There is a lawyer in this very town who gets drunk two or three times every week but you look at him. He is successful. He makes money and dresses well. With me everything is a muddle. To tell the truth I made a mistake in being a soldier and going back on my father and brothers. I have always been making mistakes. Being a man is not so easy as it seems.

"I made a mistake when I married. I love my wife but I have been able to do nothing for her. Now she shall see me as I am. My children shall see me as I am. What do I care?"

Dick had worked himself into a state. He began to talk, addressing not his children or his wife but the kitchen stove that stood in a corner of the room. The children were eating in silence. All had grown white.

Tar turned to look at the stove. How odd, he thought, that a grown man should be talking to a stove. It was a thing such as a child like himself might have done when alone in a room but a man was a man. As his father talked he saw in fancy and quite distinctly the faces of people appearing and disappearing in the darkness back of the stove. The faces, called into being by the voice of his father, emerged quite distinctly out of the darkness back of the stove and then as rapidly disappeared. They danced in the air, became large and then small.

Dick Moorehead talked as though making a speech. There were certain men who, when he lived in another town and owned a harness shop, when he was a man of business and not, as now, a mere workman, had not paid for harnesses bought in his shop. "How can I get along if they do not pay?" he asked aloud. Now he held a small baked potato balanced on the end of a fork and began waving it about. Tar's mother was looking at her plate but his brother John, his sister Margaret and his younger brother Robert were all looking at their father with staring eyes. As for Tar's mother, when something happened she did not [understand or of which she did not] approve she went about the house with a strange lost look in her eyes. The eyes frightened. They frightened Dick Moorehead as well as the children. All became self-conscious, afraid. It was as though she had been struck a blow and when you looked at her you felt at once that your hand had delivered the blow.

The room in which the Mooreheads now sat was lighted only by a small oil lamp on the table and by the glow from the stove. As it was already late in the fall darkness had come. In the kitchen stove were many cracks through which ashes and bits of burning coal sometimes fell. The stove was bound together with wires. The Mooreheads were indeed very hard up just at that time. They had reached the low stage in all the memories Tar afterward kept of his childhood.[50]

Dick Moorehead declared his position in life a terrible one. In the house [sitting] at the table he kept looking into the darkness back of the kitchen stove and thinking of the men who owed him money. "Look at me. I am in a certain position. Well I have a wife and children. I have these children to feed and men owe me money they do not pay. I am down and out and they laugh at me. I want to do my part like a man but how can I manage?"

The drunken man began calling out a long list of names of men who he declared owed him money and Tar listened filled with wonder. It was an odd circumstance that when he grew to be a man and became a writer of tales Tar remembered many of the names called out by his father that evening. Many of them were afterwards attached to characters in stories of his.

His father called off names and condemned the men who had not paid for harnesses bought when he was prosperous and owned a shop of his own but Tar did not afterward connect the names with his father or with any injustice done to his father.

Something had happened [to Tar]. [*Tar] sat on a chair near his mother facing the stove in the corner.

Light appeared and disappeared on the wall. As Dick talked he held the small baked potato balanced on the end of a fork.

50. For parallel accounts of this low point, see *A Story Teller's Story*, p. 44; and *Memoirs*, p. 21.

The baked potato made dancing shadows on the face of the wall.

The outline of faces began to appear. As Dick Moorehead talked a movement began in the shadows.

One by one the names were called and then the faces appeared. Where had Tar seen the faces before? They were the faces of men seen passing the Moorehead house, faces seen traveling on trains, faces seen from the seat of the buggy that time Tar went into the country.

There was a man with a gold tooth and an old man with his hat pulled down over his eyes and these were followed by others. The man who had balanced the board on his [*shoulder] and who had called Tar's father "the Major" came out of the shadows to stand looking at Tar. The illness from which Tar had been suffering and from which he had begun to recover was now coming back. The cracks in the stove made dancing lights on the floor.

The faces Tar saw emerging so suddenly out of darkness and then so quickly disappearing he did not connect with his father. Each face as it appeared had for him a life of its own.

His father kept talking in the thick angry voice and the faces kept appearing and disappearing. The meal progressed but Tar did not eat. The faces seen in the shadows did not frighten, they filled the child with wonder.

He sat by the table looking occasionally at his angry father and from him to the men who had so mysteriously come into the room. How glad he was his mother was there. Did the others see what he saw?

The faces now dancing on the walls of the room were the faces of men. Sometime he would himself be a man. He watched and waited but as his father talked did not connect the faces with the words of condemnation that were coming from his lips.

Jim Gibson, Curtis Brown, Andrew Hartnett, Jacob Wills— men of an Ohio countryside, who had bought harnesses of a small harness maker and then had not paid. Names were themselves something to think about. Names were like houses, they were like pictures people hang on the walls of a room. When you see a picture you do not see what the man saw who painted the picture. When you go into a house you do not feel what the people feel who live in the house.

Names called out make a certain impression. Sounds also make pictures. There are too many pictures. When you are a child and ill the pictures crowd in upon each other too fast.

Now that he was ill Tar sat too much alone. On rainy days he sat by a window inside the house and on fair days sat on a chair on the porch.

His illness had made him habitually silent. All during his illness Tar's older brother John and his sister Margaret had been kind. John, who nowdays had much business going on, in the yard and in the road, and who was often visited by other boys, came to bring him marbles and Margaret came to sit with him and tell him happenings at school.

Tar sat staring about and saying nothing. How could he tell anyone what was going on inside? There was too much going on inside. With his weak body he could do nothing but inside his body there was intense activity.

Something peculiar there was, down inside, something constantly being torn apart and then joined together again. Tar did not understand and never did understand.

For one thing everything kept going far away. There was a tree at the side of the road before the Moorehead house that kept coming out of the ground and floating away into the sky. Tar's mother came to sit in the room with him. She was always at work. When she was not bending over the wash tub or over the ironing board, she was sewing.[51] She also, the chair in which she sat, even the walls of the room, seemed to float away. Something inside Tar struggled constantly to bring everything back and put everything in its place. If things would only stay in their places how calm and nice life would be.

Tar knew nothing of death but was afraid. Things that should be small became large, things that should remain large became small. Often Tar's own hands, white and small, seemed to leave his arms and float away. They floated away over the

51. Anderson does not in A Story Teller's Story or in Tar emphasize that his mother had to wash and sew for others, but that such was the condition appears in Memoirs, pp. 20, 26–27.

tops of the trees seen through the window, almost disappeared into the sky.

Not to have everything disappear was Tar's problem. It was a problem he could not explain to anyone, and absorbed him completely. Often the tree that had come out of the ground and had floated away became merely a black dot in the sky but it was his problem not to lose sight of it. If it happened that you lost sight of the tree you lost sight of everything. Tar did not know why that was true but it was. Grimly he held on.

If he held on the tree would come back, everything would come back. Someday he would get all adjusted again.

If Tar held on things would at last be all right. Of that he was quite sure.[52]

The faces in the street before the houses in which the Mooreheads had lived had sometimes floated across the fancy of the sick boy as now in the kitchen of the Moorehead house the faces were floating on the wall back of the stove.

Tar's father kept calling new names and new faces kept coming. Tar had grown very white.

The faces on the wall appeared and disappeared faster than ever. Tar's white small hands gripped the edges of his chair.

Had it become a test for him to follow with his fancy all of the faces, must he keep track of them as he did of the trees when they seemed to float into the sky?

The faces had become a whirling mass. His father's voice seemed far away.

Something slipped. Tar's hands that had been gripping so tightly the edges of his chair let go their hold and with a little sigh he slipped from the chair to the floor, into the darkness.

52. A similar mystic episode is described in *Memoirs*, pp. 39–40.

CHAPTER V

In the tenement districts of American cities, among the poor in small towns, strange things to be seen by a boy. Most of the houses in small Middle-western towns are without dignity. They are cheaply made, thrown together. The walls are thin. Everything was done in a hurry. What goes on in one room is known to the child who is ill in the next room. Well, he knows nothing. What he feels is another matter. He cannot tell what he feels.

At times Tar resented his father as he resented the fact of younger children. While he was still weak with illness, that time after the drunken episode, his mother was pregnant. He did not know the word, did not know definitely that another child was coming. Still he did know.

Sometimes, on warm clear days, he sat in a rocking-chair on the front porch. At night he lay on a cot in a room next to the father and mother's room, downstairs. John, Margaret and Robert were asleep upstairs. The baby lay in the bed with the father and mother. There was another baby in there, not born yet.

Tar had already seen things, heard things.

Before he became ill his mother was tall and slender. When she worked in the kitchen there was a babe lying on a chair, among pillows. For a time the baby fed at the breast. Then he began feeding from a bottle.

What a little pig! The eyes of the baby were screwed up in a peculiar way. He was crying before he got the bottle and then, when he had got it into his mouth, he stopped at once. The tiny face got red. When the bottle was empty the baby slept.

When there is a baby in the house there are always unpleasant smells. Women and girls do not mind.

When your mother becomes suddenly round like a barrel there is a reason. John and Margaret knew. It had happened before. Some children do not apply what they see and hear going on around them to their [own] lives. Others do. The three older children did not speak to each other of what was in the air. Robert was too young to know.

When you are a child and ill, as Tar was at that time, you get human things all mixed up in the mind with the animal life about. Cats screamed at night, cows bawled in the barns, dogs ran in packs along the road before the house. Something always stirring—in people, in animals, trees, flowers, grasses. How are you going to tell what is gross, what is fine? Kittens were born, calves, colts. Neighbor women had babies. A woman who lived near the Mooreheads had two at one time [—twins]. Judging from what people said hardly anything more tragic [than that] could happen.

Boys in small towns, after they begin going to school, write things on fences with chalk they steal from the schoolroom. They make pictures on the sides of barns and on the sidewalks.[53]

Even before he began going to school Tar [*knew things]. [*How had he found out?] His being ill may have made him more [*aware]. There was a queer feeling down inside—fear growing [in him]. His mother, his own relation to the tall woman going about the Moorehead house doing her housework, was in some way involved.

Tar's being ill made things difficult. He could not run about the yard, play ball, go off on adventurous trips to nearby fields. When the baby had his bottle and was asleep his mother brought her sewing and sat beside him. All was still in the house. If things could only stay like that. Now and then her hand stroked his hair and when she stopped he wanted to ask her to go on doing it always but could not get his lips to form the words.

Two boys of the town, John's age, went one day to a place where a small creek crossed a street. There was a wooden

53. Sherwood Anderson enrolled in "C Primary" (second grade) October 1, 1884, not the next grade in 1885–86, and in "D Grammar" in 1886–87 (repeated for absence, from illness perhaps). In high school, Anderson attended only from September through March, 1891–92, and January through February, 1893. See A Story Teller's Story, p. 115.

bridge with cracks between the boards and the boys crawled down under the bridge and lay quietly for a long time. They wanted to see something. Afterwards they came into the Moorehead yard and talked to John. Their being under the bridge had something to do with women crossing above. When they came to the Moorehead house Tar was sitting among pillows in the sun on the front porch and when they began to talk he pretended to be asleep. The boy who told John about the adventure whispered when he came to the important part but to Tar, who lay back among the pillows with his eyes closed, just the sound of the boy's voice whispering was like cloth being torn. It was like a curtain being torn so that you stand facing—what? [Nakedness perhaps. It takes time and maturity to get strength to face nakedness. Some never get it. Why should they? The dream may be more important than the fact. It depends on what you want.]

On another day Tar was in the same chair on the porch and Robert was playing in the street [outside]. He went off down the road to where there was a field and presently came running back. In the field he had seen something he wanted Tar to see. He could not tell what it was but his eyes were large and round and he whispered one word over and over. "Come, come on," he whispered and Tar got up out of the chair and went with him.

Tar was at that time so weak that as he hurried along at Robert's heels he had to stop several times to sit beside the road. Robert danced restlessly about in the dust in the middle of the road. "What is it?" Tar kept asking but his younger brother could not tell. If Mary Moorehead had not been so occupied with the babe already born and the one about to be born she might have kept Tar at home. Among so many children one child gets lost.

The two children came to the edge of a field surrounded by a rail fence. Elders and berry bushes grew thick between the fence and the road and they were in bloom [now]. Tar and his brother crawled in among the bushes and looked through the fence, between the rails.

What they saw was startling enough. No wonder Robert was excited. A sow had just given birth to a litter of pigs. It

must have happened while Robert was running to the house
[*to bring Tar].[54]

The mother pig stood facing the road and the two [wide-
eyed] children. Tar could look directly into her eyes. It was
all a part of the day's work with her, a part of the female pig's
life. It happened just as the trees happened to put on green
leaves in the spring, just as the berry bushes happened to bloom
and later bear fruit.

Only with trees, grasses, berry bushes, things were hidden
from sight. Trees and bushes did not have eyes across which
the shadows of pain flitted.

The mother pig stood for a moment and then lay down. She
still [*seemed looking] directly at Tar. There was something
on the grass beside her, a squirming mass of life. The secret
inner life of pigs was being revealed to [*the children]. The
mother pig had stiff white hairs growing on her nose and her
eyes were heavy with weariness. Often Tar's mother's eyes
looked like that. The children were so near the [mother] pig
that Tar could have put out his hand and touched her hairy
snout. Always, after that morning, he remembered the look in
[*her] eyes, the squirming things beside her. When he grew
to be a man and was himself tired or ill he walked in city
streets and saw [many] people with that look in their eyes.
People crowded into city streets, into tenements in cities, were
like squirming things on the grass at the edge of an Ohio field.
When he turned his eyes to the sidewalk or closed them for a
moment he saw again a mother pig trying to stand on her
trembling legs, lying down on the grass and then getting
wearily up.

For a moment Tar watched the scene before him and then,
lying down on the grass under the elders, closed his eyes. His
brother Robert went away. He crawled away to where the
bushes grew thicker, already looking for some new adventure.

Time passed. The elders in bloom beside the fence were very
fragrant and bees came in swarms. They made a droning soft
sound in the air above Tar's head. He felt very weak and sick
and wondered if he would be able to make his way back

54. In *Memoirs*, pp. 18–19, Anderson watches the pigs' birth with
his sister Stella.

[°home]. As he lay thus a man came along the road and, as
though sensing the boy's presence under the bushes, stopped
and stood staring.

The man was a half witted fellow who lived several doors
away from the Mooreheads and on the same street. He was
thirty years old but had the mind of a child of four. All
Middle-western towns have such fellows.[55] All their lives they
remain gentle or one of them becomes suddenly vicious. In
small towns they live with relatives who are usually working
people and [they] are neglected by everyone. People give them
old clothes, too large or too small for their bodies.

[Well, they are of no use. They earn nothing. They must be
fed and have a place to sleep until they die.]

The half witted man did not see Tar. He may have heard
the mother pig moving about in the field beyond the bushes.
Now she had got to her feet and the little pigs—five of them—
were being cleansed and prepared for life. Already they were
at the business of being fed. When feeding little pigs make a
sound like a baby. They screw up their eyes in the same way.
Their faces get red and after they have been fed they sleep.

Some sense in feeding little pigs. They grow big rapidly
and may be sold for money.

The half witted man stood looking toward the field. Life may
be a comedy half witted people understand. The man opened
his mouth and laughed softly. In Tar's memory the scene and
the moment remained unique. It seemed to him afterward that,
at the moment, the sky overhead, the bushes with their blossoms, the bees droning in the air, even the ground on which he
lay had begun to laugh.

[°And then] the new [°Moorehead] baby was born.[56] It
happened at night. Such things usually do. Tar was in the
front room of the [Moorehead] house, wide awake, but he
managed to create the impression that he was asleep.

At first, that night when it began, there was the sound of

55. Such a character, Mook, appears in "'Queer'," *Winesburg, Ohio*,
pp. 190–91; and a similar one in *Memoirs*, pp. 28–29.

56. This is the birth of Sherwood's brother Earl, herein called "Joe,"
in 1885.

someone groaning. It did not sound like Tar's mother. She never groaned. Then someone moved restlessly in the bed in the next room. Dick Moorehead [*was awake]. "Had I better get up?" A low voice answered and there was another groan. Dick hurried about getting into his clothes. He came into the front room, carrying a lamp, and stood by Tar's cot. "He's asleep in [*here]. Had I better wake him up and take him upstairs?" More whispered words intercepted by [more] groans. The lamp in the bedroom shed a faint light through the open door into the room.

They had decided to let him remain. Dick put on his overcoat and went out the back way, through the kitchen door. He had put on the coat because it was raining. The rain made a steady pounding sound on the side of the house. Tar could hear his footsteps on the boards leading round the house to the front gate. The boards were merely thrown on the ground and some of them had become old and warped. When you stepped on them you had to be careful. In the darkness Dick had bad luck. There was a low muttered curse. He was standing [out there] in the rain rubbing his shin. Tar heard his footsteps on the sidewalk outside and then the sound grew faint. It could not be heard above the steady sound of the rain on the side walls of the house.

[*Tar lay], listening intensely. He was like a young quail crouched [down] under leaves when a dog is ranging a field. Not a muscle of his body moved. In a household like the Mooreheads' a child does not run instinctively to the mother. Love, warmth, the natural expression of [*tenderness], all such [*impulses] are buried away. Tar had to live his own life, lie quiet and wait. Most Middle-western families [*of the old days] were like that.

Tar lay [in the bed] listening [a long time]. His mother groaned softly. She stirred [about] in her bed. What was going on?

Tar knew because he had seen the pigs born in the field, [he] knew because what was happening in the Moorehead house was always happening in some house on a street in which the Mooreheads lived. It happened to neighbor women and to horses, to dogs, to cows. Chickens, turkeys and birds got born out of eggs. That was much better. The mother bird did not groan with pain [*while it was going on].

It would have been better[, *Tar thought,] if he had not seen the thing in the field, if he had not seen the look of pain in a mother pig's eyes. His own illness had been something special. His body was weak sometimes but there was no pain. It was a thing of dreams, of distorted dreams that would not come to an end. He always, when the bad times were on, had to hold onto something to keep from falling [*away] into nothingness, into some black cold [*dismal] place.

If Tar had not seen the mother pig in the field, if older boys had not come into the yard and talked [to John]. . . .

The mother pig, standing in the field, had a look of pain in her eyes. She made a sound that was like a groan.

She had long dirty white hairs on her nose.

The sound coming from the nearby room did not seem to come from Tar's mother. She was to him something lovely. [Birth was ugly, shocking. It could not be her.] [*He clung to that thought. What was going on was shocking. It could not happen to her.] That was a comforting thought [*when it came]. He held onto [*the thought]. There was a trick his illness had taught him. When [*he felt he was] about to fall into darkness, into nothingness, [*he] just hung on. There was something inside him that helped.

Once that night, during the period of waiting, Tar crept out of bed. He was quite sure his mother was not in the next room, that it was not her he heard groaning [*in there] but he wanted to be [*quite sure]. He would creep to the door and look. When he had got his feet to the floor and stood upright the groans in the room stopped. "Well, you see," [*he told himself,] "what I heard was just made up." He got silently back into bed and the groans started again.

His father came with the doctor. He had never been to the house before. Such things happen unexpectedly. The doctor you plan to get is out of town. He had gone off to [*a] patient in the country. You do the best you can.

The doctor [who had come] was a large man with a great voice. He came into the house with his booming voice and a neighbor woman also came. Tar's father came and closed the door that led into the bedroom.

Again he got out of bed but did not go toward the door leading to the bedroom. He knelt beside the cot and felt around until he had got hold of the pillow and then buried his face. He pressed the pillow against his cheeks. In that way it was possible to shut out all sounds.

What Tar achieved [by pressing the soft pillow against his ear, by burying his face in the worn pillow] was a sense of nearness to his mother. She could not be in the next room groaning. Where was she? Birth was a thing belonging to the world of pigs, [*to] cows and horses[, *and to other women]. What was happening in the next room was not happening to her. His own breath, after his face had been for a few moments buried in the pillow, made [it] a warm place. The dreary sound of the rain outside the house, the booming sound of the doctor's voice, the queer apologetic voice of his father, the neighbor woman's voice—all sounds were shut out. His mother had gone away somewhere but he could hold onto his [own] thoughts of her. It was a trick his illness had taught him.

Once or twice, since he had been old enough to be conscious of such things, and in particular since he had been ill, his mother had taken him into her arms and had pressed his face [down thus] against her body. That was at a moment when the younger baby in the house was asleep. If there were no babies it would happen oftener.

With his face buried in the pillow, his arms embracing it, he achieved the illusion.

[*Well, he] did not want his mother to have another baby. He did not want her lying groaning in a bed. He wanted her in the dark [front] room with himself.

In fancy he [*could bring] her there. When you have an illusion hang on[to it].

Tar hung on grimly. Time passed. When at last he lifted his face from the pillow all was quiet in the house. The silence frightened him a little. Now he thought himself quite convinced nothing had happened.

He went softly to the bedroom door and opened it softly.

There was a lamp on a table and his mother was lying in the
bed with her eyes closed. She was very white. Dick Moorehead
was in the kitchen sitting in a chair by the stove. He had got
wet going out into the rain and was drying his clothes.

The neighbor woman had water in a pan and was washing
something.

Tar stood by the door until the new baby cried. It had to be
dressed now. Now it would begin to wear clothes. It would not
be like a little pig, a puppy, a kitten. Its clothes would not
grow on it. It would have to be taken care of, dressed, washed.
After a time it would begin to dress itself, wash itself. Tar
already did that.

Now he could accept the fact of the new baby. It was the
matter of being born he could not bear. Now it was done.
[Nothing to do about it now.]

He stood by the door trembling and when the baby cried
his mother opened her eyes. It had cried before but with the
pillow pressed against his ears Tar had not heard. His father
sitting in the kitchen did not move [or look up]. He sat staring at the lighted stove[, a discouraged looking figure]. Steam
arose from his [wet] clothes.

Nothing moved but the eyes of Tar's mother and he did not
know whether or not she saw him standing there. The eyes
seemed to be looking reproachfully at him and he backed
softly out of the room into the darkness [of the front room].

In the morning Tar went into the bedroom with John, Robert
and Margaret. Margaret went at once to the new baby. She
kissed it. Tar did not look. He, John and Robert stood at the
foot of the bed and said nothing. There was something stirring,
under the covers, beside the mother. They were told it was a
boy.

They went outside. After the rain of the night the morning
was bright and clear. Fortunately for John a boy of his own
age came along the street and he called to him and hurried off.

Robert went into the woodshed at the back of the house. He
had [some sort of] business going on in there with wooden
blocks.

Well, he was all right and so was Tar [now]. The worst was

over. Dick Moorehead would go uptown and into a saloon. He had been through a hard night and would want a drink. While he was drinking he would tell the bartender the news and the bartender would smile. John would tell the neighbor boy. It might be he already knew. Such news travels fast in a small town. [*For a few days] the boys and the father would alike be [*half] ashamed, [*with] a kind of queer secret shame, and then it would pass off.

In time they would [all] accept the new baby as one of themselves.

Tar was weak from his night's adventure but so also was his mother. John and Robert felt the same way. [*It had been a strange hard night in the house and now that it was over Tar was relieved.] He wouldn't have to think about it [*again]. A baby is just a baby but [*to a boy] an unborn baby in the house is something [*he is glad to see come out into the light].

PART II

CHAPTER VI

HENRY FULTON was a thick-shouldered, thick-headed boy much larger than Tar. They lived in the same part of an Ohio town and when Tar went to school he had to walk right past the Fulton place. There was a small frame house, on the bank of a creek and near a bridge, and back of it, in the little valley made by the creek, was a corn field and a thicket of uncleared land. Henry's mother was a stout red-faced woman who went about the back yard in her bare feet. Her husband drove a dray. Tar could go to school another way. He could walk along a railroad embankment or go clear around by the waterworks pond, nearly a half mile out of the way.

The railroad embankment was fun. There was a certain risk. Tar had to cross the railroad bridge, built high up over the creek, and when he was in the middle of it he looked down. Then he glanced nervously up and down the tracks and shivers ran through his body. What if a train should come? He planned what he would do. Well, he would lie flat on the tracks, letting the train pass over him. A boy at school had told him of another boy who did that. It took nerve, I tell you. You have to lie flat as a pancake and must not move a muscle.

And so along comes the train. The engineer sees you but cannot stop his train. It rushes on. If you keep your nerve now what a tale you will have to tell. Not so many boys have been run over by trains and not got a scratch either. Sometimes when Tar went to school by the railroad embankment he almost wished a train would come. It should be a fast passenger train going at sixty miles an hour. There is a thing called "suction" you have to watch out for. Tar and a boy friend at school had discussed that. "There was a boy once who stood close beside the tracks when the train went through. He got too close. The suction drew him right under the train. Suction is a thing that pulls at you. It hasn't got any hands but you'd better look out."

Why had Henry Fulton got it in for Tar? John Moorehead walked right past his house, never thinking. Even little Robert

Moorehead, who was now in the baby room, the primary, went that way without thinking anything about it. Whether or not Henry really wanted to punch Tar was the question. How could Tar tell? When Henry saw Tar he shouted and made for him. Henry had strange-looking small grey eyes. His hair was red and stood straight up on his head and when he rushed at Tar he laughed and the laugh gave Tar the shivers, like walking over the railroad bridge.

About the suction now, when you have been caught walking across a railroad bridge. When the train is coming you want to tuck your shirt down tight inside your pants. If an end of your shirt sticks up it catches on some whirling thing under the train and you are drawn right up. Talk about sausage!

The best part is when the train has passed. At last the engineer has stopped his engine. The passengers climb off. Everyone is pale, of course. Tar would lie still for a little while because now he wasn't scared. He would fool 'em a little just for a joke. When they got to where he was, the white anxious people, up he would jump and walk off as cool as a cucumber. The story would get all over town. After that happened, if a boy like Henry Fulton took after him, there would always be a big boy around to take Tar's part. "Well, he's got moral courage, that's it. It's a thing generals have in battle. They don't fight. Sometimes they are little fellows. You could put Napoleon Bonaparte in the neck of a bottle—almost."

Tar knew a lot about "moral courage" because his father often spoke of it. It's something like suction. You couldn't describe it or see it but it was as strong as a horse.

As it was Tar might have asked John Moorehead to take his part against Henry [*Fulton] but after all he couldn't. You can't let on about things like that to an older brother.

There was another thing he might do about being run over by a train, if he had the nerve. He might wait until the train was almost upon him. Then he could drop through between two of the railroad ties and hang by his hands like a bat. Maybe that would be the best way.

The house in which the Mooreheads now lived was larger than any during Tar's time. Things had changed. Tar's mother caressed her children more than she used to, she talked more and Dick Moorehead spent more time at home. Nowdays he was always taking some of the children with him when he went house or sign painting on Saturdays.[1] He drank some but not so much as he did, just enough to make him talk well. It didn't take much for that.

As for Tar, he was now all right. He was in the third room at school. Robert was in the primary. There had been two new babies, little Fern, who died within a month after she was born, Will, still a baby almost, and Joe. Although Tar did not know it Fern was to be the last baby born to the family.[2] For some reason, and although he had always resented Robert, Will and the baby Joe were great fun. Tar even liked to take care of Joe, not too often but now and then. You could tickle his toes and he made the funniest sounds. It made you laugh to think you had once been like that, couldn't talk, couldn't walk about, had to have someone feed you.

A boy could not understand older people most of the time, no use trying. Sometimes Tar's parents were one way, sometimes another. If he depended on his mother it wouldn't work. She had babies and had to think about them, after they came. The first two or three years a baby isn't any good, while a horse, big as he is, can work and everything when he is three.

Sometimes Tar's father was all right and then again he was all wrong. When Tar and Robert went with him, sign painting on fences on Saturdays, and when there were no older people about he was o. k. Sometimes he told about the battle of Vicksburg. He really won the battle. Well, anyway he told General Grant what to do and he did it but afterward General Grant never gave Dick any credit. The fact is that after the city was won General Grant left Tar's father out West with the army of occupation while he took General Sherman, Sheridan and a lot of other officers with him down East, and let them have chances Dick never had. Dick never even got promoted. He

1. Anderson recalls accompanying his father on painting trips in A Story Teller's Story, pp. 5–7, 72–75, 93–94; and Memoirs, p. 26.
2. Fern Anderson, the last of Sherwood's brothers and sisters, may have died in December, 1892, making her almost two years old at her death.

was a captain before the battle of Vicksburg and a captain afterwards. It would have been better if he had never told General Grant how to win the battle. If Grant had taken Dick down East he wouldn't have been so long licking General Lee. Dick would have thought up a plan. He did think up one but he never told anyone.

"I tell you what. If you tell another man how to do something and he does it and it works then, afterwards, he doesn't like you much. He wants all the credit for himself. As though there weren't enough to go around. That's the way men are."

Dick Moorehead was all right when there were no other men about but let another man come along and then what? They talked and talked, about nothing mostly. You never got hardly any sign painting done.

The best thing, Tar thought, would be to have a friend who was another boy nearly ten years older. Tar was smart. He had skipped a whole grade in school already and he could skip another grade if he wanted to. Maybe he would. The best thing would be to have a boy friend who was strong as an ox but dumb. Tar would get his lessons for him and he would do Tar's fighting. Well, in the morning he would come around Tar's way to go to school with him. Tar and he would walk right past Henry Fulton's house. Henry had better keep out of sight.

Older people got strange ideas into their heads. When Tar was in the first grade at school, the primary (he stayed there only two or three weeks because his mother had taught him his letters and how to read when he was sick that time) when he was in the primary Tar told a lie. He said he did not throw a stone that broke a window in the school house when everyone knew he did.

Tar said he did not do it and stuck to the lie. What a fuss was made. The teacher came to the Moorehead house to talk to Tar's mother. What everyone said was that if he would confess, own up, he would feel better.

Tar had stuck it out for a long time. He wasn't allowed to go to school for three days. How strangely his mother acted, so unreasonable. You wouldn't have expected it from her. He would go into the house all cheered up to see if she had forgotten the whole nonsensical business but she never had. She agreed with the teacher that if he would own up everything would be all right. Even Margaret got to talking that way. John had more sense. He kept out of it, never said a word.

And it was all foolishness. Finally Tar did own up. The truth was that by that time there had been such a fuss made that he could not rightly remember whether he had thrown the stone or not. And what if he did? What of it? Another glass had already been put in the window. It was only a small stone. Tar wasn't throwing at the window. That was the whole point.

If he owned up to a thing like that he got credit for something he never intended doing at all.

Tar had finally confessed. Of course he had felt badly during the three days. No one knew how he did feel. What you've got at such a time is moral courage and that's what people can't understand. When everyone is against you what are you going to do? Sometimes, during the three days, he cried when no one was looking.

It was his mother who really got him to own up. He was sitting with her on the back porch and she said again that if he would own up he would feel all right. How had she known he wasn't feeling all right?

He did own up, all of a sudden, without thinking.

Then his mother was satisfied, the teacher was satisfied, everyone was satisfied. After he had told what they thought was the truth he went out to the barn. His mother had put her arms about him but that one time her arms did not feel so good. It was better not to tell a lie like that when everyone is going to make such a fuss [*about it] [but] after you have told it. . . . Anyway, during the three days; everyone had found out something. Tar could stick to a thing when he had made up his mind.

The best part of the place where the Mooreheads now lived was that it had a barn. Of course there wasn't any horse or cow but a barn is a barn.

After Tar confessed that time he went out to the barn and crawled up into the empty loft. What an empty feeling inside too—the lie gone. When he was holding out even Margaret, who had to go and preach, had a kind of admiration for him. If, when Tar grew to be a man, he ever became a great criminal like Jesse James or someone and got caught, they would never get any confession out of him. He had made up his mind to that. He would defy them all. "Well, go ahead, hang me then." As he stood upon the gallows he would smile and wave his hand. If they let him he would wear his Sunday suit—all white. "Ladies and gentlemen, I, the notorious Jesse James, am about to die. I've something I want to say. You think you can make me come down off my perch. Well, try it.

"You can all go to hell, that's where you can go."

That's the way to do a thing like that. Grown people have such mixed-up ideas. There are a lot of things they never get straight.

When you have a boy friend ten years older who is stout but dumb you are all right. There was a boy named Elmer Cowley Tar thought might almost have done for the place but he was too dumb.[3] And then besides he never paid any attention to Tar. He wanted to be John's friend but John would not have him. "Ah, he's a block-head," John said. If he hadn't been quite so dumb and had taken a notion to Tar it might have been just the thing.

The trouble with a boy like that, who was too dumb, was that he would never get the point. Let Henry Fulton get after Tar when they were going to school in the morning and like as not Elmer would only laugh. If Henry really started pounding Tar he might rush in but that wasn't the point either. Pounding isn't the worst part. It's expecting to be pounded that is the worst of all. If a boy isn't smart enough to know that, what good is he?

The trouble with going around by the railroad bridge or by the waterworks pond was that it made Tar out a coward to himself. What if no one knew? What difference did that make?

Henry Fulton had a gift Tar would have given much to pos-

3. Elmer Cowley appears as the central figure in " 'Queer,' " *Winesburg, Ohio*, pp. 190–201.

sess. The chances were he only wanted to scare Tar because Tar had caught up with him in school. Henry was nearly two years older, but they were both in the same room and both by ill luck lived at the same end of town.

About Henry's special gift. He was a born "butter." Some are born that way. Tar wished he had been. Henry could put down his head and run against anything and it did not seem to hurt his head at all.

In the school house yard there was a high board fence and Henry could stand back and take a flying run, hitting the fence with all his might and afterwards only smile. You could hear the boards of the fence crack. Once, at home in the barn, Tar gave the thing a trial. He did not run full speed and afterwards he was glad he didn't. His head was sore enough as it was. If you haven't a gift you haven't it. You might as well give the matter up.

The only gift Tar had was that he was smart. It isn't anything at all to get such lessons as they give you in school. There are always a lot of dumb boys in your class and the whole class has to wait for them. If you've got any sense you don't have to work much. It isn't any fun though to be smart. What good does it do?

A boy like Henry Fulton had more fun than a dozen smart boys. At the recess time all the other boys gathered around. Tar kept in the background only because Henry had got that notion of taking after him.

In the school yard there was a high board fence. At the recess time the girls played on one side the fence, the boys on the other. Margaret was over there on the other side with the girls. On the fence the boys drew pictures. They threw stones and, in the winter[time], snowballs over the fence.

What Henry Fulton did was to knock loose one of the boards with his head. Some older boys put him up to it. Henry was really dumb. He would have been a good one to be Tar's friend, the best one in school, counting the talent he had, but it wasn't to be.

Henry ran against the fence full tilt, then he ran again. The board had begun to give a little. It began to creak. The girls on their side knew what was going on and all the boys were gathered around. Tar was so jealous of Henry that it made him ache inside.

Bang, Henry's head went against the fence and then he drew back and, bang, it went again. He said it didn't hurt at all. Maybe he lied, still his head must have been tough. Other boys went up to feel of it. There wasn't any bump raised at all.

And then the board gave way. It was a wide board and Henry had knocked it right out of the fence. You could have crawled right through to the girls' side.

Afterwards when they were all back in the room the superintendent of the school came to the door of the room in which both Tar and Henry sat. He, the superintendent, was a large man with a black beard and he admired Tar. All the older Mooreheads, John, Margaret and Tar, had a record for being smart and that is what a man like a superintendent [*admires].

"Another one of Mary Moorehead's children. And you jumped a grade. Well, you're a smart lot."

The whole school room had heard him say that. It put a boy in bad. Why didn't the man keep his mouth shut?

He, the superintendent, was always lending books to John and Margaret. He told all three of the older Moorehead children to come to his house anytime and get any book they wanted.

It was fun to read books all right. *Rob Roy, Robinson Crusoe, The Swiss Family Robinson.* Margaret read the Elsie Books but she did not get them from the superintendent. A dark pale woman who clerked in the post office started lending them to her.[4] They made her cry but she liked it. Girls like nothing better than crying. In the Elsie Books a girl, about Margaret's age, was sitting at a piano. Her mother was dead and she was afraid her papa was going to marry another woman, an adventuress, who was sitting right in the room. She, the adventuress, was the kind of woman who would make a fuss over a little girl, kiss her and pet her when her father was around, and then

---

4. Elsie Dinsmook, heroine of twenty-eight novels by Martha Foley (1828–1909), most popular childrens' author of the nineteenth century. The postmistress, Gertrude Wilmot, appears briefly in *Winesburg, Ohio*, p. 245.

maybe hit her a clip over the head when her papa wasn't looking, that is to say after she'd married the papa.

Margaret read that part of one of the Elsie Books to Tar. She
just had to read it to someone. "It was so full of feeling," she
said. She cried when she read it.

Books are all right but it's better not to let other boys know
you like them. It's all right to be smart but when the superintendent of the school gives you away, right before everyone,
what fun is there in that?

That day when Henry Fulton butted the board out of the
fence at the recess time the superintendent came to the door of
the room with a whip in his hand and called Henry Fulton out.
There was a dead silence in the room.

Henry was going to get a beating and Tar was glad. At the
same time he wasn't glad.

What would happen would be that Henry would walk right
out and take it as cool as you please.

He would get a lot of credit he did not deserve. If Tar's head
had been made like that he could have butted a board out of
the fence too. If they would whip a boy for being smart, for
having his lessons so he could reel them right off, he'd get as
many lickings as any boy in school.

In the school room the woman teacher was silent, all the
children were silent while Henry got up and went to the door.
He made a loud clattering sound with his feet.

Tar could not help hating him because he was so brave. He
wanted to lean over to the boy who sat in the next seat and ask
a question. "Do you suppose . . . ?"

What Tar wanted to ask the boy was rather hard to put into
words. There was a hypothetical question to be asked. "If you
were a boy, born with a thick head and could knock boards out
of fences and if the superintendent found you out (probably
because some girl told) and you were going to be whipped and
were in a hall alone with the superintendent, would the same
kind of nerve that led you not to let on it hurt your head to the
other boys when you butted a fence, would the same kind of
nerve you had then lead you to butt the superintendent?"

Standing up and just taking a licking without crying wasn't
anything. Even Tar could do that, maybe.

Now Tar had got himself into one of his thinking times, one

of his questioning moods. One of the reasons it was fun to read books was that while you were reading, if the book was any good and had any good exciting places in it, you did not think or ask questions while you were reading. At other times—oh well.

Tar now was in one of his bad times. What he did when he was in such times was to make himself do, in imagination, what maybe he never would do if he had the chance. Then sometimes he was betrayed into telling others what he had imagined as a fact. That was all right too but nearly every time someone caught him. It was the kind of thing Tar's father was always doing but his mother did not do it. That was why nearly everyone respected his mother so much while they liked his father and did not respect him hardly at all. Even Tar knew the difference.

Tar wanted to be like his mother but had a secret fear he was growing more like his father all the time. It made him sick inside to realize it sometimes and still he could not help being as he was.[5]

He was doing the thing now. Instead of Henry Fulton, he, Tar Moorehead, had just marched out of the room. He was not born to be a butter, try as hard as he might, he never could knock a board out of a fence with his head but here he was pretending he could.

He had in fancy just been marched out of the school room and was alone with the superintendent in a hall where the children hung up their hats and coats.

There was a stairway leading down. Tar's room was on the second floor.

The superintendent went along as cool as you please. It was all [*a] part of the day's work with him. You caught a boy doing something and whipped him. If he cried all right. If he did not cry, was one of the stubborn kind that would not cry, you just hit him a few extra clips for good luck and let him go. What else could you do?

There was a place right at the head of the stairs, an open space. That was where the superintendent did the whipping.

5. The same fear occurs in *A Story Teller's Story*, pp. 57–58.

All right for Henry Fulton but what about Tar?

When he, Tar, was out there, in fancy, what a difference. What he did was to walk along, just as Henry would have done, but he was thinking and planning. Here's where smartness comes in. If you've got a thick head that will knock boards out of fences you get credit all right but you can't think.

Tar was thinking about the time when the superintendent went and called the attention of the whole room to his Moorehead smartness. Now was the time to get even.

The superintendent wouldn't be expecting nothing at all, not from a Moorehead. He would be thinking, because they were smart, they were a lot of sissies. Well, they weren't. Maybe Margaret was one but John wasn't. You ought to see him clip Elmer Cowley on the chin.

If you can't butt fences that doesn't mean you can't butt people. People are pretty soft, right in the middle. What made Napoleon Bonaparte such a great man, Dick said, was that he was always doing what no one expected.

What Tar did, in fancy, was to walk along before the superintendent right to that place at the head of the stairs. He had got a little ahead, just enough to give him a flying start, and then he turned. He used just the technique Henry used on fences. Well, he had watched often enough. He knew how it was done.

He took a flying start and aimed right for the soft place in the superintendent's middle and he hit it too.

He knocked the superintendent down a flight of stairs. It made a racket. People, women teachers and scholars, came running into the hall from all the rooms. Tar was trembling all over. Imaginative people, when they do anything like that, always tremble afterward.

Tar was trembling as he sat in the school room, having done nothing. When he got through thinking a thing like that out he was trembling so that when he tried to write something on a slate he couldn't. His hand trembled so he could hardly hold a pencil. If anyone wanted to know why he was so sick that time Dick came home drunk there it was. If you're made that way you are.

Henry Fulton had come back into the room as cool as you please. Of course all the others were looking at him.

What had he done? He had taken a licking without crying. People thought he was brave.

Had he knocked a superintendent down a flight of stairs as Tar had? Had he used his brains? What was the good having a head that was good for butting boards out of fences when you didn't know enough to butt the right thing at the right time?

CHAPTER VII

WHAT was really hardest for Tar, the bitterest thing of all to face, was that a fellow like himself hardly ever worked any of his fine schemes out into facts. Tar did once.

He was coming home from school and Robert was with him. It was spring and there was a flood. Over by the Fulton house the creek was full and was tearing under the bridge that stood right near the house.

Tar had not wanted to go home that way but Robert was with him. You can't be always explaining.

The two boys went along the street down through the little valley that led up to the part of the town where they lived and there was Henry Fulton with two other boys, Tar did not know, standing on the bridge and throwing sticks into the creek.

They threw them in on the upside and then ran across the bridge to see them shoot out. Maybe, that time, Henry never intended to take after Tar and show him up for a coward.

Who knows what anyone thinks, what they intend? How can you tell?

What Tar did was to walk along with Robert as though there wasn't any such person as Henry. Robert was talking and chattering away. One of the boys threw a large stick into the creek and it went bounding under the bridge. Suddenly all three of the boys turned and looked at Tar and Robert. Robert was all for joining in the fun, getting some sticks and throwing them in.

Tar was in one of his bad times again. If you are the kind that has such times you are always thinking—"Now so and so is going to do so and so." Maybe they aren't at all. How do you know? If you are that kind what you think people are going to do is just as bad as what they do. Henry, when he saw Tar alone, was always putting down his head, squinting up his eyes and taking after him. Tar ran like a scared cat and then Henry stopped running and laughed. Everyone who saw it laughed. He couldn't catch Tar running and knew he couldn't.

At the edge of the bridge Tar stopped. The other boys were

not looking and Robert wasn't paying any attention but Henry was looking. What funny eyes he had. He was leaning against the railing of the bridge.

The two boys stood looking at each other. What a situation! Tar was then as he was all through his life. Let him alone, let him think and have fancies and he could work you out a perfect scheme for anything. That's what later made him able to tell stories. When you write or tell stories you can make things come out just fine. What do you suppose Dick would have done if he had been compelled to stay around where General Grant was after the Civil War? It would have crabbed his style something awful.

A writer is all right writing and a story teller is all right telling stories but what if you put him in a position where he has to act? Such a person is always doing either the right thing at the wrong time or the wrong thing at the right time.

Maybe, that time, Henry Fulton did not intend to take after Tar and show him up for a coward before Robert and the two strange boys. Maybe Henry wasn't thinking of anything but throwing sticks in the creek.

How was Tar to know? He was thinking, "Now he is going to put down his head and butt me. If I run Robert and the others will begin to laugh. Like as not Robert will go home and tell John." Robert was a pretty good sport, for a kid, but you can't expect a young kid to use good judgment. You can't expect him to know when to keep his mouth shut.

Tar moved a few steps across the bridge toward Henry. Pshaw, now he was trembling again. What was the matter with him? What was he going to do?

It all came of being smart, of thinking you are going to do something when you aren't. At school Tar had been thinking about that soft spot in people's middle, about butting the superintendent down [*the] stairs—a thing he would never have had the nerve to try to do really—and now.

Was he going to try to butt the champion butter? What a foolish notion. Tar almost felt like laughing at himself. Of course Henry did not expect any such thing. He would have had to be pretty smart to ever expect any boy to butt him and he wasn't smart. That wasn't his line.

Another step, another and another. Tar was in the middle of the bridge. He made a quick dive and—great Scott—he had done it. He had butted Henry, had hit him right in the middle.

The worse time came when it was done. What happened was that Henry, expecting nothing, was caught off guard. He doubled up and went right through the bridge railing into the creek. He was on the up[stream] side of the bridge and at once his body disappeared. Whether he could swim or not Tar did not know. As there was a flood the creek was fairly raging along.

As it turned out it was one of the few times in his life Tar ever did anything that really turned out pretty well. At first he just stood trembling. All the other boys were struck dumb with amazement and did not do a thing. Henry had disappeared. It may have been that only a second passed before he appeared again but it seemed to Tar hours. He ran to the railing of the bridge as did all the others. One of the strange boys ran toward the Fulton house to tell Henry's mother. In another minute or two Henry's dead body would be dragged ashore. Henry's mother would be leaning over it and crying.[6]

What would Tar do? Of course the town marshal would come for him.

After all it might not be so bad—if he kept his nerve and did not run or cry. He would be led right up through town, everyone looking, everyone pointing. "That's Tar Moorehead, the murderer. He murdered Henry Fulton, the champion butter. He butted him to his death."

It would not be half bad if it weren't for the hanging in the end.

What happened was that Henry got out of the creek by himself. It wasn't nearly as deep as it looked and he could swim.

The whole thing would have turned out fine for Tar if he hadn't been so trembly. Instead of staying where the two strange boys could see how cool and collected he was he had to [*leave].

He did not even want to be with Robert, not for a time. "You

6. The death of a child by drowning appears in *Memoirs*, p. 50.

cut on home and you keep your mouth shut," he managed to say. He hoped Robert would not know how upset he was, would not notice how his voice trembled.

Tar went over by the waterworks pond and sat under a tree. He was disgusted with himself. Henry Fulton had a scared look on his face when he crawled out of the creek and Tar thought maybe now Henry would be scared of him all the time. For just a second Henry had stood on the bank of the creek looking at Tar. [*Tar] wasn't crying [*anyway]. What Henry's eyes were saying was this—"You're crazy. Sure I'm afraid of you. You're crazy. A fellow can't tell what you'll do."

"It was all right and a gain," Tar thought. Ever since he had been going to school he had been planning something and now he had done it.

If you are a boy and read aren't you always reading about such things? There is a bully in the school and a smart boy, who is pale and not very well. One day, to everyone's surprise, he licks the bully of the school. What he has is a thing called "moral courage." It's like "suction." That's what carries him through. He uses his head, learns to box. When the two boys meet it is a contest between brains and brawn and brains win.

That was all right, Tar thought. It was just the sort of thing he was always planning to do and never doing.

What it came down to was this—if he had planned in advance to out-butt Henry Fulton, if he had practised up, say on Robert or Elmer Cowley, and then if, in front of everyone in school, during the recess time, he had walked right up to Henry and had challenged him. . . .

What was the use? Tar stayed over by the waterworks pond a while, until his nerves got less trembly, and then went home. Robert was there and so was John and Robert had told John.

It was pretty fine. Tar was a hero after all. John made a fuss over him and wanted him to tell about it and he did.

When he told he was all right. Well, he could put in certain flourishes. The thoughts he had been having when he was alone went away. He could make it sound pretty good.

After all the story would get around. If Henry Fulton thought he, Tar, was a little crazy and a desperate fellow he would keep his hands off. Older boys who did not know what Tar knew would think he, Tar, had planned it all out and had done it all with cool determination. Bigger boys would begin to want to be his friend. That's the way boys are.

It was pretty good after all, Tar thought, and he began to strut a little. Not too much. He had to be careful now. John was pretty foxy. If he put it on too thick he would be found out.

Doing a thing is one thing and telling about it is another.

At the telling Tar thought he wasn't so bad.

Anyway, when you tell about it you can use your brains. The trouble with Dick Moorehead, Tar had even then begun to suspect, was that when he told his stories he laid it on a little too thick. Better let others do most of the talking. If others lay it on a little thick, as Robert was now doing, shrug your shoulders. Deny it. Pretend not to want any credit. "Ah, I never did nothing."

That was the way. Tar had now got ground under his feet. The story of what had happened at the bridge, when he had done something without thinking, in a crazy kind of way, had begun to re-shape itself in his fancy. If he could keep the truth down for a time it would be all right. He could reconstruct the whole thing to his liking.

There were only John and his mother to fear. If his mother heard of the story she might smile one of her smiles.

Tar thought he would be all right if only Robert would keep still. If Robert would not get too excited and just because, temporarily, he thought Tar a hero, would not talk too much.

As for John—there was a good deal of the mother in him. That he had seemed to swallow the story as Robert had told it was a comfort to Tar.

CHAPTER VIII

HORSES trotting around a race track in an Ohio town on a Sunday morning, in the summer squirrels running along the top of a worn fence, apples getting ripe in orchards.

Some of the Moorehead children went to Sunday school on Sundays, others did not. When Tar had a clean suit of Sunday clothes he sometimes went. The teacher talked of how David slew Goliath and of how Jonah fled from the Lord and concealed himself in a ship bound for Tarshish.[7]

What a strange place that must be, that Tarshish. Words [*making] pictures in Tar's head. The teacher had said little enough about Tarshish. That was a mistake. Thinking of Tarshish Tar couldn't pay attention to the rest of the lesson. If his father had been teaching the class he might have spread himself about the town, or country, or whatever it was. Why had Jonah wanted to go to Tarshish? Just at that time a passion for race horses had taken possession of Tar. He saw in fancy a wild place of yellow sand and bushes—wind swept. Men were racing horses at the edge of the sea. He may have got the notion out of a picture book.

Most places that are any fun are wicked places. Jonah was fleeing from the Lord. Maybe Tarshish was the name of a race course. It would be a good name.

The Mooreheads never owned any horses and cows but there were horses pastured in a field near the Moorehead house.[8]

A horse had funny thick lips. When Tar held an apple in his hand and put his hand through the fence the lips of the horse closed over the apple so gently he hardly felt anything at all.

7. This Bible story provides the analogy for "Godliness," *Winesburg, Ohio*, pp. 63–102.

8. On Anderson's love for horses, see *A Story Teller's Story*, pp. 101–2, 118–25, 178–81, 195, 313–14; "Here They Come," *Esquire*, XIII (March, 1940), 80–81; and *Memoirs*, pp. 34–35, 79. Besides the stories in *Horses and Men*, consult Linda Carol Traynham, "The Horse as Symbol in Sherwood Anderson's Fiction," M.A. Thesis, University of South Carolina, 1966.

Yes, he did. The funny hairy thick lips of the horse tickled the inside of the hand.

Animals were funny creatures but so were people. Tar spoke to his friend Jim Moore on the subject of dogs.[9] "A strange dog, if you run from him and are afraid, will take after you and act as though he was going to eat you up but if you stand still and look him right in the eye he won't do anything. No animal can stand the steady penetrating gaze of the human eye." Some people have a more penetrating gaze than others. It's a good thing to have.

A boy at school had told Tar that when a strange fierce dog took after you the best thing to do was to turn your back, stoop down and look at the dog through your legs. Tar never tried it, but when he grew to be a man he read the same thing in an old book. Boys were telling other boys that same tale on the way to school in the time of the old Norse sagas.[10] Tar asked Jim if he had ever tried it. They both agreed they would, sometime. It would be a ridiculous position to be caught in though, if it did not work. It would sure be a cinch for the dog.

"A better scheme is to pretend to pick up stones. There are hardly ever any good stones around when a fierce dog gets after you but a dog is easily bluffed. It's better to pretend to pick up a stone than to actually pick up one. If you throw your stone and miss, where are you?"

You've got to get used to people in towns. Some are one way, some another. Older people act so strangely.

When Tar was sick that time there was an old man, a doctor, who used to come to the house. He had a good deal to do with straightening the Mooreheads out. What was wrong with Mary Moorehead was that she was almost too good.

If you are too good you think— "Well now, I'll be patient and kind. I won't scold, whatever happens." In the saloons sometimes, when Dick Moorehead was spending money he

9. Jim Moore appears in *Memoirs*, pp. 33–34.
10. Anderson retells a Norse saga, that of Fredis, in *A Story Teller's Story*, pp. 237–40.

should have taken home, he heard other men speaking of their wives. Most men are afraid of their wives.

The men used to say things. "I don't want the old woman on my neck." That was just a way of speaking. Women don't really get on men's necks. A panther, when he is after a deer, jumps on her neck and pins her to earth but that wasn't what the man in the saloon meant. He meant he would get Hail Columbia when he got home and Dick hardly ever did get Hail Columbia. Doctor Reefy said he should get it more often. Maybe he gave it to Dick himself. He might have given Mary Moorehead a stiff talking to.[11] Tar never heard any of it. He might have said, "Look here woman, that husband of yours needs to have the gaff put to him now and then."

In the Moorehead house things changed, got better. Not that Dick became good. No one expected that.

Dick stayed more at home, brought more of his money home. Neighbors came in more. Dick could tell his war stories on the front porch in the presence of some neighbor man, a drayman, a man who was section boss on the Wheeling Railroad, and the children could sit and listen.

Tar's mother had a way, she always kept, of knocking the props out from under people sometimes with little side re-marks but she held herself back more and more. There are some people that, when they smile, make the whole [*world] smile. When they freeze up everyone around freezes up. Robert Moorehead got to be a good deal like his mother when he grew older. John and Will were the steady ones. The youngest one of all, little Joe Moorehead, was to be the artist of the family. Later he was what people call a genius and had a hard time making a living.

After his childhood was over, and after she had died, Tar thought his mother must have been smart. He was in love with her all his life. This trick of thinking someone is perfect does not give them much chance. Tar always, after he grew up, let his father alone—just as he was. He enjoyed thinking of him as a lovable improvident fellow. It may even have been that he afterwards attributed to Dick a lot of sins he never committed.

11. See "Death," *Winesburg, Ohio,* pp. 220–32.

Dick wouldn't have objected. "Well, take some notice of me. If you can't figure me out to be good, figure me out to be bad. Whatever you do, pay me some attention." Something of that sort Dick would have felt. Tar was always a good deal like Dick. He liked the notion of being always in the limelight and hated it too.

It may be that you are most likely to love someone you can't possibly be like. After Doctor Reefy began coming to the Moorehead house Mary Moorehead changed but not so much. She went to the children's room after they had gone to bed and kissed them all. She was like a young girl about it, did not seem able to caress them in the daylight. None of her children ever saw her kiss Dick and the sight would have startled them— shocked them a little.

If you have a mother like Mary Moorehead and she is lovely to look at—or you think she is, which is the same thing—and she dies when you are young, what you do all your life afterwards is to use her as material for dreams. It is unfair to her but you do it.

Very likely you make her sweeter than she was, kinder than she was, wiser than she was. What's the harm?

You are always wanting someone almost perfect to think about because you know you can't be that way yourself. If you ever do try you give up after a time.

Little Fern Moorehead died when she was three weeks old. Tar was sick in bed that time too.[12] After that night when Joe was born he had a fever. Then he wasn't much good for another year. That was what brought Doctor Reefy to the house. He was the only man Tar ever knew who talked up to his mother. He made her cry. The doctor had big funny-looking hands. He looked like pictures of Abraham Lincoln.

When Fern died Tar did not even have a chance to go to the funeral but he did not mind, was in fact glad. "If you have to die it's too bad but the fuss people make is awful. It makes everything so public and kind of terrible."

12. Anderson refers to this illness in "Stolen Day," *This Week*, April 27, 1941, pp. 6, 23; *Memoirs*, pp. 55–56.

Tar escaped it all. It would be the kind of time when Dick would be at his worst and Dick at his worst would be pretty bad.

By being sick Tar missed everything and his sister Margaret had to stay at home with him and she missed it too. A boy always gets the best side of girls and women when he is sick. "It's their chief time," Tar thought. He thought about it sometimes in bed. "That may be why men and boys are always getting sick."

When Tar was sick and had a fever he was out of his head a part of the time and all he ever knew of his sister Fern was a sound sometimes at night in the next room, a sound something like a tree toad. It got into the dreams of his fever time and stayed in his dreams. Afterwards he thought Fern was more real to him than any of the others.

Even when he grew to be a man Tar used to walk along the street sometimes thinking of her. He would be walking and talking with some other man and there she would be, just ahead of him. He saw her in every lovely gesture other women made. If, when he was a young man and very susceptible to women's charms, he said to some woman, "You make me think of my sister Fern who died," it was the finest compliment he could pay but the woman did not seem to appreciate it. Pretty women want to stand on their own feet. They do not want to remind you of anyone.

If a child in the family dies and you knew the child alive you always think of him as he was when he died. A child dies in spasms. It is terrible to think about.

But if you have never seen the child.

Tar could think of Fern as fourteen when he was fourteen. He could think of her as forty when he was forty.

Imagine Tar as a grown man. He has had a quarrel with his wife and goes out of the house in a huff. Time now to think of Fern. She is a grown woman. A little now he has got her confused in his mind with the figure of his dead mother.

When he grew older—up around forty—Tar always fancied Fern as about eighteen. Older men like the notion of some woman about eighteen with the wisdom of forty and the physical beauty and sweetness of girlhood. They like to think of such a one as attached to them with iron bands. It's the way older men are.

CHAPTER IX

Ohio [*in the spring or summer,] race horses trotting on a race track, corn growing in fields, little streams in narrow valleys, men going out in the spring to plow, in the fall, the nuts getting ripe in the woods about an Ohio town. Over in Europe they clean everything up. They have a lot of people and not too much land. When he grew to be a man Tar saw Europe and liked it, but all the time he was there he had an American hunger and it wasn't a "Star Spangled Banner" hunger either.[13]

What he hungered for was waste places, roominess. He wanted to see weeds growing, neglected old orchards, empty haunted houses.

An old worm fence where the elders and berries grow wild wastes a lot of land a barbed wire fence saves but it is nice. It's a place for a boy to crawl under and hide for a while. A man, if he is any good, never gets over being a boy.

In the woods about Middle-western towns in Tar's time a world of waste places. From the top of the hill where the Mooreheads lived, after Tar got well and began to go to school, you only had to walk across a corn field and a meadow where the Shepards kept their cow to get to the woods along Squirrel Creek. John was selling papers and was pretty busy so maybe he couldn't go along and Robert was too young.

Jim Moore lived down the road in a white, freshly-painted house and could nearly always get away. The other boys at school called him "Pee-Wee Moore" but Tar didn't. Jim was a year older and was pretty strong but that wasn't the only reason. Tar and Jim went through the standing corn, they went across the meadow.

If Jim could not go it was all right.

What Tar did when he went alone was to imagine things. His imagination made him afraid sometimes, it made him glad and happy sometimes.

13. Anderson visited Europe in 1921 as the guest of Paul Rosenfeld, again in 1926, and finally in 1932. See *A Story Teller's Story*, pp. 139, 286, 307–17.

The corn, when it grew high, was like a forest down under which there was always a strange soft light. It was hot down under the corn and made Tar sweat. At night his mother made him wash his feet and hands before he went to bed so he got as dirty as he wanted to. There was nothing saved [*by] keeping clean.

Sometimes he sprawled on the ground and lay for a long time sweating and watching the ants and bugs on the ground under the corn.

Ants, grasshoppers and bugs in general had a world of their own, birds had their world, wild animals and tame animals had their worlds. What does a pig think? Tame ducks in someone's yard are the funniest things in the world. They are scattered around and one of them makes a honking sound and they all begin to run. The back part of a duck wobbles up and down when he runs. Their flat feet go pitter-patter, pitter-patter, the funniest sound. And then they all get together and there isn't anything special going on. They stand looking at each other. "Well, what were you honking for? What'd you call us for, you fool?"

In the woods along a creek in a wasteful country logs lie about rotting. There is first a cleared place and then a place so filled with brush and berry bushes you can't see into it. It makes a good kind of place for rabbits—or snakes.

In a woods like that there are paths everywhere, leading just nowhere. You sit on a log. If there is a rabbit in the pile of brush in front, what do you suppose he is thinking about? He sees you and you can't see him. If there is a man and a woman rabbit what are they saying to each other? Do you suppose a man rabbit ever gets a little lit-up and comes home to sit around bragging to the neighbors about when he was in the army, the neighbors having been only privates while he was a captain? If the man rabbit does that he certainly talks pretty low. You can't hear a word he says.

CHAPTER X

TAR had got, through Doctor Reefy, who came to the house when he was ill, a man friend. His name was Tom Whitehead and he was fat and forty-two and owned race horses and a farm and had a fat wife and no children.

He was a friend of Doctor Reefy who also had no children. The doctor had married, when he was past forty, a young woman of twenty, but she only lived for a year. After his wife's death and when he was not at work the doctor went around with Tom Whitehead, with an old tree nurseryman named John Spaniard, with Judge Blair and with a young dudish fellow who got drunk a lot but who said funny, sarcastic things [when he was drunk].[14] The young man was the son of a United States Senator, now dead, and had been left some money, everyone said he was fooling away as fast as he could.

All of the men who were the doctor's friends had taken a sudden fancy for the Moorehead children and the race horse man seemed to have picked out Tar.

The others helped John make money and gave presents to Margaret and Robert. The doctor did it all. He managed everything without any fuss.

What happened to Tar was that in the late afternoons or on Saturdays or sometimes on Sundays Tom Whitehead drove along the road past the Moorehead place and stopped for him.

He was in a jogging cart and Tar sat on his knees.

First they went along a dusty road past waterworks pond, then up a little hill and in at the fair ground gate. Tom Whitehead had a stable over near the fair ground and a house near it but it was more fun to go to the race track itself.

Not many boys had such chances Tar thought. John didn't because he had to work so much and Jim Moore didn't. Jim

14. Dr. Reefy's wife appears in *Winesburg, Ohio*, pp. 35–38; John Spaniard, p. 36. Judge Blair may be the same person as Judge Turner, who appears in *A Story Teller's Story*, pp. 120–38, 139, 141, 144, 183–84, 185, 191.

lived alone with his mother who was a widow and she fussed over him a lot. When he went anywhere with Tar his mother gave a lot of directions. "Now it's early in the spring and the ground is damp. Don't sit on the ground.

"No, you can't go in swimming, not yet. I don't want you little fellows to be going in swimming when there are no older people about. You might get cramps. Don't go into the woods. There are always hunters around shooting off guns. I read in the paper only last week where a boy got killed."

Better to get killed right out than to fussed at all the time. If you've got such a mother, the loving fussy kind, you've got to stand for it but it's tough luck. A good thing Mary Moorehead had so many children. It kept her busy. She could not be thinking up a lot of things for a boy not to do.

Jim and Tar had talked it over. The Moores had some money. Mrs. Moore owned a farm. In some ways it is fine to be the only child a woman has but on the whole you lose by it. "It's the same way with a hen and chicks," Tar said to Jim and Jim agreed. Jim did not know how it hurts sometimes—when you want your mother to fuss over you and she is so busy with one of the other kids she can't pay you any attention.

Not many boys had the chance Tar had after Tom Whitehead took him up. After Tom called for him a few times he did not wait to be asked but went almost every day. If he went to the stables there were always men sitting around. Tom had a farm in the country where he raised some colts and others he bought as yearlings at the Cleveland sale in the spring. At such a sale other men who raise racing colts bring them in and they are sold at auction. You stand around and bid. That's where a good horse eye comes in.

You buy a colt that hasn't had any training, or two or four or maybe a dozen colts. Some will turn out corkers and some will be dubs. As good an eye as Tom Whitehead had, and he was known to horsemen all over the state, he made a lot of mistakes. When a colt turned out no good he said to the men sitting around, "I'm slipping. I thought that bay was all right. He has good blood in him but he won't ever go fast. He hasn't got that little extra something. It ain't in him. I guess I better go to an eye doctor and get my eyes fixed up. Maybe I'm getting old and a little blind."

It was good fun over at the Whitehead stables but better fun at the fair ground tracks where Tom trained his colts. At the stables Doctor Reefy came and sat around, Will Truesdale, the young swell who was good to Margaret and gave her presents, came, Judge Blair came.

A lot of men sitting and talking—always of horses. There was a bench along the front. Neighbor women told Mary Moorehead she shouldn't let her boy keep such company but she went right on. Many times Tar couldn't understand the talk. The men were always making little sarcastic cracks at each other, like his mother did sometimes to people.

The men talked of religion and politics and whether or not a man has a soul and a horse hasn't. Some of the men held to one set of opinions, some to another. The best thing, Tar thought, was to go back into the stable itself.

There was a board floor and a long row of box stalls on each side and in the front of each stall there was an opening with iron bars so he could look through but the horse inside could not get out. A good thing, too. Tar walked along slow, looking in.

"Fassig's Irish Maid; Old Hundred; Tipton Ten; Willing-to-Please; Saul The First; Passenger Boy; Holy Mackerel."

The names were on little tickets fastened on the front of the stalls.

Passenger Boy was as black as a black cat and went like a cat when he was going fast. One of the stablemen, Henry Bardshare, said he could kick the crown off a king's head if he got a chance. "Say, he'd kick the stars out of the flag, he'd kick the beard off your face. When he gets through racing I'm going to set him up for a barber."

On the bench in front of the stable, on summer afternoons when there weren't any horses being worked at the track, the men talked—sometimes of women, sometimes of why God lets certain things happen, sometimes of why is a farmer always growling. Tar soon grew tired of the talk. There was too much talk in his head already, he thought.

CHAPTER XI

AT the track in the morning what a difference. Now the horses held the stage. Passenger Boy was out and Old Hundred and Holy Mackerel. Tom was tooling Passenger Boy himself. He and Holy Mackerel, a gelding, and a three year old Tom reckoned was the fastest thing he had, were going to do a mile together after they got warmed up.

Passenger Boy was old, fourteen years old, but you would never have guessed it. He had a funny cat-like way of going—smooth and low and fast when it did not look fast.

Tar went over to where there were some trees in the center of the track. Sometimes, when Tom didn't come for him and paid [him] no attention, he went alone afoot and got there early in the morning. If he had to go without breakfast it was all right. You wait around for breakfast and what happens? Your sister Margaret says, "Get some wood in Tar, get some water, mind the house while I go to the store."

Old horses like Passenger Boy are like some old men, Tar knew long afterwards, when he was a man. You've got to warm the old ones up a lot—prod 'em—but when they get going the right kinds—boy, look out. What you've got to do is heat them up. At the stables Tar once heard young Bill Truesdale say that a lot of men, of what he called antiquity, were the same way. "Look at King David, now. They had a lot of trouble trying to heat him up at the last." Men and horses don't change much.

Will Truesdale was always talking of antiquity. People said he was a born scholar but he got soused about three times a week. He claimed there was plenty of precedent for it. "A lot of the smartest men the world ever knew could have put me under the table. I haven't got the stomach they had."

That kind of talk, half in fun, half serious, at the stables where the men sat around, but over at the track mostly silence. When a good horse is going fast even a talky man can't talk much.

Out in the very center, inside the oval track, there was a big tree, an oak, and when you sat under it and edged slowly around you could see a horse every step of the mile.

Tar went over there once in the early morning and sat down. It was a Sunday morning and that, he thought, was a good time to go. If he stayed at home Margaret would say, "You might as well go to Sunday school." Margaret wanted Tar to learn everything. She was ambitious for him but you learn things at the tracks too.

On Sunday, when you dress up, your mother has to wash your shirt afterwards. You can't help getting it dirty. She has enough to do as it is.

When Tar got to the tracks early Tom and his men and the horses were already there. One by one they brought the horses out. Some they worked fast, others they just jogged for miles and miles. That was to harden up their legs.

Then Passenger Boy came, a little stiff at first, but, after they had jogged him a long time, getting more and more into that easy cat-like way of going. Holy Mackerel went high and proud. The trouble with him was that when he was in his speed he would, if you weren't mighty careful and pressed him a little too much, break and spoil everything.

Now Tar had got it all down fine, the words of racing, the slang. He loved to say over horses' names, racing words, horse words.

When he sat that way, alone over under the tree, he kept talking to the horses in a low voice. "Easy boy now, now . . . get along there now . . . hi boy . . . hi boy . . . [*hi, boy . . . hi, boy]" . . . pretending he was driving.

The "hi boy" came when you wanted a horse to flatten himself out into his stride.

If you aren't a man yet and can't do what men do you can have almost as much fun pretending you are doing it . . . if there isn't anyone around looking and listening.

Tar watched the horses, he indulged in dreams of someday being a horseman. On the Sunday when he went to the tracks something happened.

When he got there, in the early morning light, it began

[being] a grey day, as so many Sundays are, and it rained a little. At first he thought the rain might spoil the fun but it didn't last long. The rain only laid the dust on the track.

Tar had come away from home without his breakfast but, as it was getting late summer and soon Tom would be sending some of his horses to the races, some of his men were living at the tracks, keeping the horses over there and eating there themselves.

They cooked out of doors and had a little fire. After the rain the day half cleared, making a soft light.

On the Sunday morning Tom saw Tar coming in at the fair ground gate and calling to him gave him some fried bacon and bread. How good it tasted, better out of doors that way—than anything Tar could ever get at home. Maybe his mother had told Tom Whitehead how he was so crazy about being at the tracks that he often left home without his breakfast.

After he gave Tar the bacon and bread—Tar made into a sandwich—Tom did not pay any more attention to him. It was just as well. Tar did not want attention[, *not that day]. There are certain days when, if everyone leaves you alone, it just suits. They don't come often in a life. For some the best day is when they marry, for some when they get rich, have a lot of money left them or something like that.

Anyway there are days that just seem to go high and fine, like Holy Mackerel when he don't break in the stretch, or like old Passenger Boy when he finally gets into that soft cat-like stride of his. Such days are as rare as ripe apples on a tree in the winter.

As soon as he had bolted the bacon and bread Tar went over to the tree where he could look all around the track. The grass was wet going over but it was dry under the tree.

He was glad Jim Moore wasn't along, glad his brother John, or Robert, wasn't there.

Well, he wanted to be alone, that was all.

He made up his mind early in the morning he wasn't going home all day, not 'till night.

He lay on the ground under the oak tree and watched the horses work. When Holy Mackerel and Passenger Boy got down to business, Tom Whitehead standing over by the judges' stand with a stop watch in his hand and letting a lighter man drive, it was exciting of course. A lot of people think it's great when one horse nips the other right at the wire but if you are any horseman you ought to know pretty well which horse is likely to do the nipping. It isn't settled at the wire but probably over on the back stretch where there isn't anyone to see. Tar knew that was true because he had heard Tom Whitehead say so. It was a shame Tom was so fat and heavy. He would have been as good a driver as Pop Geers or Walter Cox if he hadn't been so fat.

It is settled on the back stretch which horse is which because back there one horse says to another, "Come on you big mutt, let's see what you've got." Races are won by the little extra something that you've got or you haven't.

What happens is that these wire-nippers always get in the papers and stories. A newspaper writer likes that stuff, "nipped at the wire, the wind sobbing through the mighty lungs," you know. Newspaper men like it and the crowd at the races likes it. [Some drivers and riders are always working for that grandstand stuff.] Tar reckoned sometimes that, had he been a driver, his dad would have been that kind and maybe he would himself but the thought made him ashamed.

And then sometimes a man like Tom Whitehead says to one of his drivers, "You let Holy Mackerel get down in front. Take old Passenger Boy back a little up there at the head of the stretch. Then let him come on."

You get the idea. It doesn't mean Passenger Boy couldn't have won. It means he couldn't win, given the handicap he had, being taken back that way. It was to give Holy Mackerel the habit of landing in front. Old Passenger Boy maybe didn't care quite so much. He knew he'd get his oats all right anyway. If you've been down in front a lot of times and heard the cheering and all that, what do you care?

If you know a lot about racing or anything it takes something out of it but you gain something too. It's all bunk winning anything if you don't win it right. "There's about three people in Ohio know that and four of them are dead," Tar once heard

Will Truesdale say. Tar [*did not quite] know what it meant
and yet he did know, in a way.

The point is that the way a horse moves is something in itself.

Anyway, on the Sunday morning, Holy Mackerel won, after
Passenger Boy had been taken back at the head of the stretch,
and Tar saw the taking back and then the way Passenger Boy
ate up the space between and almost made Holy Mackerel
break at the critical moment. He might have broken had
Charlie Friedly, driving Passenger Boy, given a certain kind of
a whoop at the right moment as he would have done in a race.

He saw that and the movements of the horses all around the
track.

Then some other horses, colts mostly, worked out and noon
came and afternoon and Tar did not move.

He felt all right. It was just a day when he did not want to
see anyone.

After the horsemen got through their work he did not go
back over to where the men were. Some of them went away.
They were Irish and Catholics and could maybe get to a mass.

Tar was lying on his back under the oak. Anyone in the
world any good has had such a day. Such days make a person
wonder when they come why they are so scarce.

It may have been just a feeling of peace. Tar was lying on
his back under the tree looking up at the sky. Birds flew overhead. Now and then a bird landed in the tree. For a time he
could hear the voices of the men at work with the horses but
could not make out any words.

"Well, a big tree is something in itself. A tree can laugh
sometimes, smile sometimes, frown sometimes. Suppose you are
a big tree and a long dry time comes. A big tree must need a
lot to drink. There isn't any worse feeling than being thirsty
and knowing you can't get anything to drink.

"A tree is something, and grass is something else. Some days
you aren't hungry at all. Put food before you and you don't
even want it. If a mother sees you just sitting around and sitting
around and not saying anything [she's likely, if she hasn't a lot
of other kids to keep her busy, to begin fussing. It's] likely as
not the first thing she thinks of is food. 'You'd better eat some-

thing.' Jim Moore's mother is like that. She's stuffed him until
he [*is] so fat he [*can't] hardly climb a fence."

Tar stayed for a long time under the tree and then he heard
a sound far off, a low humming sound that occasionally grew
louder and then died down again.

What a funny sound for Sunday!

Tar thought he knew what it was and presently got up and
walked slowly across the field, climbed a fence, crossed the
tracks and then climbed another fence. When he crossed the
tracks he looked up and down. When he stood on the tracks he
always wished he was a horse, young like Holy Mackerel and
full of wisdom and speed and meanness like Passenger Boy.

Tar had got outside the race track now. He crossed a stumpy
field and climbed a wire fence and got into a road.

It wasn't a big road but a little back country road. Such roads
have deep ruts in them and often rocks sticking up.

And now he had got quite out of town. The sound he had
heard grew a little louder. He passed farm houses, went through
a wood, climbed a hill.

Presently he saw it. It was what he had thought. Some men
were threshing grain in a field.

"What the deuce! On Sunday!

"They must be some foreigners, like Germans or something.
They can't be very civilized."

It wasn't anywhere Tar had ever been and he knew none of
the men but he climbed a fence and went toward them.

The stacks of wheat were on a hill near a wood. As he got
nearer he went more slowly.

Well, there were a lot of country boys, about his own age,
standing around. Some were all dressed up, for Sunday, some
were in their everyday clothes. They were all strangers. The
men were strangers. Tar went past the machine and the engine
and sat down under a tree by a fence. There was a large old
man with a grey beard sitting there smoking a pipe.

Tar sat near him, staring at him, staring at the men at work,
staring at the country boys of his own age, standing about.

What a queer feeling he had. You've had such a feeling. You
are walking in a street you've been in a thousand times, and

suddenly it's all different [and new]. Wherever you go people are doing something. On certain days whatever they are doing is full of interest. If they aren't working out colts on a race track they are threshing wheat.

You would be surprised how the wheat runs out of a threshing machine, like a river. Wheat is ground up into flour and made into bread. A field that isn't very big and that you can walk across in no time will produce bushels [and bushels] of wheat.

When men are at work threshing wheat they are like they are when they train colts for the races. They make funny remarks. They work like the very deuce for a while and then lay off and maybe wrestle around.

Tar saw one young man, at work on the top of a stack of wheat, push another to the ground. Then he crawled back up and the two put down their forks and began to wrestle. There was a man on an elevated platform feeding the wheat into the separator and he began to dance. He took a bundle of the wheat in his hands, shook it in the air, made a motion like a bird trying to fly that can't fly, and then began to dance again.

The two men on the stack wrestled as hard as they could, laughing all the time, and the old man by the fence near Tar growled at them but you could tell he did not mean what he said.

The whole job of threshing came to a stop. All were intent on watching the struggle on the stack until one fellow had thrown the other to the ground.

Some women came along a lane bearing baskets and all the men went away from the machine to sit by the fence. It was in the middle of the afternoon but in the country, when threshing is going on, people do like that. They eat and eat, just anytime. Tar had heard his father talk of it. Dick liked to be painting a house in the country when the threshers came.[15] Lots of people served wine then—some they had made themselves. A good German farmer was best. "It takes the Germans to eat and drink," Dick often said. It was funny Dick wasn't fat the way he could eat when he was away from home and could get it.

15. If Sherwood Anderson did engage in threshing work, the time would be the summer of 1899.

When the people of the farm, the visiting threshers and the neighbors who had come to help, were all sitting by the fence eating and drinking they kept offering Tar some but he would not take it. Why he did not know. It wasn't because it was Sunday and it seemed strange to see people at work. It was a queer day for him, a dumb day. One of the farm boys, of about his own age, came to sit near him, holding a large sandwich in his hand. Tar had taken nothing to eat since breakfast at the track and that was early, about six o'clock. They always work the horses as early as they can. It was now well past four in the afternoon.

Tar and the strange boy sat by an old stump that was hollow and a spider had built his web in it. A large ant crawled up the farm boy's leg and when he knocked it off it fell in the web. It struggled furiously. If you looked close at the web you could see, away back in a kind of cone-like place, the old fat spider looking out.

Tar and the strange boy looked at the spider, they looked at the struggling ant, they looked at each other. It's queer that on some days you can't talk to save you. "He's a goner," the farm boy said, pointing at the struggling ant. "You bet," Tar said.

The men went back to work and the boy disappeared. The old man who had been sitting by the fence smoking his pipe went to work. He had left his matches lying on the ground.

Tar went and got them. He gathered up some loose straw and shoved it into the front of his shirt. Why he wanted the matches and the straw he did not know. On some days a boy just likes to touch things. He picks up stones and carries them when he doesn't want them at all.

"There are days when you like everything and days you don't. Other people hardly ever know just how you feel."

Tar went away from the threshers, drifted down along the fence and got into a meadow below. He could see the farm house now. At a farm house, when there are threshers, a lot of neighbor women come in. More come than need to come. They cook a lot of food but they fool around a lot too. What they like to do is talk. You never heard such chatter.

It was funny though, their doing it on Sunday.

Tar walked across a meadow and then crossed a creek on a fallen log. He knew in a general way the direction in which lay the town and the Moorehead house. What would his mother think of his being gone all day? Suppose it should turn out like Rip Van Winkle and he had gone for years. Usually when he went off to the race tracks alone in the early morning he was back at home by ten. If it was Saturday there were always a lot of things to do. Saturday was John's big paper day and Tar was expected to get busy.

He had to split and bring in wood, get water, go to the store.

Sunday was, after all, a lot better. This one was a queer day for him, an exceptional day. When an exceptional day comes you've got to do just what comes into your head. If you don't everything is spoiled. If you want to eat you eat, if you don't want to eat you don't. Other people and what they want don't count, not for that day.

Tar went up a slight hill and sat by another fence in a wood. When he came out of the wood he could see the fair ground fence and knew that in ten or fifteen minutes he could get home—if he wanted to go. He didn't.

What did he want? It was growing late now. He must have been in the woods at least two hours. How quickly the time went—sometimes.

He went down a hill and came to the creek that led to waterworks pond. At the pond they had built a dam and backed the water up. There was an engine house near the pond that put on full steam when there was a fire in town and that also furnished the town with electric lights. When it was moonlight they did not turn on the lights. Dick Moorehead was always grumbling about it. He did not pay any taxes and a man who doesn't pay any taxes is always the best grumbler. Dick was always saying the tax payers ought to furnish the school books, too. "A soldier serves his country and that makes up for not paying taxes," Dick said. Tar sometimes wondered what Dick would have done if he hadn't got the chance to be a soldier. It had given him so much to grumble about, brag about, talk about. He had enjoyed being a soldier, too. "It was a life just made for me. If I had been to West Point I'd have stayed in the army. If you aren't a West Point man the others look down on you," Dick said.

At the waterworks engine house they had an engine with a wheel twice as high as your head. It whirled round and round, so fast you could hardly see the spokes. The engineer never said anything. If you went to the door and stood looking in he never looked at you. You never saw a man with so much grease on one pair of pants.

Up the creek, at the place to which Tar had now come, there had been a house once but it had burned down. There was an old apple orchard, the trees all let go, so many little shoots growing out of the limbs you could hardly climb up. The orchard was on the side of a hill that led right down to the creek. Beside it was a corn field.

Tar sat down by the creek at the edge of the corn field and the orchard. When he had been sitting there a long time a ground hog on the opposite bank of the creek came out of his hole, stood on his hind legs and looked at Tar.

Tar did not move. It was a queer notion carrying that straw around inside his shirt. It tickled.

He took it out and the ground hog disappeared into his hole. It was growing dusk now. Pretty soon he would have to go home. Sunday was a funny kind of a day, some people going to church, others staying at home.

The ones that stayed at home dressed up anyway.

Tar had been told it was God's day. He gathered some dry leaves along the fence by the orchard and then went a little way into the corn. When corn is almost ripe there are always some outer leaves that have dried and withered.

"Barren corn makes bitter bread." Tar heard Will Truesdale say that one day as he sat with the other men on the bench before Tom Whitehead's stable. He wondered what it meant. It was poetry Will was quoting. It would be nice to be educated like Will but not a souse and to know all the words there are and what they mean. If you put words together in just a certain way they sound nice even though you don't know what they mean. They go well together like some people. Afterwards you are walking along alone and you say the words to yourself, liking the sound they make.

Nice sounds at night by an old orchard and a corn field too, about the best sound you can hear. The crickets are going it and the frogs and the grasshoppers.

Tar lit the little pile of leaves, dry corn leaves and straw. Then he put some sticks on. The leaves weren't very dry. There wasn't a big quick fire just a gentle one with white smoke. The smoke curled up through the branches of one of the old apple trees in the orchard, some man had planted, thinking he would make a home there by the creek. He had got tired or discouraged, Tar thought, and after his house burned had moved away. People were always leaving one place and moving to another.

The smoke went lazily up, into the branches of the trees. When a little breeze came some of it was blown through the standing corn.

People talked about God. There wasn't anything very definite in Tar's mind. Lots of times you do something—like carrying that straw from the threshing inside your shirt all afternoon (it tickling you)—and you don't know why you do it.

There is a lot to think about you never can really think about. If you talk about God to a boy he gets all mixed up. Once some of the kids were talking about death and Jim Moore said that when he died he wanted them to sing at his funeral a song called "Let's Go to the Fair in an Automobile" and a big boy that was standing near laughed fit to kill.

He didn't have sense enough to know that Jim did not mean what he said. He meant he liked the sound. Maybe he heard someone sing that song who had a nice voice.

A preacher who came to the Mooreheads' house once and talked a lot about God and hell scared Tar and made Mary Moorehead mad. What's the use getting all worked up? [16]

If you sit at the edge of a corn field and an orchard and you have a little fire and it is almost night and there is a corn field and the smoke goes up lazy and slow toward the sky and you look up. . . .

16. Conventional religion was of no importance in Sherwood Anderson's life. In *Memoirs*, p. 26. he states that his parents did not attend church.

Tar waited until the fire had all burned out and then went home.

It was dark when he got there. If your mother has any sense she knows enough to know that certain days are certain days. If you do what she doesn't expect on such a day she never says a word.

Tar's mother said nothing. When he got home his father had gone away and so had John. Supper was over but his mother got him some. Margaret was talking with a neighbor girl in the back yard and Robert was just sitting around. The baby was asleep.

What Tar did, after he had his supper, was just to sit on the front porch with his mother. She was sitting near and now and then touched him with her fingers. [He felt as though he had been going through some kind of a ceremony. It's just because things in general are so good and all right, for the time being. They liked to make a fire and watch the smoke go up in Bible times. That was a long time ago. When you have a fire like that, all by yourself, and the smoke is going up, lazy that way, through the branches of old apple trees and in among corn that has grown up higher than your head and when you look up it is late evening and almost dark it's a long ways up to the sky where the stars are, all right.]

PART III

CHAPTER XII

SHE was an old woman and lived on a farm near the town in which the Mooreheads lived.[1] All country and small town people have seen such old women but no one knows much about them. Such an old woman comes into town driving an old worn-out horse or she comes afoot, carrying a basket. She may own a few hens and have eggs to sell. She brings them in a basket and takes them to a grocer. There she trades them in. She gets some salt pork and some beans. Then she gets a pound or two of sugar and some flour.

Afterward she goes to the butcher and asks for some dog meat. She might spend ten or fifteen cents but when she does she asks for something. In Tar's day the butchers gave liver to anyone who wanted to carry it away. In the Moorehead family they were always having it. [Once] one of Tar's brothers got a whole cow's liver out at the slaughter hourse near the fair grounds. He came staggering home with it and afterwards the Mooreheads had it until they were sick of it. It never cost a cent. Tar hated the thought of it all the rest of his life.

The old farm woman got her some liver and a soup bone. She never visited with anyone and as soon as she had got what she wanted lit out for home. It made quite a load for such an old body. No one gave her a lift. People drive right down a road and never notice such an old woman.

The old woman used to come into town past the Moorehead house during the summer and fall when Tar was sick. She went home later carrying a heavy pack on her back. Two or three large gaunt-looking dogs followed at her heels.

Well, she was nothing special. She was one of the sort hardly anyone knows but she got into Tar's thoughts. Her name was Grimes and she lived, with her husband and son, in a small un-

1. This is Anderson's famous "Death in the Woods," which was published in *The American Mercury*, IX (September, 1926), 7–13; and in *Death in the Woods*, pp. 3–24. See *A Story Teller's Story*, p. 92.

painted house on the bank of a small creek four miles from town.

The husband and son were a tough pair. Although the son was but twenty-one he had already served a term in jail. It was whispered about that the woman's husband stole horses and ran them off to some other county. Now and then, when a horse turned up missing, the man had also disappeared. No one ever caught him.

Once later when Tar was loafing at Tom Whitehead's barn the man came there and sat on the bench in front. Judge Blair and two or three other men were there but not one spoke to him. He sat for a few minutes and then got up and went away. When he was leaving he turned and stared at the men. There was a look of defiance in his eyes. "Well, I have tried to be friendly. You do not want to talk to me. It has always been so wherever I have gone in this town. If, someday, one of your fine horses turns up missing, well, then what?"

He did not say anything actually. "I'd like to bust one of you on the jaw" was about what his eyes said. Tar remembered afterwards how the look in his eyes made the shivers run down his back.

The man belonged to a family that had had money once. His father John Grimes had owned a sawmill when the country was new and had made money. Then he got to drinking and running after women. When he died there wasn't much left.

Jake Grimes blew in the rest. Pretty soon there wasn't any more lumber to cut and his land was nearly all gone.

He had got his wife off a German farmer, where he went to work one June day in the wheat harvest. She was a young thing then and scared to death.

You see the farmer was up to something with the girl who was what is called "a bound girl"—and his wife had her suspicions.[2] She took it out on the girl when the man wasn't around. Then, when the wife had to go off to town for supplies, the farmer got after her. She told young Jake that nothing really

2. The "bound girl" reference is similar to those Anderson made to his mother's girlhood, but there is no evidence to support Emma Smith's having been "bound out."

ever happened but he did not know whether to believe her
or not.

He got her pretty easy himself, the first time he was out
with her. Well, he wouldn't have married her if the German
farmer hadn't tried to tell him where to get off. Jake got her to
go riding with him in his buggy one night, when he was threshing on the place, and then he came for her the next Sunday
night.

She managed to get out of the house without her employer's
seeing her and then, when she was getting into the buggy, he
showed up. It was almost dark and he just popped up suddenly
at the horse's head. He grabbed the horse by the bridle and
Jake got out his buggy whip.

They had it out right there. The German was a tough one.
Maybe he didn't care whether his wife knew or not. Jake hit
him over the face and shoulders with the buggy whip but the
horse got to acting up and he had to climb out.

Then the two men went for it. The girl didn't see it. The
horse started to run away and went nearly a mile down the
road before the girl got him stopped. Then she [*managed]
to tie him to a tree beside the road. Tar later knew all about
it. It must have stuck in his mind from small town tales, heard
when he loitered about where men talked. Jake found her after
he got through with the German. She was huddled up in the
buggy seat, crying, scared to death. She told Jake a lot of stuff,
how the German had tried to get her, how he chased her once
in the barn, how another time, when they happened to be alone
in the house together, he tore her dress open clear down the
front. The German, she said, might have got her that time if
he hadn't heard his old woman drive in at the gate. The wife
had been off to town for supplies. Well, she would be putting
the horse in the barn. The German managed to sneak off to
the fields without her seeing. He told the girl he would kill her
if she told. What could she do? She told a lie about ripping
her dress in the barn when she was feeding the stock. She was
a bound girl and didn't know who or where her father and
mother were. Maybe she did not have any father. The reader
will understand.

She married Jake and had a son and a daughter by him but
the daughter died young.

Then the woman settled down to feed stock. That was her
job. At the German's place she had cooked the food for the
German and his wife. The German's wife was a strong woman
with big hips and worked most of the time in the fields with
her husband. [*The girl] fed them and fed the cows in the
barn, fed the pigs, the horses and the chickens. Every moment
of every day as a young girl was spent feeding something.

Then she married Jake Grimes and he had to be fed. She
was a slight thing and when she had been married for three
or four years, and after the two children were born, her slender
shoulders became stooped.

Jake always had a lot of big dogs around the house that
stood near the unused old sawmill near the creek. He was
always trading horses when he wasn't stealing something and
had a lot of poor bony ones about. Also he kept three or four
pigs and a cow. They were all pastured in the few acres left
of the Grimes place and Jake did little or nothing.

He went into debt for a threshing outfit and ran that for
several years but it did not pay. People would not trust him.
They were afraid he would steal the grain at night. He had
to go a long way off to get work and it cost too much to get
there. In the winter he hunted and cut a little firewood, to be
sold in some nearby town. When his boy grew up he was just
like his father. They got drunk together. If there wasn't anything to eat in the house when they came home the old man
gave his old woman a [*clip] over the head. She had a few
chickens of her own and had to kill one of them in a hurry.
When they were all killed she would not have any eggs to sell
when she went to town and then what would she do?

She had to scheme all her life about getting things fed,
getting the pigs fed so they would grow fat and could be
butchered in the fall. When they were butchered her husband
took most of the meat off to town and sold it. If he did not
do it first the boy did it. They fought sometimes and when
they fought the old woman stood aside trembling.

She had got the habit of silence anyway—that was fixed.

Sometimes, when she began to look old—she wasn't forty yet—
and when the husband and son were both gone off, trading
horses, or drinking or hunting or stealing, she went around the
house and the barn yard muttering to herself.

How was she going to get everything fed—that was her
problem. The dogs had to be fed. There wasn't enough hay in
the barn for the horses and the cow. If she did not feed the
chickens how could they lay eggs? Without eggs to sell how
could she get things in town, things she had to have to keep
the place going? Thank Heavens she did not have to feed her
husband—in a certain way. That hadn't lasted long after their
marriage and after the babies came. Where he went on his
long trips she did not know. Sometimes he was gone from home
for weeks at a time and after the boy grew up they went off
together.

They left everything at home for her to manage and she
had no money. She knew no one. No one ever talked to her.
When it was winter she had to gather sticks of wood for her
fire, had to try to manage to keep the stock fed with very little
grain, very little hay.

The stock in the barn cried to her hungrily, the dogs followed
her about. In the winter the hens laid few enough eggs. They
huddled in corners of the barn and she kept watching them.
If a hen lays an egg in the barn in the winter and you do not
find it, it freezes and breaks.

One day in the winter the old woman went off to town with
a few eggs and the dogs followed her. She didn't get started
until nearly three o'clock and the snow was heavy. She hadn't
been feeling very well for several days and so she went muttering along, scantily clad, her shoulders stooped. She had an old
grain bag in which she carried her eggs, tucked away down in
the bottom. There weren't many of them but in the winter the
price of eggs is up. She would get a little meat [*in exchange
for the eggs], some salt pork, a little sugar, and coffee perhaps.
It might be the butcher would give her a piece of liver.

When she had got to town and was trading in the eggs the
dogs lay by the door outside. She did pretty well, got the
things she needed, more than she had hoped. Then she went to

the butcher and he gave her some liver and some dog meat.

It was the first time anyone had spoken to her in a friendly way for a long time. The butcher was alone in his shop when she went in and was annoyed by the thought of such a sick-looking old woman out on such a day. It was bitter cold and the snow, that had let up during the afternoon, was falling again. The butcher said something about her husband and her son, swore at them, and the old woman stared at him, a look of mild surprise in her eyes. He said that if either the husband or the son was going to get any of the liver or the heavy bones with scraps of meat hanging to them, he had put into the grain bag, he'd see [*him] starve first.

Starve, eh? Well, things had to be fed. Men had to be fed, and horses that aren't any good but maybe can be traded off, and a poor thin cow that hadn't given any milk for three months.

Horses, cows, pigs, dogs, men.

The old woman had to get back home before darkness came if she could. The dogs followed at her heels, sniffing at the heavy grain bag she had fastened on her back. When she got to the edge of town she stopped by a fence and tied the bag [on]to her back with a piece of rope she had carried in her dress pocket for just that purpose. That was an easier way to carry it. Her arms ached. It was hard when she had to crawl over fences and once she fell over and landed in the snow. The dogs went frisking about. She had to struggle to get to her feet again but she made it. The point of climbing over the fences was that there was a short cut over a hill and through a wood. She might have gone around by the road but it was a mile farther that way. She was afraid she couldn't make it. And then besides the stock had to be fed. There was a little hay left, a little corn. Perhaps her husband and son would bring some home when they came. They had driven off in the only buggy the Grimes family had, a rickety thing, a rickety horse hitched to the buggy, two other rickety horses led by halters. They were going to trade horses, get a little money if they could. They might come home drunk. It would be well to have something in the house when they got back.

The son had an affair on with a woman at the county seat, fifteen miles away. She was a bad woman, a tough one. Once, in the summer, the son had brought her to the house. Both she and the son had been drinking. Jake Grimes was away and the son and his woman ordered the old woman about like a servant. She did not mind much, was used to it. Whatever happened she never said anything. That was her way of getting along. She had managed that way when she was a young girl at the German's and ever since she had married Jake. That time her son brought his woman to the house they stayed all night, sleeping together just as though they were married. It hadn't shocked the old woman, not much. She had got past being shocked early in life.

With the pack on her back she went painfully along across an open field, wading in the deep snow, and got into the wood. She had to go up a little hill. There wasn't so much snow in the woods.

There was a path but it was hard to follow. Just beyond the top of the hill, where the woods was thickest, there was a small clearing. Had someone once thought of building a house there? The clearing was as large as a building lot in town, large enough for a house and a garden. The path ran along the side of the clearing and when she got there the old woman sat down to rest at the foot of a tree.

It was a foolish thing to do. When she got herself placed, the pack against the tree's trunk, it was nice but what about getting up again? She worried about that for a moment and then closed her eyes.

She must have slept for a time. When you are about so cold you can't get any colder. The afternoon grew a little warmer and the snow came thicker than ever. Then after a time the weather cleared. The moon even came out.

There were four Grimes dogs that had followed Mrs. Grimes into town, all tall gaunt fellows. Such men as Jake Grimes and his son always keep just such dogs. They kick and abuse them but they stay. The Grimes dogs, in order to keep from starving, had to do a lot of foraging for themselves and they had been at it while the old woman slept with her back to the tree at the side of the clearing. They had been chasing rabbits in the woods and in adjoining fields and in their ranging had picked up three other farm dogs.

All the dogs came back to the clearing after a time. They were excited about something. Such nights, cold and clear and with a moon, do things to dogs. It may be that some old instinct, come down from the time when they were wolves and ranged the woods in packs on winter nights, comes back into them.

The dogs in the clearing, before the old woman, had caught two or three rabbits and their immediate hunger had been satisfied. They began to play, running in circles in the clearing. Round and round they ran, each dog's nose at the tail of the next dog. In the clearing, under the snowladen trees and under the wintry moon, they made a strange picture, running thus silently in a circle their running had beaten in the soft snow. The dogs made no sound. They ran and ran in the circle.

It may have been that the old woman saw them doing that before she died. She may have awakened once or twice and looked at the strange sight with dim old eyes.

She would not be very cold now, just drowsy. Life hangs on a long time. Perhaps the old woman was out of her head. She may have dreamed of her girlhood at the German's, and before that when she was a child and before her mother lit out and left her.

Her dreams couldn't have been very pleasant. Not many pleasant things had happened to her. Now and then one of the Grimes dogs left the running circle and came to stand before her. The dog thrust his face close to hers. His red tongue was hanging out.

The running of the dogs may have been a kind of death ceremony. It may have been that the primitive instinct of the wolf, having been aroused in the dogs by the night and the running, they were afraid.

"Now we are no longer wolves. We are dogs, the servants of men. Keep alive man. When man dies we become wolves again."

When one of the dogs came to where the old woman sat with her back against the tree and had thrust his nose close to her face he seemed satisfied and [*went] back to run with the pack. All the Grimes dogs did it at some time, during the evening, before she died. Tar Moorehead knew all about it afterwards, when he grew to be a man, because once in a wood on another winter night he saw a pack of dogs act [*just] that way. The dogs were waiting for him to die as they had waited for the old woman that night when he was a child [but] when it happened to him he was a young man and had no intention of dying.[3]

The old woman died softly and quietly. When she was dead and when one of the Grimes dogs had come to her and had found her dead all the dogs stopped running.

They gathered about her.

Well, she was dead now. She had fed the Grimes dogs when she was alive, what about now?

There was the pack on her back, the grain bag containing the piece of salt pork, the liver the butcher had given her, the dog meat, the soup bones. The butcher in town, having been suddenly overcome with a feeling of pity, had loaded her grain bag heavily. It had been a big haul for the old woman.

A big haul for the dogs now.

One of the Grimes dogs sprang suddenly out from among the others and began worrying the pack on the old woman's back. Had the dogs really been wolves that one would have been the leader of the pack. What he did all the others did.

All of them sank their teeth into the grain bag the old woman had fastened with ropes to her back.

They dragged the old woman's body out into the open clearing. The worn-out old dress was quickly torn from her shoulders. When she was found, a day or two later, the dress had been torn from her body clear to the hips but the dogs had not touched the body. They had got the meat out of the grain bag, that was all. Her body was frozen stiff when it was found and the shoulders were so narrow and the body so slight that in death it looked like the body of a young girl.

Such things happening in towns of the Middle West, on farms near town, when Tar Moorehead was a child. A hunter

3. Anderson describes his own experience in *Memoirs*, pp. 310–12.

out after rabbits found the old woman's body and did not touch it. Something, the beaten [round] path in the little snow covered clearing, the silence of the place, the place where the dogs had worried the body trying to pull the grain bag away or tear it open—something startled the man and he hurried off to town.

Tar was on Main Street with his brother John who was taking the afternoon papers to the stores. It was almost night.

The hunter came into a grocery and told his story. Then he went to a hardware shop and into a drug store. Men began to gather on the sidewalks. Then they started out along the road to the place in the wood.

Of course John Moorehead should have gone on about his business of distributing papers but he didn't. Everyone was going to the woods. The undertaker went and the town marshal. Several men got on a dray and rode out to where the path left the road but the horses weren't very sharply shod and slid about on the slippery roads. They made no better time than those who walked.

The town marshal was a large man whose leg had been injured in the Civil War. He carried a heavy cane and limped rapidly along the road. John and Tar Moorehead followed at his heels and as they went other boys and men joined the crowd.

It had grown dark by the time they got to where the old woman had turned out of the road but the moon had come out. The marshal was thinking there might have been a murder. He kept asking the hunter questions. The hunter went along with his gun across his shoulder, a dog following at his heels. It isn't often a rabbit hunter has a chance to be so conspicuous. He was taking full advantage of it, leading the procession with the town marshal. "I did not see any wounds. She was a young girl. Her face was buried in the snow. No, I didn't know her." As a matter of fact the hunter had not looked closely at the body. He had been frightened. She might have been murdered and someone might spring out from behind a tree and murder him. In a woods, in the late afternoon, when the trees are all bare and there is white snow on the ground, when all is silent, something creepy steals over the body. If something strange or

uncanny has happened in the neighborhood all you think about
is getting away from there as fast as you can.

The crowd of men and boys had got to where the old woman
had crossed the field and went, following the marshal and the
hunter, up the slight incline and into the woods.

Tar and John Moorehead were both silent. John had his
bundle of papers in a bag slung across his shoulder. When he
got back to town he would have to go on distributing his
papers before he went home to supper. If Tar went with him,
as John had no doubt already determined he should, they
would both be late. Either Tar's mother or his sister would
have to warm their supper.

Well, they would have something to tell. A boy did not
get such a chance often. It was lucky they just happened to
be in the grocery when the hunter came in. The hunter was a
country fellow. Neither of the boys had ever seen him before.

Now the crowd of men and boys had got to the clearing.
Darkness comes quickly on such winter nights but the full
moon made everything clear. The two Moorehead boys stood
near the tree, beneath which the old woman had died.

She did not look old, lying there frozen, [not] in that light.
One of the men turned her over in the snow and Tar saw everything. His body trembled and so did his brother's. It might
have been the cold.

Neither of them had ever before seen a woman's body. It
may have been the snow, clinging to the frozen flesh, that made
it look so white, so like marble. No woman had come with
the party from town but one of the men, he was the town
blacksmith, took off his overcoat and spread it over her. Then
he gathered her into his arms and started off to town, all the
others following silently. At that time no one knew who she
was.

Tar had seen everything, had seen the round [*track] in the
snow, like a miniature race track, where the dogs had run, had
seen how the men were mystified, had seen the white bare
young-looking shoulders, had heard the whispered comments
of the men.

The men were simply mystified. They took the body to the

undertaker's and when the blacksmith, the hunter, the marshal and several others had got inside they closed the door. If Dick Moorehead had been there perhaps he could have got in and could have seen and heard everything, but the [*two] Moorehead boys couldn't.

Tar went with his brother John to distribute the [rest of his] papers and when they got home it was John who told the story.

Tar kept silent and went to bed early. It may have been he was not satisfied with the way John told the story.

Later, in the town, he must have heard other fragments of the old woman's story. He remembered her going past the Moorehead house when he was ill. She was recognized the next day and there was an investigation. The husband and son were found somewhere and brought to town and there was an attempt to connect them with the woman's death but it did not work. They had perfect enough alibis.

The town was however against them. They had to get out. Where they went Tar never heard.

He remembered only the picture there in the forest, the men standing about, the naked, girlish-looking figure, face down in the snow, the [*circle] made by the running dogs and the clear cold winter sky above. White fragments of clouds were drifting across the sky. They went racing across the little open space among the trees.

The scene in the forest had become for Tar, without his knowing it, the foundation for a story a child could not understand and it needed understanding. The fragments had to be picked up slowly long afterwards.

Things happened. When Tar was a young man he went to work on the farm of a German.[4] There was a hired girl and she was afraid of her employer. The farmer's wife hated her.

Tar saw things at that place. Once later, on a winter night, he had a half uncanny, mystical sort of adventure with dogs in a forest on a clear moonlit night. When he was a school boy, and on a summer day, he went with a boy friend out along a creek some miles from town and came to the house where the old woman had lived. No one had lived in the house since her

4. Again Sherwood Anderson refers to the summer of 1899, after his discharge from the army.

death. The doors were broken from the hinges, the window lights were all broken. As the boy and Tar stood in the road outside two dogs, just roving farm dogs no doubt, came running around a corner of the house. The dogs were tall gaunt fellows and came to the fence and glared through at the boys standing in the road.

The whole thing, the story of the old woman's death, was to Tar as he grew older like music heard from far off. The notes had to be picked up slowly one at a time. Something had to be understood.

The woman who died was one of those who feed [*animals]. From childhood she had been feeding animal life, in men, in cows, in chickens, in pigs, in horses, in dogs. She spent her life feeding all sorts of [*animals]. The experience with her husband was a purely animal experience. Her having children was an animal experience. Her daughter had died in childhood and with her one son she had apparently no human relations. She fed him as she fed her husband. When her son grew up he brought a woman to the house and the old woman fed them, saying nothing. On the night when she died she was hurrying homeward, bearing on her body food for animals.

She died in the clearing in the woods and even after her death continued feeding the animal life in the dogs that had trotted out of the town at her heels.

CHAPTER XIII

SOMETHING had been bothering Tar for a long time. It got worse during the summer of his thirteenth year. His mother had not been very well for a long time but that summer she seemed to get better. [*Now Tar, rather than John, sold the papers] but that did not take much time.⁵ As his mother wasn't very well and had other younger children to take her time she couldn't pay much attention to [*Tar].

He and Jim Moore went off to the woods on afternoons. Sometimes they just lazied around and sometimes they went fishing or swimming. Up along the creek farmers were working in the fields. When they went swimming, in a place called "Mama Culver's Hole," other boys from town came.⁶ Young men sometimes came down across the fields to the creek. There was one young man who was subject to fits. His father was the town blacksmith [*who had carried the dead woman out of the woods]. He went in swimming, just as the others did, but someone had to watch him [all the time]. Once he had a fit in the water and had to be pulled out so he wouldn't drown. Tar saw that, saw the man lying naked on the bank of the creek, saw the queer look in his eyes, the queer jerky movements of his legs, arms and body.

The man muttered words Tar couldn't understand. It might have been like a bad dream you have sometimes at night. [*He] only looked for a moment. Pretty soon the man got up and dressed. He walked slowly about in a field, his head hanging down, went to sit with his back against a tree. How pale he was.⁷

When the older boys and young men came to the swimming hole Tar and Jim Moore lit out. Older boys in such a place like to take it out on the youngsters. They throw mud on small boys' bodies after they come out from swimming and are partly

5. In *Memoirs*, p. 36, Anderson describes his boyhood job as newsboy.
6. This swimming hole is described in *Memoirs*, pp. 30–31.
7. *Ibid.*

dressed. When it hits you you have to go in and wash yourself off again. Sometimes they do it a dozen times.

Then they hide your clothes or dip them in the water and tie knots in the sleeve of your shirt. When you want to dress and go away you can't.

[*A gentle lot—small-town boys—sometimes.] They take a shirt sleeve and dip it in the water. Then they tie a hard knot and pull as hard as they can and a boy has a hard time getting it untied. If he has to take his teeth to it the older boys in the water laugh and shout. There is a song about it full of words worse than you could hear in any livery stable. "Chaw beef," the older boys yell.[8] Then they shout out the song. The whole place rings with it. It isn't any fancy singing.

The thing that troubled Tar troubled Jim Moore too. Sometimes when they were alone together, in the woods away up the creek beyond the regular swimming hole, they went in together. Then they came out and lay naked on the bank of the creek on the grass in the sun. It felt good.

[*Then] they began to talk about things they had heard, at school, among the young men at the swimming hole.

"Suppose you ever got a chance with a girl, what then?" Maybe little girls going home together from school, no boys about, talk the same way.

"Oh, I won't get any such chance. I'd be afraid, I guess, wouldn't you?"

"I guess you get over being afraid. Let's go."[9]

You can talk and think about a lot of things and then, when you come home where your mother and sister are, it doesn't seem to count much against you. If you had a chance and did something it might be different.

Sometimes when Tar and Jim were lying like that, on the creek bank, one of them touched the other's body. It was a queer feeling. When it happened they both sprang up and began to run about. Some young trees grew by the creek bank up that way and they climbed the trees. The trees were small,

8. The exact scene occurs in *Memoirs*, p. 31.
9. On Anderson's early interest in sex, see *Memoirs*, pp. 61–74. Compare the ensuing episodes with "Nobody Knows," *Winesburg, Ohio*, pp. 58–62.

smooth and slender and the boys pretended they were monkeys or some other kind of wild young animals. They kept on doing it for a long time, both acting rather crazy.

Once when they were doing it a man came along and they had to run and hide in some bushes. They were in a close place and had to lie close together. After the man passed they went at once to get their clothes, both feeling strange.

Strange about what? Well, how are you going to tell? All boys are that way sometimes.

There was a boy Jim and Tar both knew, who had the nerve to do anything. Once he was with a girl and they went into a barn. The girl's mother saw them go in and followed. The girl got a whipping. Neither Tar nor Jim thought anything really happened but the boy said it did. He bragged about it. "It isn't the first time."

Such talk. Tar and Jim thought the boy lied. "He wouldn't have the nerve—do you think?"

They talked about such things more than they wanted to. They couldn't help it. When they had talked a lot they both felt uncomfortable. Well, how are you going to find out anything? When men are talking you listen all you can. If the men see you hanging around they tell you to get out.

Tar saw things, taking papers to houses in the evening. There was a man used to come with a horse and buggy and wait in a certain place in a dark street and after a while he was joined by a woman. The woman was married and so was the man. Before the woman came the man had put on the side curtains to his buggy. They drove away together.

Tar knew who they were and after a time the man knew he knew. One day he met Tar on the street. The man stopped. He bought a paper. Then he stood looking at Tar with his hands thrust into his pockets. The man owned a large farm, several miles from town, and his wife and children lived out there but he was in town nearly all the time. He was a buyer of farm products, shipping them off to nearby cities. The woman Tar had seen get into the buggy was the wife of a merchant.

The man put a five dollar bill into Tar's hand. "I guess you know enough to keep your mouth shut," he said. That was all.

After he said it the man turned and went away. Tar had never had so much money, had never before had any money he did not expect to account for. It was an easy way to get it. When any of the Moorehead children made any money they gave it to their mother. She never asked anything of the sort. It just seemed the natural thing to do.

Tar bought himself a quarter's worth of candy, he bought a package of Sweet Caporal cigarettes. He and Jim Moore would try smoking them sometime when they were off in the woods. Then he bought a swell necktie that cost fifty cents.

That was all right. He had a little more than four dollars in his pocket. He had got the change in silver dollars. Ernest Wright, who kept a small hotel in town, was always standing in front of his hotel with a pile of silver dollars in his hands, playing with them. At the fair, in the fall, when there were a lot of fakers from out of town come for the fair, they set up little booths for gambling. You could get a cane by throwing a ring over it or a gold watch or a revolver by picking out the right number on a wheel. There were lots of such places. One year Dick Moorehead, being out of work, got a job in one of them.

At all such places little piles of silver dollars were stacked about up where everyone could see them. Dick Moorehead said a farmer or a hired man had about as much chance to win any of the money as a snowball had in hell.

It was nice though to see the silver dollars piled up, nice to see Ernest Wright jingling silver dollars in his hands as he stood on the sidewalk before his hotel.

Nice for Tar to have four big silver dollars he did not feel he had to account for. They had just come down into his hand, out of the sky, as it were. The candy he could eat, the cigarettes he and Jim Moore would try smoking someday soon. The new necktie would be a little difficult. Where would he tell the others at home he had got it? Most boys of his age in town never got any fifty cent neckties. Dick didn't get but about two new ones a year—when there was a G.A.R. convention or something. Tar might say he had found it and found the four silver dollars, too. Then he could give the money to his mother and forget it. It was fine to feel the heavy silver dollars in his pocket but he had got them in a strange way. Silver is much better to have than bills. It feels like more.

When a man is married you see him with his wife and you do not think anything [about it] but a man like that, waiting in a buggy in a side street, and then a woman coming along, trying to act as though she is going to call on some neighbor— it being night and supper over and her husband gone back to his store. Then the woman looking around and getting, quick, into the buggy. They driving off with the curtains drawn, that way.

Plenty Madame Bovaries in American small towns—what! [10]

Tar wanted to tell Jim Moore but didn't dare. There was a kind of agreement between himself and the man from whom he had taken the five dollars.

The woman knew he knew as well as the man. He had come out of an alleyway bare-footed, making no sound, with a bundle of papers under his arm, had popped right out on them.

Maybe he did it purposely.

The woman's husband took a morning paper at his store and had an afternoon paper delivered at his house. It was a funny feeling to go into his store afterwards and see him there, talking to some man, knowing nothing, Tar, just a kid, knowing such a lot.

Well, what did he know?

The trouble is that such things set a boy thinking. You want to see a lot and when you see something it stirs you up and makes you almost wish you hadn't. The woman, when Tar took the paper to her house, never let on. She had a nerve all right.

Why did they go sneaking out that way? A boy knows but doesn't know. If Tar could only have talked it over with John or Jim Moore it would have been a relief. You can't talk about such things to someone in your own family. You have to go outside.

Tar saw other things. Win Connell, who worked in Cary's drug store, married Mrs. Grey, after her first husband died.

---

10. Gustave Flaubert (1821–80) published *Madame Bovary* in 1857.

She was taller than he was. They took a house and furnished it with her first husband's furniture. One evening, when it was raining and dark, only about seven o'clock, Tar went along back of their house on his paper route and they had forgot to close the window blinds. They didn't have a thing on, either of them, and he was chasing her around. You would never think grown people could act like that.[11]

Tar was in the alleyway, just as he was that time he saw the people in the buggy. By cutting through alleyways you save time [*delivering papers] when a train is late. There he stood, holding his papers under his coat so they wouldn't get wet, and there were the two grown people acting like that.

There was a kind of living room and a stairway going upstairs and then some other rooms on the ground floor, without any lights in them.

What Tar saw first was the woman running like that, without any clothes on, across the room and her husband after her. It made Tar laugh. They were like monkeys. The woman ran upstairs and he after her. Then down she came again. They dodged into the dark rooms and then out again. He caught her sometimes but she must have been slippery. She got away every time. They kept it up and kept it up. Such a crazy thing to see. There was a couch in the room Tar was looking into and once she got behind it and he was in front. He put his hands on the top of the couch and sprang clear over. You wouldn't have thought [*a drug clerk] could do it.

Then he chased her into one of the dark rooms. Tar waited and waited but they did not come out.

A fellow like Win Connell had to work, after supper, at the store. He would get dressed and go down there. People coming in to get prescriptions put up, to buy a cigar maybe. Win standing back of the counter smiling. "Is there anything else? Certainly, if it is not satisfactory bring it back. We aim to please."

Tar going away out of his way, being later than ever to supper, to go past Cary's drug store and look in, to see Win

11. A similar scene of innocent voyeurism occurs in "Girl by the Stove," *Decision*, I (January, 1942), 19–22.

in there, just like any other man, doing what he did all the
time every day. And less than an hour ago. . . .

Win wasn't so very old but he was already baldheaded.

The world of older people opening out gradually to a boy
going around with his papers. Some older ones seemed to have
a lot of dignity. Others hadn't. Boys, Tar's own age, had secret
vices. Some of the boys at the swimming hole did things, said
things. When men get older they grow sentimental about the
old swimming hole. They remember only the pleasant things
that happened. There is a trick of the mind that makes you
forget [*the] unpleasant [things]. It's just as well. If you
could see life clear and straight maybe you couldn't live.

A boy goes around town filled with curiosity. He knows
where the vicious dogs are, what people speak kindly to him.
There are soreheads everywhere. You can't get a thing out of
them. If the paper is an hour late they growl and fuss at you.
What the deuce. You don't run the railroad. If the train is
late it isn't your fault.

That Win Connell doing that. Tar laughed about it sometimes at night in bed. How many other people cutting up all
kinds of capers behind the blinds of houses? In some houses
men and women were always quarreling. Tar came along the
street and opening a gate went into a yard. He was going to
put the paper under the back door. Some wanted it put there.
As he went around the house the sound of quarreling inside.
"I didn't either. You're a liar. I'll knock your damn head off.
Try it once." The low growling voice of a man, the sharp
cutting voice of an angry woman.

Tar tapped on the back door. It might be his collection
night. Both the man and woman came to the door. They both
thought it might be some neighbor and that they had been
caught quarreling. [*"Well, it's only a boy."] When they saw
it was only [*Tar] a look of relief on the two faces. The man
paid Tar with a growl. "You've been late twice this week. I
want my paper to be here when I get home."

The door was slammed and Tar hung about for a moment.
Would they start quarreling again? They did. Maybe they
liked it.

At night streets of houses with closed blinds. Men coming out at the front door to go uptown. They went into saloons, into the drug store, into the barber shop or the cigar store. There they sat bragging, sometimes, sometimes just being quiet. Dick Moorehead did not quarrel with his wife but just the same he was one thing at home and another when he was out in the evening among men. Tar had slid in among groups of men when his father was holding forth. He slid out pretty fast. Dick had to sing pretty low at home. Tar wondered why. It wasn't because Mary Moorehead scolded him.

In nearly every house he visited either the man or woman ruled the roost. Downtown, among the other men, [*a man was] always trying to create the impression [*he was] boss. "I said to my old woman—look here, I said—you do so and so. You bet she did it."

Did it eh? In most of the houses Tar visited it was as at the Moorehead house—the women were the strong ones. Sometimes they ruled by bitter words, sometimes by tears, sometimes by silence. Silence was Mary Moorehead's way.

PART IV

CHAPTER XIV

There was a girl, Tar's age, came to visit Colonel Farley's house on Maumee Street. The street went out past the Farley place and ended at the town cemetery. The Farley Place was the last one on the street but one, an old [rickety] house where the Thompsons lived.

The Farley house was large and had a cupola on top. There was a low hedge in front facing the road and an apple orchard at the side. At the back of the apple orchard was a large red barn. It was one of the swellest places in town.

The Farleys were people who were always nice to Tar after he began selling papers but he did not see them often. Colonel Farley had been in the war like Tar's father and was a married man when he went in. He had two sons, both of whom had gone to college. Then they went away to live in some city and they must have got rich. Some said they had married rich women. They sent money home to the Colonel and his wife, plenty of it. The Colonel was a lawyer but hadn't much practise—just fooled around getting pensions for old soldiers and that sort of thing. Sometimes he did not go to his office all day. Tar saw him sitting on the front porch of the house reading a book. His wife sat sewing. She was small and fat. When he collected for the paper the Colonel always gave Tar an extra nickel. Such people, Tar thought, [*were] all right.

They had another old couple living with them. The man took care of their carriage and drove the Colonel and his wife out on fine afternoons and the woman cooked and did the housework. Everyone had it pretty soft at that house, Tar thought.

They weren't much like the Thompsons who lived beyond them out that street, right by the cemetery gate.

The Thompsons were a tough lot. There were three grown sons and a girl Tar's age. Tar hardly ever saw old Boss Thompson or the boys. They went every summer with a circus or a street fair. One year they had a stuffed whale on a box car.

They had canvas all around it and went around to towns and charged ten cents to look at it.[1]

When they were at home the Thompsons, father and sons, hung around the saloons and bragged. Old Boss Thompson always seemed to have plenty of money but he made his women folks live like dogs. His old woman never had a new dress and looked all worn out while the old man and the boys were always strutting in Main Street. That year they had the whale old Thompson wore a plug hat and always had on a fancy vest. He liked to go into a saloon or a store and take out a big roll of bills. If he had a nickel in his pocket when he wanted some beer he never showed it. He took out a ten dollar bill, peeled it off a big roll and threw it on the bar. Some men said most of the roll was made up of one dollar bills. The boys were the same sort but they did not have so much money to strut with. The old man kept everything for himself.

The girl that came to visit the Farleys in the summer was their son's daughter. Her father and mother had gone to Europe so she was going to stay until they came back. Tar heard about it before she came—such things get about town pretty fast— and [there he] was on hand at the railroad station to get his bundle of papers, when she came in.

She was pretty all right. Well, she had blue eyes and yellow hair and wore a white dress and white stockings. The Colonel and his wife and the old man who drove their carriage met her at the station.

Tar had got his papers—the baggage man always threw them off on the station platform at his feet—and he hustled to see if he could sell some to people getting off and on the train. When the girl got off—she had been put in charge of the conductor and he [*handed] her off himself—the Colonel came over to where Tar stood and asked for his paper. "I can just as well save you coming clear out our way," he said. He was holding the girl's hand. "This is my [*granddaughter], Miss Ester Farley," [he said]. Tar went all red. It was the first time anyone had ever introduced him to a lady. He did

---

1. This girl reappears in *Memoirs*, pp. 61–66.

not know what to do so he took off his cap but did not say a word.

The girl didn't even blush. What she did was just to stare at him.

"Lordy," Tar thought. He didn't want to wait to see her again until he had to take the paper to the Farleys' the next day, [*so] he went out that way in the afternoon, but never saw a thing. The worst was that when he went out past the Farleys' he had to do one of two things. The street did not go anywhere, just went to the cemetery gate and stopped and he had to go on into the cemetery, through it and out over a fence [*and] into another street, or come back again past the Farleys'. Well, he did not want the Colonel, his wife or the girl to think he was hanging around.

The girl had got him all stirred up, right off. It was the first time that had happened. He dreamed of her at night and did[*n't] even dare speak of her to Jim Moore. One day Jim said something about her. Tar got red. He had to begin talking of something else [quick]. He couldn't think what to say.

[*Tar] began going off by himself. It he went out the rail-road tracks a mile—toward the little town of Greenville—then turned off through the fields, he came to a creek that did not run through [his] town at all.

He could go that way clear to Greenville if he wanted to. He did once. It was only five miles. It was nice to be in a town where he did not know a soul. The main street was only half as long as the one in his own town. People he had never seen were standing in the store doors, strange people walking in the streets. They looked at him with curiosity in their eyes. In his own town he had now become a familiar figure, running around with the papers mornings and evenings.

The reason he liked to go off by himself that summer was that, when he was alone, he could fancy the new girl was with him. Sometimes when he took the paper he saw her at the Farley house. She even came out sometimes to take the paper from him and did it with a self-possessed smile on her face. If he was disconcerted in her presence she wasn't.

She said "good morning" to him and all he could do was

to mutter something she could not hear. Often when he was going around with the papers in the afternoon he saw her riding with her grandfather and grandmother. They all spoke to him and he took off his cap, awkwardly.

After all, she was only a girl like his sister Margaret.

When he went out of town alone, in the summer afternoons, he could imagine she was with him. He took hold of her hand as they walked along. He wasn't afraid then.

The best place to go was to a beech woods about a half mile back from the tracks.

The beech trees grew in a little grassy gully that led down to the creek and on the hill above. There was a branch of the creek in the gully in the early spring but during the summer it dried up.

There isn't any woods like a beech woods, Tar thought. Under the trees the ground was clear, no small bushes growing, and there were places among the big roots that stuck up out of the ground where he could lie as in a bed. Everywhere squirrels and chipmunks darted about. When he had been still a long time they came [pretty] close. Tar could have shot any number of squirrels that summer and perhaps if he had and had taken them home to be cooked it would have helped the Mooreheads a good deal, but he never took a gun [with him].

John had one. He had got it cheap second-handed. Tar could have borrowed it easy enough. He did not want to.

He wanted to go to the beech woods because he wanted to dream of the new girl in town, wanted to pretend she was with him. When he got to the place he settled his body down in a good comfortable place among the roots and closed his eyes.

There was the girl, close beside him, in fancy[, *of course]. He did not talk [to her] much. What was to be said? He took her hand in his, held her hand against his cheek. Her fingers were so soft and small that when he held her hand his own looked big like the hand of a man.

He was going to marry the Farley girl when he grew up. That he had decided. He did not know just what marriage meant. Yes he did. The reason he was so ashamed and blushed

so when he went near her was because he was always having
such thoughts when she wasn't [*near]. First he would have
to grow up and go to the city. He would have to get as rich
as she was. That would take time but not so long. Tar made
four dollars a week selling papers. He was in a town where
there weren't many people. If the town were twice as large he
would make twice as much—if four times as [*large] four
times as much. Four times four is sixteen. In a year there are
fifty-two weeks. Four times fifty-two is two hundred and eight
dollars. Lordy, that's a lot.

And he wouldn't be selling just papers. Maybe he'd get him
a store. Then he would have him a carriage or an automobile.
He would ride up in front of her house.

Tar tried to imagine what the city house the girl lived in
when she was at home could be like. The Farley house on
Maumee Street was about the grandest place in town but the
wealth of Colonel Farley didn't amount to anything against
that of his sons in the city. Everyone in town said that.

In the beech woods, during the summer afternoons, Tar
closed his eyes and dreamed the hours away. Sometimes he
went to sleep. Nowdays he was always lying awake in bed at
night. In the woods he could hardly tell the difference between
sleeping and waking. All that summer no one in his own family
seemed to pay any attention to him. He just came and went
at the Moorehead house, mostly in silence. Sometimes John
or Margaret spoke to him. "What's the matter with you?" "Ah,
nothing." It may have been that his mother was a little puzzled
by his state. She however said nothing. Tar was glad of that.

In the beech woods he lay on his back and closed his eyes.
Then he opened them slowly. The beech trees near the foot
of the ravine were heavy-bodied great fellows. Their coats were
patched with color, the white bark alternating with torn brown
places. Up the side of the hill, in one spot, there was a group
of young beech trees. Tar could imagine the forest above going
on and on indefinitely.

In books things were always happening in forests. A young
girl got lost in such a place. She was very beautiful, like the
new girl in town. Well, there she was in the forest alone and
night came on. She had to sleep in a hollow tree, or in a place

among tree roots. As she lay there and just as darkness was coming she saw something. Some men rode into the forest and stopped near her. She kept very still. One of the men got off his horse and said strange words—"Open Sesame"—and the ground opened at his feet. There was a great door, so cleverly covered with leaves sticks [stones] and earth that you would never guess it was there.

The men went down a stairway and stayed a long time. When they came out they got on their horses and the leader—a strangely handsome man—just such a man as Tar felt he would be when he grew up—said some more strange words. "Close Sesame," he said and the door closed and all was as before.

Then the girl tried it. She went to the place and said the words and the door opened. Many strange adventures followed. Tar remembered them dimly from a book Dick Moorehead read aloud to the children on winter evenings.[2]

There were other stories, other things always happening in forests. Sometimes boys or girls got changed into birds or trees or animals. The young beech trees that grew on the side of the ravine had bodies like the bodies of young girls. When a little wind blew they swayed slightly. Tar, when he kept his eyes closed, could fancy the trees were beckoning to him. There was one young [*beech]—he never knew why he singled out just that one—that might just have been Colonel Farley's granddaughter.

Once Tar went to where it stood and touched it with his finger. The feeling he had was at the moment so real that he blushed when he did it.

He became obsessed with the notion of going out to the beech grove at night and one night he did it.

He had picked out a moonlit night. Well, a neighbor was at the Mooreheads' and Dick was talking on the front porch. Mary Moorehead was there but not saying much as usual. Tar's papers were all sold. If he stayed away for a time his mother would not [*care]. She was sitting silently in a rocking chair. Everyone was listening to Dick. He usually managed to make them do that.

2. Anderson refers to "Ali Baba and the Forty Thieves" from the Arabic *Thousand and One Nights.*

Tar lit out the back way and hurried around through back streets to the railroad tracks. When he had got out of town a freight train came along. A lot of tramps were in an empty coal car. Tar saw them as plain as day. One of them was singing.

He got to the place where he had to turn off the tracks and without [any] trouble found his way to the beech grove.

[It was all different than in the daytime.] [*It was all strange.] Everything was still and spooky. He found a place where he could lie comfortably, and waited.

[*For what?] What did he expect? He did not know. Perhaps he thought the girl might come to him, that she might have got lost and would be somewhere in the woods when he got there. In the darkness he wouldn't be so embarrassed when she was near.

She wasn't there of course. [*He didn't really expect it.] No one was there. No robbers came on horseback, nothing happened. He kept perfectly still for a long time and there wasn't a sound.

Then little sounds began. He could see things more clearly as his eyes grew accustomed to the dim light. A squirrel or a rabbit ran down along the bottom of the ravine. He saw a flash of something white. There was a sound back of him, one of the little soft sounds made by tiny animals when they move about at night. His body trembled. It was as though something was running over his body, under his clothes.

It might have been an ant. He wondered whether or not ants went out at night.

The wind blew a little stronger and a little stronger—not a gale, just blowing steadily, up the ravine from the creek. He could hear the creek chattering. There was a place near where it had to run over stones.

Tar closed his eyes and held them closed a long time. Afterwards he wondered if he slept. If he did it couldn't have been long.

When he opened his eyes again he was looking right at the place where the young beeches grew. He could see the one young beech tree he had gone across the ravine to touch that time, standing out from all the others.

That time when he was sick things—trees houses and people

—were always leaving the ground and floating away from him. He had to hold onto something inside himself. If he hadn't he might have died. No one else understood about that but he did.

Now the white young beech tree was coming toward him. It might have had something to do with the light and the wind blowing and the young beech trees swaying in the wind.

He did not know. The one tree just seemed to leave the others and come toward him. He was as scared as when Colonel Farley's granddaughter spoke to him when he took the paper to their house but in a different way.

He was so scared that he jumped up and ran and when he ran he got more scared. How he got out of the woods and back to the railroad track without being hurt he never knew. He kept running after he got up onto the tracks. He was in his bare feet and the cinders hurt and once he stubbed his toe so that it bled but he never stopped running or being afraid until he got back into town, and to his own house.

He couldn't have been gone long. When he got back Dick was still going it on the front porch and the others were still listening. Tar stood out back by the woodshed a long time to get his breath and let his heart stop pounding. Then he had to wash his feet and get the dried blood off his hurt toe before he went sneaking off upstairs and to bed. He did not want to get blood on the sheets.

And after he got upstairs and into bed and after the neighbors went home and his mother came upstairs to see if he and the others were all right he could not sleep.

There were a lot of nights that summer when Tar could not sleep much.

CHAPTER XV

ANOTHER adventure of quite another sort one afternoon later during that same summer. Tar could not keep off Maumee Street. In the morning he got through selling his papers by nine o'clock. Sometimes he had a job, mowing someone's lawn. There were plenty of other boys after such jobs. They didn't come any too thick.[3]

No good fooling around home. When Tar was with his friend Jim Moore during that summer he was likely to be silent. Jim didn't like it and found someone else [*with whom to go adventuring] to the woods or to the swimming hole.

Tar went to the fair ground and watched the men work the race horses, he hung around the Whitehead barn.

There were always some old newspapers that hadn't been sold, in the woodshed at home. Tar took several under his arm and went out along Maumee Street just to be going past the Farley house. Sometimes he saw the girl, sometimes he did not. When he did, when she was on the porch with her grandmother or in the yard or the orchard, he did not dare look.

The papers under his arm were to create the impression he had business out that way.

It was pretty thin. Who was there to take a paper out that way? No one but the Thompsons.

They take a paper—huh!

Now old Boss Thompson and the boys were out somewhere with a circus. It would be fun to do that when [*Tar] grew up but circuses certainly carried a tough lot of men with them. When a circus came to the town where Tar lived he got up early and went down to the ground and saw everything, right from the start, saw the tent go up, the animals fed, everything. He saw the men get ready for the parade on Main Street. They put the bright red and purple coats on right over their old horsey, manurey clothes. The men didn't even bother to wash

3. In *Memoirs*, p. 55, Anderson describes his need for many boyhood jobs, causing him to be called "Jobby" Anderson.

their hands and faces. Some of them looked at though they had never washed.

The women in the circus and the child actors were pretty near the same way. They looked grand in the parade but you ought to see how they live. The Thompson [*women] never were with a circus that came to their own town but [*they were like that].

Tar thought that since the Farley girl had come to town he knew something of what a real swell looked like. She was always dressed in clean clothes, no matter what time of day Tar saw her. He would have wagered anything she was all washed up fresh every day. Maybe she took a bath, all over, every day. The Farleys had a bathtub, one of the few in town.

The Mooreheads were pretty clean, especially Margaret, but you can't expect too much. In the winter it's a lot of trouble to be always washing.

It's nice though when you see someone else do it—a girl you're crazy about especially.

It was a wonder Mame Thompson, old Boss Thompson's one daughter, didn't go off to the circus with her father and brothers. She might have learned to ride a horse standing up or perform on a trapeze. The young girls who did such things in circuses weren't so much. Well they rode a horse standing up. What of it? It was an old steady horse usually, anyone could ride that way. Hal Brown whose father had a grocery, and cows in the barn, had to go to a field for the cows every night.[4] He was a friend of Tar's and sometimes Tar went with him and then later he went around with Tar delivering the papers. Hal could ride a horse standing up. He could ride a cow that way. He did it lots of times.

Tar began thinking about Mame Thompson, at about the same time she began paying attention to him. [*He] may have been to her what the Farley girl was to him, someone to think

4. Hal Brown represents Herman Hurd, Anderson's closest boyhood friend in Clyde. See *A Story Teller's Story*, p. 97; and *Memoirs*, pp. 53–54. The most useful interview with Hurd is Harold Detlefsen, "Herman Hurd, of Clyde, Sherwood Anderson's Boyhood Chum," *RFD News* (Bellevue, Ohio), October 8, 1962, pp. 1–2.

about. The Thompsons, in spite of old Boss Thompson's splurging around and showing his money, didn't stand so well in town. The old woman didn't go anywhere hardly. She stayed at home like Tar's mother but not for the same reason. Mary Moorehead had a lot to do—so many children—but what did old Mrs. Thompson have to do? No one at home all summer but the girl Mame and she was big enough to help with the work. The old Thompson woman looked all fagged out. She always had on dirty clothes and so did Mame, when she was at home.

Tar began seeing a good deal of her. Two or three times a week, sometimes every day, he sneaked out that way and he couldn't help going on past the Farleys' and to their house.

When he got past the Farleys' there was a drop in the road and a bridge across a ditch that was dry all summer. Then he came to the Thompsons' barn. It stood close beside the road and the house was on the opposite side [of the road], a little farther along, right near the cemetery gate.

They had a general buried in the cemetery and a stone monument. He was standing with one foot on a cannon and with a finger pointed right at the Thompsons' [house].[5]

You'd have thought the town, if it was so blamed proud of its dead general, would have set up something fancier for him to point at.

The house was one of the small unpainted kind with a lot of the shingles gone out of the roof. It looked like the Old Harry. There had been a front porch but most of the floor was all rotted away.

The Thompsons had a barn but there wasn't a horse, not even a cow. There was just a little old half rotten hay upstairs and some chickens scratching around downstairs. The hay must have been in the barn a long time. Some of it stuck out through an open door. It was all black and mouldy looking.

Mame Thompson was a year or two older than Tar. She had

5. James Birdseye McPherson (1828–64), of Clyde, Ohio, killed in the South. From his name, Anderson got the title for his first published novel, *Windy McPherson's Son* (New York: John Lane Company, 1916). See *Memoirs*, pp. 14–15.

had more experience. At first, when he began going out that way, Tar did not think about her at all and then he did. She began to notice him.

She had begun to wonder what he was up to, always coming out that way. He didn't blame her but what was he to do? He might have turned back at the bridge but if he did his going along the street wouldn't have had any sense to it. He always carried a few papers, for a bluff. Well, he [thought he] had to keep up the bluff if he could.

Mame got so, when she saw him coming, she would cross the road and stand in the open barn door. Tar hardly ever saw old Mrs. Thompson. He had to walk right past the barn or turn back. There was Mame standing inside the barn door and pretending not to see him just as he was always pretending not to see her.

It got worse and worse.

Mame wasn't slender like the Farley girl. She was a little fat and had big legs. Nearly always she had on a dirty dress and sometimes her face was dirty. Her hair was red and she had freckles on her face.

Another boy in town, named Pete Welsh, had gone right into a barn with a girl. He had told Tar and Jim Moore about it, had bragged about it.

In spite of himself Tar began thinking about Mame Thompson. That was a fine how-de-do but how could he help it? Some of the boys at school had girls. They gave them things and when they were walking home from school some of the bold[*er] ones even walked with their girls a little ways. It took nerve. When a boy did it the others came along behind shouting and making fun.

Tar might have done that with the Farley girl if he ever had the chance. He never would have. In the first place she would be going away before school began and, even if she stayed, she maybe wouldn't want him.

He wouldn't dare ever let it be known if it happened that Mame Thompson had become his girl. What an idea! That would be just nuts for Pete Welsh and Hal Brown and Jim Moore. They would never let up.

O, Lord. Tar had begun to think of Mame Thompson at night now, had got her all mixed up with his thoughts of the Farley girl, but his thoughts about her didn't get mixed up with any beech trees or clouds in the sky or anything like that.

His thoughts got pretty definite, sometimes. Would he ever have the nerve? O, Lord. What a question to ask himself. Of course he wouldn't.

After all she wasn't so bad. He got to looking at her when he went past. Sometimes she put her hands over her face and giggled and sometimes she pretended not to see him.

One day it happened. Well, he hadn't ever intended it should. He had got clear up to the barn and hadn't seen her [at all]. She might have gone away. The Thompsons' house, across the way, looked as it always did, all closed up and dark, no wash hanging out in the yard, no cats or dogs around, no smoke going up out of a kitchen chimney. You might have thought that, when the old man and the boys were away, old Mrs. Thompson and Mame didn't ever eat—or wash either.

Tar had not seen Mame as he came along the road and over the bridge. She was always standing in the barn, pretending to do something in there. What was she pretending to do?

He stopped by the barn door and looked in. Then, hearing and seeing nothing, he went in. What made him do it he did not know. He walked half way into the barn and then, when he turned to go out [again], there she was. She had been hiding behind a door [or something].

She didn't say anything and neither did Tar. They stood looking at each other and then she went to where there was a rickety old ladder leading up to the loft.

It was up to Tar whether or not he would follow. That was what she meant all right, all right. When she had got almost up she turned and looked at him but she didn't say anything. There was something in her eyes. O, Lordy.

Tar never dreamed he could be so bold. Well, he wasn't bold. With trembling legs he went across the barn floor to the foot of the ladder. There didn't seem enough strength in his arms and legs to climb [up. In such a situation a boy is terribly frightened.] There may be boys who are naturally bold, as Pete Welsh said he was, who do not care. All they want is a chance. Tar wasn't like that.

He felt as though he had died. It couldn't be himself, Tar Moorehead, doing what he was doing. It was too bold and terrible—wonderful too.

When Tar got up into the barn loft there was Mame sitting on the little pile of black old hay near the door. The loft door was open. You could see a long ways. Tar could see along the road right into the yard of the Farley place. His legs were so weak that he sat down at once, right near the girl, but he didn't look at her, didn't dare. He looked out through the barn door. A grocery boy came with things for the Farleys. He went around the house to the back door with a basket in his hand. When he came back around the house he turned the horse [around] and drove away. It was Cal Sleshinger, who drove the delivery wagon for Wagner's store. He had red hair.

So did Mame. Well, her hair wasn't exactly red. It was sandy. Her eyebrows were sandy [too].

Now Tar wasn't thinking of the fact that her dress was dirty, her fingers dirty, her face perhaps dirty. He didn't dare look at her [face]. He was thinking. What was he thinking?

"If you saw me on Main Street I bet you wouldn't speak to me. You're too stuck up."

Mame wanted to be reassured. Tar wanted to answer but couldn't. He was right near her, could have put out his hand and touched her.

She said one or two things. "Why do you keep coming out this way if you're so stuck on yourself?" Her voice was a little harsh [now].

It was evident she did not know about Tar and the Farley girl, had not connected them in her mind. She thought his coming out that way had been to see her.

That time Pete Welsh went into a barn with a girl her mother came. Pete ran and the girl got a whipping. Tar wondered if they had gone up into [*a] barn loft. He looked down through the loft door to see how far he would have to jump. Pete hadn't said anything about jumping. He had just bragged. Jim Moore had kept saying, "I bet you never did. I bet you never did," and Pete had answered sharply, "We did too. I tell you we did."

Tar could, maybe, if he had the nerve. If you have had the nerve once then maybe you have it naturally the next time. Some boys are born with nerve [*others aren't]. Everything is easy for them.

[*Now] Tar's silence and fear had infected Mame. They sat staring out through the barn door.

Something [*else] happened. Old Mrs. Thompson came into the barn and called Mame. Had she seen Tar go in? Both children sat in silence. The old woman stood downstairs. The Thompsons kept a few hens. Mame reassured Tar. "She's looking for eggs," she whispered softly. Tar could scarcely hear her voice [now].

They were [both] [*again] silent and when the old woman went out of the barn Mame got up and began crawling down the ladder.

It may have been she had become contemptuous of Tar. She did not look at him as she went down and when she had gone and when Tar heard her go out of the barn he sat for several minutes staring out through the loft door.

He wanted to cry.

The worst was that the Farley girl came out of the Farley house and stood looking along the road [toward the barn]. She [*might] have been looking through a window and might have seen him and Mame go [*into the barn]. Now, if Tar got the chance, he wouldn't ever speak to her, wouldn't dare be where she was.

He wouldn't ever get either girl. It was the way things turn out if you haven't any nerve. He would have liked to beat himself, hurt himself in some way.

When the Farley girl had gone back into the house he went to the loft door and let himself down, as far as he could hang, and then dropped. He had brought a few old newspapers with him, for the sake of his bluff, and had left them in the loft.

Good Gracious. There wasn't any way to get out of the hole he was in [now] except to cut across lots. Along where the little dry ditch ran there was some low ground where you sank in almost to your knee. It was the only way [*he] could go now without going past either the Thompsons' or the Farleys'.

Tar went that way, sinking into the soft mud. Then he had to go through a tangled berry patch where the briers tore his legs.

He was rather glad of that. The hurt places felt almost good. O, Lord! [No one knows how a boy feels sometimes, ashamed of everything.] If he had only had the nerve. [*If he had only had the nerve.]

Tar couldn't help wondering how [*it] would have been if. . . .

O, Lord!

To go home after that and to see Margaret and his mother and everyone. When he was alone with Jim Moore [perhaps] he could ask questions, but the answers he would get [likely] wouldn't be much. "If you had a chance. . . . If you were in a barn with a girl like Pete was that time. . . ."

What was the use asking questions? Jim Moore would only laugh. "Ah, I won't ever have no such a chance. I bet Pete didn't. I bet he's just a liar."

The worst for Tar wasn't at home. No one knew anything. Maybe the strange girl in town, the Farley girl, knew. Tar couldn't tell. It might be she thought a lot of things that weren't true. [*Nothing had happened.] You could never tell what a girl like that, a good girl, would be thinking.

The worst for Tar would be when he saw the Farleys on the street, driving in the carriage, the girl sitting with them. If it was on Main Street he [*could] dodge into a store [and] if on a residence street go right into someone's yard. [*He would go right into any yard] dog or no dog. Better be bit by a dog than meet her face to face now, he thought.

He would not take the paper out to the Farleys' until after dark and he [*would] let the Colonel pay him when they met on Main Street.

Well, the Colonel might complain. "You used to be so prompt. The train can't be late every day."

Tar would keep right on being late with the paper, and sneaking in at odd times, until fall came and the strange girl went back to the city. Then he would be all right. [He figured] he

could dodge Mame Thompson all right. She didn't come uptown very often and when school started she would be in another grade.

It would be all right about her because maybe she was
ashamed too.

It might be that sometimes when they did meet, when they
were both older, she would laugh at him. That was an almost
unbearable thought [*to Tar but he put it aside. It might come
back at night—for a while] [but it didn't come often. When it
came was mostly at night when he was in bed.]

[*Perhaps the feeling of shame wouldn't last very long.
When it came at night he would soon go to sleep or get to
thinking of something else.

[*Now he was thinking of what might have happened if he
had had the nerve. When that thought came at night he would
be a good deal longer time getting to sleep.]

PART V

CHAPTER XVI

DAYS of snow followed by rain, with deep mud in the unpaved streets of Tar's Ohio town. In March always a few warm days. Tar, with Jim Moore, Hal Brown and a few others, lit out for the swimming hole. The water was high. Along the bank of the creek the pussy-willows were blossoming. To the boys it seemed that all nature was shouting, "Spring has come, spring has come." What fun to take off heavy coats, heavy boots. The Moorehead boys had to wear cheap boots that by March were full of holes. On cold days the snow worked its way through broken soles.

The boys stood on the creek bank looking at each other. A few insects were out. A bee flew past Tar's face. "Lordy! I dare you! You go in and I will."

The boys took off their clothes and plunged in. What a disappointment! How icy cold the swift-running water! They got out quickly and dressed shivering.

Fun though to go wandering along creek banks, through leafless strips of forest, the clear sun shining. A grand day to play hookey from school. Suppose a boy gets a hiding from the superintendent. What's the difs?

During the cold winter months Tar's father managed to stay away from home a good deal. The slender girl he had married had been the mother of seven children. You know what that does to a woman. When she isn't very well she looks like the devil. Gaunt cheeks, stooped shoulders, hands always trembling.

Men like Tar's father take life as it comes. Life rolls off them like water off a duck's back. What's the use hanging around where there is sadness in the air, trouble you can't remedy, being what you are?

Dick Moorehead liked people and people liked him. He told stories, drank hard cider at farm houses. All his life afterwards Tar remembered a few trips he took with Dick to the country.

There was one house where he saw two great German women, one married, the other single and living with her sister. The German woman's husband was also large. They had a whole keg of beer on tap, oceans of food on the table. Dick seemed more at home there than in town, in the Moorehead house. In the evening some neighbors came in and they all danced. Dick was like a kid, swinging the big girls around. He could crack such jokes that all the men whooped with laughter and the women giggled and blushed. Tar couldn't understand the jokes. He sat in a corner staring.

At another time in the country in the summer a lot of men camped in the woods at the edge of a creek. They were ex-soldiers, making a night of it.

And again, with the coming of darkness, women came. That was when Dick began to shine. People liked to have him because he made everything lively. That night by the camp fire, when everyone thought Tar was asleep, both the men and women got a little lit up. Dick went with a woman back into the darkness.[1] You couldn't tell who the women were, who the men were. Dick knew all kinds of people. He had one kind of life at home in town and another when he was abroad. Why did he take his son on such expeditions? It may have been that Mary Moorehead asked him to take the boy and he did not know how to get out of it. Tar couldn't stay away long. He had to get back to town and tend up to his papers. Both times they left town in the evening and Dick brought him back the next day. Then Dick cut out again, alone. Two kinds of lives led by the man who was Tar's father, two kinds of lives led by a lot of quiet-seeming men of the town.

Tar got onto a lot of things, slowly. When you are a boy you don't go around selling papers with your eyes shut. The more you can see the better you like it.

Maybe, later, you lead several kinds of lives yourself. You are one thing today and another tomorrow, changing like the weather.

1. In *A Story Teller's Story*, pp. 32–33, Anderson describes his father's fidelity to his mother; but in *Memoirs*, p. 17, the father is described as unfaithful.

There are solid people and people not so solid. It's more fun on the whole not to be too solid. Solid good people miss a lot.

It might have been that Tar's mother knew things she never let on to know. What she knew or didn't know left something for Tar to think about and wonder about all the rest of his life. Hatred of his father came and then, a long time afterwards, understanding [began to come]. A lot of women are like mothers with their husbands. They have to be. Some men can't grow up. A woman has a lot of kids and she gets so and so. What she wanted from a man, at first, she doesn't want any more. Better let him go and have his fling. Life isn't so gay for any of us, when we are poor anyway. There comes a time when a woman wants her children to have their chance and that is about all she asks. She would like to live long enough to see that happen, and then. . . .

Tar's mother must have been glad most of her children were boys. The cards are stacked better for boys. No denying that.

The Moorehead house, with Tar's mother nowadays always half ill and growing constantly weaker, was no place for such a one as Dick. Now the woman of the house was living on her nerve. She was living because she did not want to die, not yet.

Such a woman grows very determined and silent. The husband, more than the children, feels her silence as a kind of reproach. God, what can a man do?

Some obscure disease eating at Mary Moorehead's body. She did her work in the house, with Margaret's assistance, and still took in family washings but she grew constantly paler and her hands trembled more and more. John worked every day in a factory.[2] He too was growing habitually silent. The work may have been too heavy for his young body. In Tar's childhood no one spoke of laws about children in factories.

The slender long work-roughened fingers of Tar's mother fascinated him. He remembered them clearly long afterward when her figure began to grow dim in his mind. It may have

2. A bicycle factory came to Clyde, Ohio, in 1894. Sherwood himself worked in the factory, as described in *A Story Teller's Story*, pp. 148–50; and *Memoirs*, pp. 82–89.

been the memory of his mother's hands that made him think so much about other people's hands. With their hands young lovers touched each other tenderly, painters spent a long life-time training the hands to follow the dictates of their fancies, men in workshops grasped tools with their hands. Hands young and strong, boneless soft hands at the ends of the arms of bone-less soft men, hands of fighters, knocking other men down, the steady quiet hands of railroad engineers at the throttles of huge engines, soft hands creeping toward bodies in the night, hands beginning to age, to tremble, the hands of a mother that touches the babe, the hands of a mother remembered clearly, the hands of a father forgotten. A father remembered as a half rebellious man, telling tales, grabbing huge German women boldly, grab-bing what he could get his hands on, going along. Well, what's a man to do anyway?

During the winter after the summer of his adventure in the barn with Mame Thompson, Tar got to hating a lot of things and people he had never before thought much about.

Sometimes he hated his father, sometimes a man called [Hog] Hawkins. Sometimes it was a traveling man who lived in town but only came back home about once a month. Some-times it was a man named Whaley who was a lawyer but, Tar thought, not much good.

Tar's hatreds were nearly all concerned with money. He had got a money hunger that ate at him night and day. The feeling had grown in him because of his mother's illness. If the Moore-heads had money, if they had a big warm house, if his mother had warm clothes, lots of them, like some women to whose houses he went delivering papers. . . .

Well, Tar's father might have been another sort of man. The gay kind are all right when you don't need them for anything special, just want to be entertained. They can make you laugh all right.

Suppose you don't feel much like laughing.

In the winter after John went to the factory he came home after dark at night. Tar was out in the dark delivering papers. Margaret hurried home from school and helped her mother. Margaret was O. K.

Tar thought much about money. He thought of food and clothes. There was a man came from the city and went skating on waterworks pond. He was the father of the girl who came to visit Colonel Farley. Tar had a lot of nerve thinking maybe he might get in with such a girl, from such a family. Mr. Farley was skating on the pond and he asked Tar to hold his overcoat. When he came to get it he gave Tar fifty cents. He did not know who Tar was, no more than if he had been a post on which he had hung his coat.

The coat, Tar held for perhaps twenty minutes, was lined with fur. It was made of such cloth as Tar had never seen before. Such a man, although he might be as old as Tar's father, was like a boy. All the clothes he wore were such as it made you glad and sad to feel. A king might have worn such a coat. "If you have money enough you're as good as a king and don't have all the bother," Tar thought.

If Tar's mother had such a coat. What was the use thinking? You get to thinking and you get bluer and bluer. What good does it do? If you keep it up you'll maybe get to acting the baby. Another kid comes along and says, "What's the matter, Tar?" What are you going to answer?

Tar spent hours going about trying to think of new ways to make money. There are jobs to be had in a town but there are a lot of boys after them. He saw traveling men get off trains wearing fine warm clothes, women warmly clad. The traveling man who lived in town came home to see his wife. He stood in Shooter's bar drinking with two other men and when Tar tackled him for the money he owed for his paper he took a large roll of bills out of his pocket.

"Oh, hell, boy, I ain't got the change. Let it go 'till the next time."

Let it go indeed! A man like that doesn't know what forty cents means. Such fellows, strutting around with someone else's money in their pockets! If you get sore and insist they'll stop the paper. You can't afford to lose customers.

One evening Tar waited two hours in Lawyer Whaley's office, trying to collect some money. It was getting near Christmas. Lawyer Whaley owed him fifty cents. He saw a man going up the stairway to the lawyer's office and figured out maybe the man was a client. He had to watch such fellows [*as Lawyer Whaley] pretty close. [*He] owed money all over town. Such a man, when he has any money, will shovel it out but he doesn't get any very often. You've got to be on the spot.

On that particular evening, a week before Christmas, Tar saw the man, a farmer, go up to the office and as his paper train was late he went right up after him. There was a small dark outer office and an inner one with a fire where the lawyer sat.

If you had to wait outside you got cold all right. Two or three cheap chairs, a rickety kind of a cheap table. Not even a magazine to look at. If there had been one it was so dark you couldn't see.

Tar sat in the office waiting, filled with contempt. He thought about other lawyers in town. There was Lawyer King who had a big fine neat office. People said he fooled around with other men's wives. Well, he was sharp, had about all the good practise in town. If such a man owed you money you didn't spend any time being worried. Someday you met him on the street and he paid you up without your saying a word, thought of it himself and like as not gave you a quarter extra. At Christmas time such a man was good for a dollar. If it was two weeks after Christmas before he thought of it he forked it right over when he saw you.

Such a man might be free with other men's wives, he might be up to sharp practise. Maybe other lawyers only said he was because they were jealous and anyway his wife was pretty sloppy. Sometimes when Tar went around with the afternoon paper she didn't even have her hair put up. The grass wasn't ever cut in the yard, nothing was tended up to but Lawyer King made up for it the way he fixed his office. It might be his liking to stay in his office rather than in his house was what made him such a good lawyer.

Tar sat a long time in Lawyer Whaley's office. Inside he could hear the voices. When at last the farmer started to come out the two men stood a moment by the outer door and then the farmer took some money out of his pocket and gave it to the lawyer. When he went away he almost fell over Tar who was thinking that if he had any law business he would take it to Lawyer King, not to such a man as Whaley.

He got up and went into Lawyer Whaley's office. "No chance now his telling me to wait 'till some other day." The man was standing by the front window, still holding the money in his hand.

He knew what Tar wanted. "How much do I owe you?" he asked. It was fifty cents. He shoved out a two dollar bill and Tar had to think fast. If a boy had the luck to catch him flush such a man might give a dollar for Christmas or he might not give anything at all. Tar decided to say he hadn't any change. The man might think of Christmas coming and give him an extra fifty cents or he might say, "Well, come around next week," and Tar would have all his waiting for nothing. He would have to do it again.

"I haven't got any change," Tar said. Anyway he had taken the plunge. The man hesitated for a moment. There was a wavering uncertain light in his eyes. When a boy needs money as Tar did he learns to watch people's eyes. After all Lawyer Whaley had three or four kids and he didn't get a client very often. He was thinking about Christmas for his own kids, maybe.

When such a man can't make up his mind he is likely to do something foolish. That's what makes him what he is. Tar stood with the two dollar bill in his hand waiting, not offering to give it back, and the man did not know what to do. At first he made a little motion with his hand, not very strong, and then he made it stronger.

He had taken the plunge. Tar felt a little ashamed and a little proud. He had worked the man just right. "Ah, keep the change. It's for Christmas," the man said. Tar was so surprised getting the whole dollar and a half extra that way he could not answer. When he had got down into the street he realized he hadn't even thanked Lawyer Whaley. He felt a little like going back and putting the [*extra] dollar on the lawyer's table. "Fifty cents is enough at Christmas from such a man as you." Likely as not, when Christmas time came, he wouldn't have a cent to get presents for his own kids. The lawyer had on a black coat all worn shiny and a little black tie, also shiny. Tar did not want to go back and he did want to keep the money. He did not know what to do. He had worked a game on the man, saying he had no change when he did have it, and the game had worked too well. If he had got but fifty cents, as he had planned, it would have been all right.

He kept the dollar and a half, took it home to his mother, but for several days every time he thought of the incident he was ashamed.

It's the way things work out. You think up a slick scheme to get something for nothing and you get it [and] then, when you do get it, it isn't half as nice as you hoped.

CHAPTER XVII

EVERYONE eating food. [Tar Moorehead thought a lot about foods.] Dick Moorehead, when he went off to the country, fared pretty well. Lots of people came out all right about food. Some women were naturally good cooks, others weren't. A groceryman sold food in his store and could bring things home. John, working in the factory, had to have something substantial. He had grown tall now and looked almost a man. When he was at home, nights and on Sundays, he was silent like the mother. It may have been because he was worried, maybe he had to work too hard. He worked in a place where they made bicycles but he did not have one. Tar often went past the long brick factory. In the winter all the windows were closed and there were iron bars across the windows. That was to prevent thieves breaking in at night but it made the building look like the town jail, only much larger. After a time Tar would [*have to] go there to work and Robert would take care of the paper selling. It was almost time.

Tar dreaded the thought of the time coming when he would be a factory hand. He went around having queer dreams. Suppose it should turn out he wasn't a Moorehead at all.[3] He might have been the son of a rich man who was leaving for foreign parts. The man had come to his mother and had said, "Here is my child. Its mother is dead and I must leave for foreign parts. If I do not return you may keep him as your own child. Do not ever let him know. Someday I may return and then we shall see what we shall see."

When he had been having some such dream Tar looked at his mother closely. He looked at his father, at John, Robert and Margaret. Well, he tried to imagine he did not look like the others. The dream made him feel a little disloyal. He felt his

3. Anderson's boyish fancies of his birth occur in *A Story Teller's Story*, pp. 71–78, 81–90, and 92–96.

nose with his fingers. It wasn't the same shape as John or Margaret's nose.

When the fact that he was of different stock was finally made known he would never take advantage of the others. He would have money, oodles of it, and all the Mooreheads would be treated exactly as though they were his equals. Perhaps he would go to his mother and say—"Do not let the others know. The secret is buried in my breast. It shall stay there sealed forever. John shall go to college, Margaret shall have fine clothes, Robert a bicycle."

Having such thoughts made Tar feel very tender about all the other Mooreheads. What fine things he would buy for his mother. He had to smile to think of how Dick Moorehead would go about town cutting a swath. He could have fancy vests, a fur-lined overcoat. He wouldn't have to work, could just put in his time being leader of the town band or something like that.

Of course John and Margaret would laugh if they knew what was going on in Tar's head but no one need know. It wasn't true of course, just something to think about nights after he got into bed and when he was going through dark side streets on winter evenings with his papers.

Sometimes when a well-dressed man got off a train it almost seemed to Tar that his dream was about to come true. If the man had walked right up to him and had said, "My son, my son. I am your father. I have been in foreign parts and have accumulated a huge fortune. Now I have come to make you rich. You shall have everything your heart desires." If something of that sort should happen Tar thought he would not be too much surprised. He was ready for it to happen anyway, had thought it all out.

Tar's mother and his sister Margaret always had to be figuring on food. Three meals every day for hungry boys. Things to clean up. Sometimes when Dick had been away in the country a long time, he came home bringing a lot of country sausage or pork.

At other times, in the winter specially, the Mooreheads got pretty low. They only had meat about once a week, no butter, no pie, even on Sundays. They had corn meal baked into cakes and cabbage soup with pieces of fat pork floating in it. You can soak your bread in that.[4]

Mary Moorehead got pieces of salt pork and fried the grease out of it. Then she made gravy. That was good on bread. Beans go a long way. You make a stew with some salt pork in it. It isn't half bad and fills you up, anyway.

Hal Brown and Jim Moore sometimes urged Tar to go home with them to their houses to eat. Small town people are always doing that. Perhaps Tar had helped Hal do his chores and Hal had gone with him on his paper route. It's all right to go to someone else's house, now and then, but if you do it often you ought to be able to ask them to your house. Corn meal mush or cabbage soup will do at a pinch but you don't want to ask a guest to sit down to it. If you're poor and hard up you don't want the whole town to know and be talking.

Beans or cabbage stew, eaten maybe at the table in the kitchen by the kitchen stove, huh! Some winters the Mooreheads couldn't afford to have more than one fire. They had to eat, get their lessons, undress for bed, do everything in the kitchen. When they were eating Tar's mother got Margaret to dish things up. It was so the children couldn't see how much her hands trembled after a day's washing.

At the Browns', when Tar went there, such an abundance. You wouldn't think there was so much in the world. If you took all you could stuff, no one ever noticed. Just to look around the table made your eyes ache.

They had big dishes of mashed potatoes, fried chicken with good gravy—maybe little pieces of good meat floating in it— not thin either—a dozen kinds of jams and jellies in glasses—it looked pretty that way, so pretty you couldn't bear hardly to take a spoonful and spoil the way it looked—sweet potatoes baked in brown sugar—the sugar melting and making a thick kind of candy over it—big bowls full of apples bananas and oranges, beans baked in a big dish—all brown over the top— turkey sometimes when it wasn't Christmas, Thanksgiving or

4. For Anderson's stories of cabbage soup, see *A Story Teller's Story*, pp. 38–43; and, especially, "Sherwood Anderson's Earliest Autobiography," *A Story Teller's Story*, pp. 345–47.

anything, three or four kinds of pie, cakes with layers and brown sweet stuff between the layers—white frosting on top with sometimes red candies stuck in it—apple dumplings.

Every time when Tar went there different kinds of stuff on the table—plenty of it and always good. It was a wonder Hal Brown wasn't fatter. He was as skinny as Tar.

If Ma Brown didn't do the cooking one of the big Brown girls did. They were all good cooks. Tar would have bet that Margaret, if she had the chance, could do some swell cooking too. You have to have the stuff to cook with, plenty of it.

No matter how cold it is, after a feed like that you feel all warm. You can go around outdoors with your coat all un-buttoned. You almost sweat, even outdoors and when it's zero weather.

Hal Brown was Tar's age in a family where all the others were grown up. The Brown girls, Kate and Sue and Sally and Jane and Mary, were all big strapping girls—five of them—and there was an older brother who worked downtown in the Browns' store. He was called Shorty Brown because he was so long and big. Well, he was six feet three. The Brown kind of eating had built him up, all right. He could take hold of the collar of Hal's coat with one hand and of Tar's collar with the other and he could lift them both off the floor, do it without half trying.

Ma Brown wasn't so big. She wasn't as tall as Tar's mother. You could never guess how she could have had such a son as Shorty or such daughters as she had. Tar and Jim Moore used to talk about it sometimes. "Gee, it doesn't seem as though it could be done," Jim said.

Shorty Brown had shoulders like a horse. Maybe it was the food. Maybe Hal would be that way sometime. Still the Moores fed pretty well and Jim wasn't as tall as Tar, if he was a little fatter. Ma Brown ate the same food the rest did. Look at her.

Pa Brown and the girls were big. When he was at home Pa Brown—he was known as "Cal"—hardly ever said a word. In the house the girls made a racket and so did Shorty, Hal and the mother. The mother was always scolding but she didn't mean a thing and no one paid any attention. The children laughed and cracked jokes and after supper some nights all of the girls got at Shorty and tried to put him on the floor. If they broke a dish or two Ma Brown scolded but no one cared much. When they were at it Hal tried to help his bigger brother but he didn't count. It was a sight to see. If the girls got their dresses torn it made no difference. No one got mad.

Cal Brown, when he got through supper, went into the front room and sat down to read a book. He was always reading books like *Ben Hur* and *Romola* and Dickens' *Works* and if one of the girls came and banged on the piano he went right on.

Such a man to always have a book in his hand when he was at home! He owned the biggest gents' clothing store in town. There must have been a thousand suits of clothes all laid out on long tables. You could have a suit for five dollars down and a dollar a week. Tar and John and Robert got theirs that way.

When there was hell going on in the Browns' house, after supper on a winter evening, Ma Brown kept screaming and saying, "Now behave yourselves. Don't you see your Pa's reading?" but no one paid any attention. Cal Brown didn't seem to care a lick. "Ah let 'em alone," he said when he said anything. Mostly he never even noticed.

Tar stood a little to one side, trying to hide himself. It was good to come to the Browns' [*house] to eat but he couldn't do it too often. Having a father like Dick Moorehead, a mother like Mary Moorehead was not like belonging to such a family as the Browns.

He couldn't invite Hal Brown or Jim Moore to come to the Moorehead's and eat cabbage soup.

Well, food isn't the only thing. Jim or Hal might not care. Mary Moorehead would though, Tar's older brother John would, Margaret would. The Mooreheads were proud. In Tar's home everything was concealed. You are in bed and your brother John is lying beside you in the same bed. In the next room Margaret is sleeping. She has to have a room by herself. That is because she is a girl.

You are in bed and you lie thinking. John may be doing the same thing, Margaret may be doing it. A Moorehead said nothing at such a time.

Concealed in his corner of the big dining room [*at the Browns'], Tar watched Hal Brown's father. The man was getting old and grey. He had little wrinkles about his eyes. When he read a book he put on spectacles. The clothing store man was the son of a large farmer who had been prosperous. He had married the daughter of another [prosperous] farmer. Then he had come to town and had started a store. When his father died he got the farm and later his wife also got money.

Such people had lived in one place always. There had always been plenty of food, clothes, warm houses. They did not drift about, living in little mean houses, leaving suddenly because the rent was due and they could not pay it.

They were not proud, did not have to be proud.

In the Browns' house the feeling of warm safety. Great strong girls wrestling with their tall brother on the floor. Dresses being torn.

The Brown girls could milk cows, could cook, do anything. They went off with young men to dances. In the house sometimes, in the presence of Tar and their own younger brother, they said things about men and women and animals that made Tar blush. If, when the girls were cutting up like that, their father was there he never even spoke.

He and Tar were the only silent ones in the Browns' house.

Was it because Tar did not want any of the Browns to know how glad he was to be in their house, to be so warm, to see all the fun going on and be so filled with food?

At the table when someone asked him to have a second helping he always shook his head and said, "No," in a faint voice, but Cal Brown, who was serving, paid no attention. "You pass his plate," he said to one of the girls and it came back to Tar heaping full. More fried chicken, gravy, another great heap of mashed potatoes, another wedge of pie. The big Brown girls and Shorty [Brown] looked at each other and smiled.

Sometimes one of the Brown girls would begin to hug and kiss Tar right in front of the others. It was after they all got up from the table and when Tar was trying to hide himself by getting into a corner. When he could do that he kept quiet and watched, saw the little wrinkles about Cal Brown's eyes as he read his book. There was always something laughing in [*the merchant's] eyes but he never laughed out loud.

Tar hoped a wrestling match would start between Shorty

and the girls. Then they would all get absorbed, and leave him alone.

He couldn't go to the Browns' or to Jim Moore's too often because he didn't feel like asking them to come to his house to eat just one dish off the kitchen table, the baby maybe crying.

When one of the girls took it into her head to kiss him he couldn't help blushing and that made the others laugh. The big girl, almost a woman, did it to tease him. The Brown girls all had strong arms and great motherly breasts. The one who was teasing him held him tight and then turning his face up kissed him while he struggled. Hal Brown whooped with laughter. They never tried to kiss Hal because he didn't blush. Tar wished he didn't. He couldn't help it.

Dick Moorehead, during the winter always going around visiting farm houses, pretending he was looking for painting and paper-hanging jobs. Maybe he was. If a big girl at some farm house, some girl like one of the Brown girls, tried to kiss him, he wouldn't ever have blushed. He would have liked it. Dick wasn't the blushing kind. Tar had seen enough to know that.

The Brown girls and Shorty Brown weren't the blushing kind but they weren't like Dick.

Dick, off in the country that way, always got plenty to eat. People liked him around because he was entertaining. Tar got invited to the Moores' and the Browns'. John and Margaret had their friends. They got invited too. Mary Moorehead stayed at home.

A woman, when she has kids, when her man isn't a very good provider, gets the worst of it, all right. Tar's mother was the blushing kind just like Tar. When Tar got a little older he would get over it maybe. Women like his mother never did.

CHAPTER XVIII

THERE was a man in town—Hog Hawkins. People called him the name right to his face. He had given the Moorehead boys a lot of trouble.

The morning Cleveland papers were two cents each but if you had your paper delivered to your house or to a store you got it for ten cents the six days. Sunday papers were special and sold for five cents. People, at their houses, usually took the evening papers but the stores, a few lawyers and others, wanted the morning paper. The morning paper came in at eight o'clock. Just time to run around with the papers and make it to school. Lots of people came down to the train to get their paper [there].

Hog Hawkins always did. He had to have a paper because he dealt in hogs, buying them from farmers and shipping to the city markets. He had to know the city market prices.

When John was selling papers Hog Hawkins got to owing him, at one time forty cents, and he said he had paid it when he hadn't. There was a quarrel and he wrote to the office of the paper in the city and tried to have John's agency taken away. In the letter he said John was dishonest and impertinent.

It caused a lot of trouble. John had to get Lawyer King and three or four merchants to write saying he was O. K. It isn't a very nice thing to have to ask. John hated it.

Then John wanted to get even with Hog Hawkins and did. The man might have saved two cents a week by being all right, and everyone knew that two cents means a lot to such a man, but John made him pay up cash every day [after that]. If he had paid by the week in advance John would have made it apply on the old debt. Hog Hawkins would never have trusted him with the ten cents. He knew better than that.

At first Hog tried to get out of buying any paper at all. They took it at the barber shop and at the hotel and it was lying around and he went into one of the two places and sat looking at it for a few mornings but that couldn't last. The old hog buyer had a little dirty white beard, he never had trimmed, and he was bald.

No money in such a man for a barber. In the barber shop they began hiding the paper when they saw him coming and the clerk at the hotel did the same thing. No one wanted him around. He smelled something awful.

When John Moorehead got his dander up you couldn't move him any more than a brick wall. He did not say much but he could [sure] stand pat. If Hog Hawkins wanted a paper he had to trot down to the station with the two cents in his hand. If he was across the street and shouted John did not pay any attention. People had to smile when they saw it. The old man always reached for the paper before he gave John the two cents but John put the paper behind his back. Sometimes they just stood like that, glaring at each other, and then the old man caved in. When it happened at the station the baggage man, the express agent and the railroad crew all laughed. They used to whisper to John when Hog had his back turned. "Don't you give in," they said. Little [enough] chance of that.

It wasn't long before [almost] everyone had it in for Hog. He had cheated a lot of people and was so stingy he hardly ever spent a cent. He lived alone in a small brick house on a street back of the cemetery and almost always had pigs turned loose in the yard. In hot weather you could smell the place a half mile. People tried to have him arrested for keeping the place so dirty but he got out of it some way. If they made a law no one could keep pigs in town it shut out a lot of other people from keeping [*pretty clean] pigs and they didn't want that. A hog can be kept clean the same as a dog or a cat but such a man would never keep anything clean. He had been married to a farmer's daughter when he was young but she never had any children and died after three or four years. Some people said that when his wife was alive he wasn't so bad.

When Tar began to sell the papers the feud between Hog Hawkins and the Mooreheads kept up.

Tar wasn't as foxy as John. He let Hog get into him for ten cents right off and that gave the old man a lot of satisfaction. It was a victory. John's method had always been never to say a word. He stood with the paper held behind his back and waited. "No cash, no paper." That was his line.

Tar tried scolding [Hog], trying to get his ten cents back, and that gave the old man a chance to laugh [at him]. In John's day the laugh had been on the other side of the fence.

[And] then something happened. Spring came and there was a long rainy time. One night a bridge got washed out east of town and the morning train did not come. At the station it was marked first three hours late and then five. The afternoon train was due at four thirty and on a late March afternoon in Ohio, when it is raining and the clouds hang low, it is pretty near dark by five.

Tar went down to see about the trains at six and then went home to supper. He went again at seven and at nine. No trains all day. The telegraph operator told him he had better go [on] home and forget it and he did go home thinking he would go to bed but Margaret got on her ear.

What was the matter with her Tar didn't know. She didn't usually act as she did that night. John had come home from work tired and had gone to bed. Mary Moorehead, pale and sick-looking, went to bed early. It wasn't very cold but the rain fell steadily and it was dark as pitch outside. Maybe the calendar said it should have been a moonlight night. The electric lights were turned off all over town.

It wasn't that Margaret was trying to tell Tar what he should do about his job. She was just nervous and excited, without any reason, and said she knew that if she went to bed she couldn't sleep. Girls get that way sometimes.[5] It might have been the spring coming on. "Ah, let's sit up until a train does come and then let's take the papers around," she kept saying. They were in the kitchen and the mother must have gone to sleep in her room. She never said a word. Margaret put on John's raincoat and his rubber boots. Tar had on a ponchoon. He could put his papers under it and keep them pretty dry.

They went to the station that night at ten and again at eleven.

5. Anderson's sister Stella died in surgery in 1917. She is the subject of a beautiful section of the *Memoirs*, pp. 90–103.

There wasn't a soul on Main Street. Even the night watchman had hid himself away. [*It was a night when even a thief wouldn't be out.] The telegraph operator had to stay but he had a grouch. After Tar asked him about the train three or four times he wouldn't answer. Well, he wanted to be at home in bed. Everyone did but Margaret. She had infected Tar with her nervousness [and excitement].

When they went to the station at eleven they decided to stay. "If we go home again like as not we'll wake mother up," Margaret said. In the station there was a fat country woman sitting on a bench asleep with her mouth open. They had left a light burning [in there] but it was pretty dim. A woman like that would be going to see her daughter in another town, a daughter who was sick or going to have a baby or something. Country people don't travel much. When they make up their minds they'll stand anything. Start them and you can't stop them. There was a woman in Tar's town went clear out to Kansas to see her daughter and she took along all her own food and sat up in the day coach all the way. Tar heard her tell about it once in a store when she got back home.

The train got in at half past one. The baggage master and the ticket man had gone home and the telegraph operator did their work. He had to stay up anyway. He thought Tar and his sister had gone crazy. "Hey, you crazy kids. What does anyone in the world care whether or not they get a paper this time a night? You ought to be spanked and sent off to bed, the both of you." The telegraph operator had a grouch that night [all right].

Margaret was all right and so was Tar. Now that he had got into it Tar enjoyed staying up as much as his sister. On a night like that you are sleepy and sleepy, so you think you can't stand it another minute, and then suddenly you aren't sleepy at all. It's like getting your second wind when you are running a race.

A town at night, away after midnight and when it's raining, is different from a town in the day or in the early evening when it's dark but the people in the houses are all awake. When Tar went around with his papers on ordinary evenings he had a lot of short-cuts he always took. Well, he knew where they had

dogs, knew how to save a lot of ground. He went through alleyways, climbed fences. Most people did not care. When a boy
went around that way he saw a lot of things going on. Tar had
seen other things besides that time when he saw Win Connell
and his new wife cutting up.

That night, with Margaret along, he wondered whether he
would go his regular way or keep to the sidewalks. As though
sensing what was going on in his mind Margaret wanted to go
the shortest and darkest way.

It was fun, puddling about in the rain and darkness, going
up to dark houses, slipping the paper under a door or back of a
blind. Old Mrs. Stevens lived alone and was afraid of disease.
She had some money and had another old woman working for
her. She was always afraid of taking cold and when it was
winter or cold weather she paid Tar an extra five cents a week
and he took the paper in the kitchen and held it over the
kitchen stove. When it was warm and dry the old woman who
worked in the kitchen ran with it into the front room. There
was a box on the front door of the house to keep the paper
dry in wet weather. Tar told Margaret about it and she laughed.

All kinds of people in a town, having all kinds of notions, and
now they were all asleep. When they came to a house Margaret stood outside while Tar crept up and put the paper in the
dryest place he could find. He knew most of the dogs [*and
anyway,] that night the ugly ones were inside out of the rain.

Everyone inside out of the rain but Tar and Margaret, all
asleep, cuddled up in beds. If you let yourself go you could
imagine just how they looked. When Tar was going around
alone he often spent his time trying to imagine what was going
on in houses. He could pretend the houses had no walls. It was
a good way to put in the time.

Walls of houses could not hide things from [*him] more
than a dark night like that. When Tar came back from taking
a paper into a house and when Margaret was waiting outside
he could not see her. Sometimes she hid behind a tree. He called
to her in a loud whisper. Then she came out and they laughed.

They came to a short-cut that Tar hardly ever took at night
except when it was warm and clear. It was right through the
cemetery, not on the Farley-Thompson side but the other way.

You got over a fence and went between the graves. Then you crawled over another fence and through an orchard and you were out in another street.

Tar told Margaret about the cemetery short-cut just to tease her. She had been so bold, had wanted to do everything. He just thought he would try her out and was surprised and a little upset when she took him up.

"Oh, come on. Let's do it," she said. After that there wasn't anything else Tar could do.

They found the place and got over the fence and there they were right in among the graves. They kept stumbling over stones but they didn't laugh now. Margaret was sorry she had been so bold. She crept close to Tar and took hold of his hand. It had got darker and darker. They couldn't see even the white gravestones.

That was where it happened. Hog Hawkins lived out that way. His hog yard backed right up against the orchard they had to cross after they got out of the cemetery.

They had got almost through and Tar was going ahead, hanging onto Margaret's hand and trying to find his way, when they almost fell over Hog kneeling over a grave.

They didn't know who it was, not at first. When they were almost on top of him he groaned and they stopped. At first they thought it was a ghost. Why they didn't both cut and run they never knew. They were too scared[, maybe].

They both stood trembling and clinging to each other and there came a stroke of lightning and Tar saw who it was. It was the only stroke of lightning that night and after it passed there wasn't hardly any thunder at all, just a low rumbling sound.

A low rumbling sound far off in the darkness somewhere and a groan from the man kneeling by the grave, almost at Tar's feet. The old hog buyer had been unable to sleep that night and had come out to the graveyard, to his wife's grave, to pray. Perhaps he did it every night when he could not sleep. That might have been the reason he lived in a house so near the graveyard.

A man like that, never having liked but one person, never having been liked by but one person. They had married and then she had died. Nothing after that but [*lonesomeness]. He had got so he hated people and wanted to die. Well, he was pretty sure his wife had gone to Heaven. He wanted to get in there [too] if he could. If she was in Heaven she might say a word for him. He was pretty sure she would.

Suppose he died some night in his house, not a living thing about but some hogs. In the town there was a story. Everyone told it. A farmer came to town looking for the hog buyer. He met Charlie Durlam, the postmaster, who pointed out the house. "You will find him down there. You can tell him from the hogs because he wears a hat."

The graveyard had become the hog buyer's church to which he went at night. To belong to a regular church would imply some kind of understanding with other people. He would have to give money now and then. It cost nothing to go at night into a graveyard.

Tar and Margaret went softly out of the presence of the kneeling man. After the one flash of lightning it was black dark but Tar managed to find the way to the fence and got Margaret over and into the orchard. Soon they were out on another street, both shaken and afraid. From the street they could hear the moaning voice of the hog buyer coming out of the darkness.

They hurried over the rest of Tar's route, keeping to the streets and sidewalks. Now Margaret wasn't so frisky. When they got to the Moorehead house [*she] tried to light a lamp in the kitchen and her hands trembled. Tar had to take the match and do the job. Margaret was pale. Tar might have laughed at her but wasn't so sure how he looked himself. When they had gone upstairs and to bed Tar was awake for a long time. It was good to get into bed with John, who had the bed all warm and who never woke up.

Tar had made up his mind to something but thought it just as well not to tell John. The battle the Mooreheads had been having with Hog Hawkins was John's battle, not his. He was out ten cents but what is ten cents?

He did not want the baggage man to know, did not want the express man or any of the people who habitually hung around the railroad station when the train came in to know that he had surrendered.

He had made up his mind to have it out with Hog Hawkins the very next day and did. He waited until there wasn't anyone looking and then went to where the man stood waiting.

Tar thrust out the paper and Hog Hawkins grabbed it. He made a bluff at fishing in his pockets for the pennies but of course he didn't find [*any]. He wasn't going to miss a chance like that. "Well, well, I forgot the change. You'll have to wait." When he said it he chuckled. He was sorry none of the men around the station had seen what had happened, how he had caught one of the Moorehead boys off guard.

Well, a victory was a victory.

He went off along the street clutching the paper and chuckling. Tar stood watching.

If Tar lost two cents a day three or four times a week it wouldn't amount to much. Now and then some traveling man got off a train and gave him a nickel, saying, "Keep the change." Two cents a day wasn't so much. Tar thought he could stand it. He thought of Hog Hawkins getting his little moments of satisfaction, beating him out of papers, and made up his mind he would let him.

[That is,] he would, [*he thought,] when there weren't too many people about.

CHAPTER XIX

[How is a boy to figure things out? Happenings in Tar's town as in all town's.] Now [*Tar] was growing large of body—tall and leggy. People were less conscious of him as a child. He went to ball games, to shows at the opera house.

There was a life going on outside his town. The train that brought the papers from the east went on west.

Life in the town was simple. There were no rich people. In the evening, in the summer, he saw couples walking under the trees. They were young men and women almost grown. Sometimes they kissed. When Tar saw it he became excited.

There weren't any bad women in town, except maybe. . . .

To the east Cleveland, Pittsburgh, Boston, New York. To the west Chicago.

A negro, son of the only negro in town, came to visit his father. He talked in the barber shop—in the livery barn. It was spring and all winter he had lived at Springfield, Ohio.

During the Civil War Springfield had been one of the stations on the underground railroad—abolitionists running off niggers. Tar's father knew all about that. Zanesville was another—and Oberlin, near Cleveland.

All such places had niggers yet—lots of them.

In Springfield there was a place called "the levee." Nigger prostitutes mostly. The nigger who came to town to visit his father told about it in the livery stable. He was a strong young fellow who wore loud flashy clothes. All winter he had been in Springfield and two nigger women had kept him. They went out into the streets, made money and brought it to him.

"They better had. I wouldn't stand for no foolishness.

"Knock 'em down. Treat 'em rough. That's my way."

The young negro's father was such a respectable old man. Even Dick Moorehead, who kept all his life the Southerner's attitude toward niggers, said, "Old Pete's all right—if he is a nigger."

The old negro man worked hard and so did his little dried-up wife. All their children had cut out, gone adventuring where there were other negroes. They rarely came home to visit the old couple and when one did he did not stay long.

The flashy nigger wouldn't stay long either. He said as much. "Nothing in this town for a nigger like me. I's a sport, I is."

Odd thing—that kind of relationship between men and women—even for niggers—women supporting a man that way. One of the men working at the livery barn said white men and women sometimes did the same thing.

The men at the barn and some at the barber shop were envious. "A man doesn't have to work. Money rolls in."

All kinds of things going on in towns and cities where the trains came from, in cities to which the trains go when they go on west.

Old Pete, the father of the young negro sport, did whitewashing, he worked in people's gardens, his wife did washing just like Mary Moorehead. On almost any day you could see the old man going through Main Street with his whitewash pail and brushes. He never swore, drank, stole. He was always cheerful, smiling, taking his hat off to white people. On Sundays he and his old wife put on their best clothes and went to the Methodist Church. They both had white kinky hair. Now and then, when there was a prayer going on, you heard the old man's voice. "Oh, Lord, save me," he groaned. "Yes, Lord, save me," echoed the wife.

Not much like his son, that old black. When he was in town that time [you bet] the flashy young black never went near any church.

At the Methodist Church, Sunday evenings—girls coming out, young fellows waiting to see them home.

"May I see you home tonight, Miss Smith?" Trying to be extra polite—speaking soft and low.

Sometimes a young fellow got the girl he wanted, sometimes he didn't. When he failed small boys standing about called to him. "Yi! Yi! She wouldn't let you! Yi! Yi!"

Children John's age, Margaret's age, were betwixt and between. They couldn't wait in the darkness to yell at [*the] older boys nor could they, as yet, stand up before all the others and ask some girl to let them see her home, be asked by some young man.

To Margaret that might be happening soon now. It wouldn't be long before John would stand up in the line before the church door with other young men.

Better to be a [*kid] than a betwixt and between.

Sometimes when a boy yelled "Yi! Yi!" he got caught. An older boy chased and caught him in the dark road—all the others laughing—gave him a clip side the head. Well, what of it? The thing was to take it without crying.

Then wait.

When the [*older boy] got far enough away—so you felt pretty sure he couldn't catch you again—you paid him out. "Yi! Yi! She wouldn't let you. Got left, didn't you. Yi! Yi!"

Tar did not want to be a betwixt and between. When he grew up he wanted to grow suddenly—go to bed a boy and wake up a man, big and strong. Sometimes he dreamed of that.

He could play ball pretty well, if he only had more time for practise, could hold down second base. The trouble was that the regular team—his age—always played on Saturdays. On Saturday afternoon he was busy selling Sunday papers. A Sunday paper was five cents. You made more than on other days.

Bill McCarthy came to work at McGovern's livery stable. He had been a prize fighter, a regular one, but now he was down and out.

Too much wine and women. He said that himself.

Well he knew things. He could teach boys how to box, teach them ring generalship. Once he had been sparring partner for Kid McAllister—the Nonpareil. A boy doesn't get a chance to be around with a man like that—not very often in life.

Bill got up a class. It was three dollars for five lessons and Tar took.[6] Bill made all the boys pay their money down, in advance. Ten boys went in. They were to be private lessons, one boy at a time, upstairs in the barn.

They all got what Tar got. It was a dirty trick. Bill sparred

6. Anderson tells a ludicrous story of his boxing in A Story Teller's Story, pp. 150–53, 160–61.

a moment with each boy and then—he pretended to let his hand slip—accidentally.

A boy got a black eye or something like that the first lesson. No one came back for more. Tar didn't. It was an easy way for Bill. You clip a boy over the head, knock him across a barn floor, and get three dollars—don't have to bother with the other [four] lessons.

The ex-prize fighter doing that and the young sporty nigger getting his living that way, on the levee in Springfield, came to about the same thing for Tar.

CHAPTER XX

[THINGS all mixed up in a boy's mind. What is sin? You hear people talking. Some who talk the most about God cheat the most in stores and horse trading.] [*In Tar's town many] men like Lawyer King and Judge Blair did not go to church. Doctor Reefy never went. They were on the square. You could trust them.

There was a "bad" woman came to town in Tar's time. Everyone said she was bad. No good woman in town would have anything to do with her.

She was living with a man and wasn't married [to him]. He may have had another wife—somewhere. No one knew.

They came to town on a Saturday and Tar was at the station selling papers. Then they went to the hotel and later to the livery barn where they got a horse and buggy.

They drove around town and then rented the Woodhouse place. It was a big old place and had been empty a long time. The Woodhouses were all dead or had moved away. Lawyer King was agent. He let them have it—of course.

They had furniture to buy, stuff for the kitchen, everything.

How everyone knew the woman was bad Tar did not know. They just did.

Of course all the merchants sold them [fast] stuff, fast enough. The man threw his money around. Old Mrs. Crowley worked for them in their kitchen. She didn't care. When a woman is old like that and poor she doesn't have to be [*so] particular.

Tar didn't either—a boy doesn't. He heard the men talking—at the station, the livery barn, the barber shop, the hotel.

The man bought everything the woman wanted and then went away. After that he [only] came weekends, about twice a month. They took the morning and afternoon papers and a Sunday paper too.

What did Tar care? It made him tired the way people talked.

Even the children, girls and boys coming home from school, made a kind of shrine of the place. They went around that way purposely and when they came to the house—it was surrounded by a high hedge—they all became suddenly silent.

It was as though someone had been murdered there. Tar went right in—with the papers.

People said she had come to town to have a baby. She wasn't married to the man, who was older than she was. He was a city man and rich. He spent money like a rich man. So did she.

At home—in the city where the man lived—he had a respectable wife and children. Everyone said so. It might be he belonged to a church, but now and then—weekends—he sneaked off to Tar's little town. He was keeping a woman.

Anyway she was pretty and lonesome.

Old Mrs. Crowley, who worked for her, wasn't much. Her husband had been a drayman and was dead. She was one of the muttering kind of cross old women but she could cook pretty good.

The woman—the "bad" woman—began to take notice of Tar. When he brought the paper she began to talk to him. It wasn't because he was anything special. It was the only chance she had.

She asked him questions about his mother and father, about John and Robert and the babies. She was lonesome. Tar sat on the back porch of the Woodhouse place talking with her. There was a man named Smoky Pete working in the yard.[7] Before she came he never had any regular job, was always hanging about saloons and cleaning out spittoons for a drink—jobs like that.

She paid him as much as though he had been any good. At the end of the week, when she settled with Tar, suppose she owed him twenty-five cents.

She gave him a half dollar. Well, she would have given him a dollar but was afraid it would be too much. She was afraid he would be ashamed or have his pride hurt and wouldn't take it.

They sat on the back porch of the house and talked. Not a

7. Smoky Pete occurs again in "Our Morning Roll Call," *The Sherwood Anderson Reader*, pp. 376–79.

woman in town had been to see her. Everyone said she had come to town just to have the baby by a man she wasn't married to but, although he watched closely, Tar saw no signs.

"I don't believe it. She's regular size—slim if anything," he said to Hal Brown.

Then she got to having a horse and buggy from the livery barn afternoons and taking Tar with her. "Do you think your mother will care?" she asked. Tar said, "No."

They went into the country and got flowers, oceans of them. Mostly she sat in the buggy and Tar gathered the flowers, crawling up hillsides, going down into gullies.

When they got home she gave him a quarter. Sometimes he helped her carry the flowers into the house. Once he went into her bedroom. Such dresses, fine flimsy things. He stood looking, wanting to go and touch, as he had always been wanting to touch the bits of lace his mother wore on her one good black Sunday dress when he was small. His mother had the same one good dress yet. The woman—the bad one—saw the look in his eyes and, getting all the dresses out of a big truck, spread them on the bed. There must have been twenty. Tar had never dreamed there could be such beautiful [splendid] things in the world.

That afternoon, when Tar was leaving, the woman kissed him. It was the only time she ever did.

The bad woman left Tar's town as suddenly as she came. No one knew where she went. She got a telegram in the afternoon and left on the night train. Everyone wanted to know what was in the telegram but of course the telegraph operator, Wash Williams, wouldn't tell.[8] What is in a telegram is a secret. You don't dast tell. An operator isn't allowed, but Wash Williams was a grouch anyway. He might have leaked a little but he enjoyed having everyone hint around and then not saying a word.

As for Tar, he got a note from the woman. It had been left with Mrs. Crowley and had five dollars in it.

Tar was a good deal upset, having her leave that way. All

8. Wash Williams is the central character in "Respectability," *Winesburg, Ohio*, pp. 121–27.

her things were to be sent to an address in Cleveland. The note said, "Good-bye, you're a good boy," nothing more.

Then later—about two weeks later—a bundle came from the city. It had in it some clothes for Margaret and Robert and Will and a new sweater for himself. Nothing else. The express was pre-paid.

[It was a month later when one day a neighbor woman came to visit Tar's mother when he was at home. There was more "bad" woman talk and Tar heard it. He was in the next room. The neighbor woman said how bad the strange woman was and blamed Mary Moorehead for letting Tar be around with her. She said how she would never have let a son of her's go near such a person.

[Mary Moorehead said nothing of course.

[There might have been that kind of talk going on all summer. Two or three men had tried to question Tar. "What does she say to you? What do you talk about?"

["None of your business."

[When they had questioned him he had said nothing and had hurried away.

[His mother merely changed the subject, switched the conversation to something else. That would be her way.

[Tar listened a moment and then tiptoed out of the house.

[He was glad about something but did not know just what it was. It might have been he was glad he had a chance to know a bad woman.

[Perhaps he was simply glad his mother had the good sense to let him alone.]

CHAPTER XXI

THE coming of death to Tar Moorehead's mother was without special dramatic intensity. She died in the night and only Doctor Reefy was in the room with her. There was no death-bed scene, the husband and children gathered about, a few last courageous words, weeping children, a struggle and then the soul taking flight. For a long time Doctor Reefy had been expecting her death and was not surprised. Having been summoned to the house and the children having been sent upstairs to bed he sat down to talk with the mother.

There were words said that Tar, lying awake in a room above, could not hear. As he afterwards became a writer he often reconstructed in his imagination the scene in the room below. There was a scene in a story by Chekhov, the Russian.[9] Readers will remember it—the scene in the Russian farm house, the anxious country doctor, the woman dying—wanting love before she died. Well, there had always been some kind of understanding between Doctor Reefy and his mother. The man never became his own friend, never talked intimately to him as Judge Blair did later, but he liked to think that the last talk of the man and woman in the little frame house in the Ohio town was full of significance to them both. Tar later found out, it is in their close relationships people live. He wanted such relationships for his mother. She had seemed, in life, such an isolated figure. Perhaps he underestimated his father. The figure of his mother, as she lived later in his fancy, seemed so delicately poised, capable of quick flashing rushes of feeling. If you do not make quick and intimate connections with the life that goes on in others about you you do not live at all. It is a difficult thing to do and causes most of the trouble in life but you must keep trying. That is your job and if you shirk it you shirk life [entirely].

9. Anderson probably is alluding to "A Dead Body" (1885) by Anton Chekhov (1860–1904).

Later thoughts of that sort in Tar, concerning himself, often transferred to the figure of his mother.

Voices in a room downstairs in a small frame house. Dick Moorehead, the husband, was away in the country on a painting job. What do two grown people talk about at such a time? The man and woman in the room below laughed softly. After the Doctor had been there for some time Mary Moorehead went to sleep. She died in her sleep.

When she was dead the doctor did not awaken the children but went out of the house and got a neighbor to drive off to the country for Dick and then coming back sat down. There were a few books about. At several times, during long winters when Dick had no money, he became a book agent—it enabled him to be abroad, going from house to house in the country, where he managed to make himself welcome though he sold but few books.[10] As would be natural the books he tried to sell were concerned mostly with the Civil War.

There would be a book about a character called "Corporal Si Klegg," who enlisted in the war as a green country boy and became a corporal. Si was full of the naïveté of the free-born American country lad, never having taken orders before. He was however brave enough. The book delighted Dick and he read it aloud to the children.[11]

There were other books, more technical, also concerned with the war. Was General Grant drunk during the first day of the battle of Shiloh? Why did not General Meade pursue Lee after the victory at Gettysburg? Did McClellan really want the South licked? Grant's *Memoirs*.

Mark Twain, the writer, became a publisher and published Grant's *Memoirs*.[12] All of Mark Twain's books were sold by agents who went from house to house. There was a special agent's copy with blank ruled pages at the front. That was where Dick set down the names of people who agreed to take one of the books when it came out. Dick might have sold more

---

10. Irwin Anderson's selling books is described in *Memoirs*, pp. 56–57.

11. Si Klegg must have been in one of the "dime novels" popular after the Civil War. In *Memoirs*, p. 57, Anderson refers to the same work.

12. Ulysses S. Grant published his *Personal Memoirs* in two volumes in 1885–86. See *A Story Teller's Story*, pp. 159–60.

books if he had not taken so much time for each sale. Often he
would stop at some farm house several days. In the evening
the family gathered about and Dick read aloud. He talked. It
was fun to hear him if you weren't depending on him for a
living.

Doctor Reefy sat in the Moorehead house, with the dead
woman in the next room, reading one of Dick's books. Doctors
see much of death at first hand. They know all people must die.
The book in his hand, in plain cloth binding so much, in
leather, half Morocco, so much more. You do not sell many
fancy bindings in a small town. Grant's *Memoirs* was the easiest
book to sell. Every family in the North thought they ought to
have it. It was a moral duty, as Dick always pointed out.

Doctor Reefy sat reading one of the books and he had himself been in the war. Like Walt Whitman he had been a nurse.[13]
He never shot anyone, never shot at anyone. What did the
doctor think[? Did he think of war,] of Dick, of Mary Moorehead? He had married a young girl when he was himself almost
an old man. There are some people you get to know a little
when you are a child that you puzzle about all your life and
you can't quite make them out. Writers have a little trick.
People think writers take their characters from life. They do
not. What they do is to find some man or woman who, for some
obscure reason, arouses their interest. Such a man or woman is
invaluable to a writer. He takes the few facts he knows and
tries to build a whole life. People are starting places for him
and when he gets through, often enough, what results has little
or nothing to do with the person he started with.

Mary Moorehead died during a night in the fall.[14] Tar was
then selling papers and John had gone to the factory. When

---

13. Anderson writes of Walt Whitman in *A Story Teller's Story*, pp.
106–7, 117, 282, 305; and in his Introduction to *Leaves of Grass* (New
York: Thomas Y. Crowell, 1933), pp. v–vii. See Viva Elizabeth Haught,
"The Influence of Walt Whitman on Sherwood Anderson and Carl Sand-
burg," M.A. Thesis, Duke University, 1936.

14. Emma Smith Anderson died May 10, 1895, whereupon Irwin
Anderson went to Indiana, married Minnie Stevens in 1901, and was
ignored by his older children. On the death of Sherwood Anderson's
mother, see *A Story Teller's Story*, pp. 21, 62–63.

Tar got home in the early evening that day, his mother was not at the table and Margaret said she was not feeling well. It was raining outside. The children ate in silence, the depression that always came with one of the mother's bad times hanging over the house. Depression is something on which the imagination feeds. When the meal was over Tar helped Margaret wash the dishes.

The children sat around. The mother had said she did not want anything to eat. John went off [early] to bed and so also did Robert, [*Will and Joe]. In the factory John was on piece work. Just when you have got your speed up and can make pretty good wages they change things on you. Instead of getting forty cents for polishing a bicycle frame they cut you down to thirty-two. What are you going to do? You['ve] got to have a job.

Neither Tar nor Margaret was a bit sleepy. Margaret made the others go upstairs softly so as not to disturb mother—if she was asleep. The two children got their school lessons, then Margaret read a book. It was a new one the woman who worked in the post office had let her have. When you sit around like that it's best to think of something outside the house. Only that afternoon Tar had been in a dispute with Jim Moore and another boy about baseball pitching. [*Jim] said Ike Freer was the best pitcher in town because he had the most speed and the best curves and Tar said Harry Green was the best. Both being on the town team they did not of course pitch against each other so you couldn't tell for sure. What you had to judge by was what you saw and felt. It was true Harry hadn't as much speed but you felt, when he pitched, surer of something. Well, he had some brains. When he knew he wasn't so good he said so and let Ike go in but if Ike wasn't so good he got bull-headed and if you took him out he got sore.

Tar thought of a lot of arguments with which to lay out Jim Moore when he saw him next day and then he went and got the dominoes.

The dominoes were slid silently across the boards of the table. Margaret had put her book aside. The two children were in the kitchen, that also served as a dining room, and there was an oil lamp on the table.

You can play a game like dominoes a long time and not think about anything much.

When Mary Moorehead was having one of her bad times she breathed irregularly. Her bedroom was right next the kitchen and at the front of the house was the parlor where the funeral was afterwards held. When you wanted to go upstairs to bed you had to go right through the mother's bedroom, but there was an offset in the wall and if you were careful you could go up without being seen. Mary Moorehead's bad times were coming more and more regularly. The children had almost got used to them. When Margaret had got home from school the mother was in bed and looked very pale and weak and Margaret wanted to send Robert off for the doctor but the mother said, "Not yet."

A grown person like that and your mother. . . . When they say "no" what are you going to do?

Tar kept pushing the dominoes across the table and now and then looked [up] at his sister. Thoughts kept coming. "Harry Green may not have as much speed as Ike Freer but he's got a head. In the long run a good head will tell. I like a man to know what he's doing. I guess there are ball players in the big league who are bone-heads all right but that makes no difference. You take a fellow who can do a lot with what little he's got. There's a fellow I like."

Dick was in the country painting the inside of a new house Harry Fitzsimmons had built. He had taken the job on a contract. When Dick took a job on a contract he hardly ever made [*any] money.

He couldn't figure [*much].

Anyway, it kept him busy.

You sit in a house, playing dominoes with your sister, on a night like that. Who cares who wins?

Now and then either Margaret or Tar went to put a stick of wood in the stove. Outside the house it rained and the wind came in through a crack under the door. There were always holes like that in the houses the Mooreheads lived in. You could throw a cat through the cracks. In the winter the mother, Tar and John went around and nailed strips of wood and pieces of cloth over the cracks. It kept out some of the cold.

Time passed, perhaps an hour. It seemed longer. The fears Tar had been having for a year John and Margaret also had. You go along thinking you are the only one who thinks and feels things but if you do you're a fool. Others are thinking the same thoughts. In General Grant's *Memoirs* it tells how, when a man asked him whether or not he was afraid when he was going into a battle he said, "Yes, but I know the other man is afraid too." Tar hadn't remembered many things about General Grant but he remembered that.

All of a sudden, that night when Mary Moorehead died, Margaret did something. As the two sat playing dominoes they could hear the mother breathing irregularly in the next room. The sound was soft and broken. Margaret got up in the middle of a game and tiptoed softly to the door. She stayed listening awhile, hidden so the mother couldn't see, then she came back into the kitchen and made a sign to Tar.

She had got all worked up just sitting there. That was it.

It was raining outside and her coat and hat were upstairs but she did not try to get them. Tar wanted her to take his cap but she wouldn't.

The two children got outside the house and Tar knew at once what was up. They went along the street to Doctor Reefy's office, not saying a word to each other.

Doctor Reefy wasn't there. There was a slate on the door and on it was written, "Back at 10 o'clock." It might have been there for two or three days. A doctor like that, who hasn't much practise and doesn't want much, is pretty careless.

"He might be at Judge Blair's," Tar said, and they went there.

At a time like that, when you are afraid something is going to happen, what you do is to remember other times when you were scared and everything turned out all right. It is the best way.

Well, you are going for the doctor and your mother is going to die, although you don't know it yet. Other people you meet in the street go along just as they always do. You can't blame them.

Tar and Margaret walked to Judge Blair's house, both getting sopping wet, Margaret without her coat and hat. There was a man buying something in Tiffany's drug store. Another man went along with a shovel on his shoulder. What do you suppose he's been digging, on a night like this? In the hallway of the City Hall two men were in an argument. They had got into the hallway to keep dry. "I said it was Easter when it happened. He denied it. He don't read his Bible."

What were they talking about?

"The reason Harry Green is a better baseball pitcher than Ike Freer is that he's more of a man. Some men are just naturally born strong. There have been famous pitchers in the big leagues who didn't have much speed or curves either. They just stood up there and used their noodles and they lasted a long time. They lasted twice as long as the ones who had nothing but strength."

The best writers [*to be found] in the newspapers Tar sold were the ones who wrote about ball players and sports. They had something to say. If you read them every day you learned something.

Margaret was getting soaking wet, through and through. If her mother knew she was out like that, without any coat or hat, she would be worried. People going along under umbrellas. It seemed long hours since Tar had come home from taking his papers. You get a feeling like that sometimes. Some days go by like a shot. Sometimes, in ten minutes, so many things happen it seems hours. It's that way when two race horses are fighting it out down the stretch, at a ball game when someone is at bat, two men out, two men maybe on bases.

Margaret and Tar got to Judge Blair's house and sure enough the doctor was there. It was warm and bright inside but they didn't go in. The Judge came to the door and Margaret said, "Tell the doctor please that mother's sick," and she had hardly got the words said when out the doctor came. He went right along with the two children and when they were leaving the Judge's house the Judge came and patted Tar on the back. "You're soaked," he said. He never spoke to Margaret at all.

The children took the doctor home with them and then went

upstairs. They wanted to pretend to the mother that the doctor had just come by accident—to make a call.

They went up the stairs as softly as they could and when Tar got into the room where he slept with John and Robert he undressed and got into dry clothes. He put on his Sunday suit. It was the only one he had that was dry.

Downstairs he could hear his mother and the doctor talking. He did not know that the doctor was telling his mother about the trip in the rain. What happened was that Doctor Reefy came to the foot of the stairs and called him down. No doubt he intended to call both children. He made a little whistling sound and Margaret came out of her room dressed in dry clothes just as Tar was. She also had to put on her best clothes. None of the other children heard the doctor call.

They went down and stood by the bed and their mother talked, a little. "I'm all right. Nothing's going to happen. Don't worry," she said. She meant it too. She must have thought she was all right, up to the last. It was a good thing, if she had to go, that she could go like that, just slip off during her sleep.

She said she would not die but she did. When she had spoken a few words to the children they went back upstairs but for a long time Tar did not sleep. Neither did Margaret. Tar never asked her afterwards but he knew she didn't.

When you are like that you can't sleep, what do you do? Some try one thing, some another. Tar had heard about the schemes of counting sheep and he tried it sometimes when he was too excited [or upset] to sleep but it wouldn't work for him. He tried a lot of other things.

You can imagine you are grown up and that you have become something you would like to be. You can imagine you are a big league baseball pitcher or a railroad engineer or a race track driver. You are an engineer and it's dark and rainy and your engine is swinging along the tracks. Best not to imagine yourself a hero in an accident or anything. Just fix your eyes on the rails in front. You are cutting right through a wall of darkness. Now you are among trees, now in an open country. Of course, when you are being an engineer like that, you are always driving a fast passenger train. You don't want to fool around with a freight.

You think of that and other things. That night, now and then, Tar heard his mother and the doctor talking. Sometimes they seemed to be laughing. He couldn't just tell. It might only have been the wind outside the house. Once he was quite sure he heard the doctor run across the kitchen floor. Then he thought he heard a door open and close softly.

It might have been he didn't hear anything at all.

The worst of all for Tar and Margaret and John and all of them was the next day and the next and the next. A house full of people, a sermon to be preached, the man coming with the coffin, the trip to the graveyard. Margaret got out of it the best. She worked around the house. They couldn't make her stop. A woman said, "No, let me do it," but Margaret did not answer. She was white and kept her lips tightly closed together. She went and did it herself.

People came to the house Tar had never seen, worlds of people.

CHAPTER XXII

THE queerest thing was what happened on the day after the funeral. Tar was going along a street, coming from school. School was out at four and the train with the papers did not come until five. He was coming along the street and had got past the vacant lot by Wilder's barn and there, in the lot, were some of the town [*boys] playing ball. Clark Wilder was there and the Richmond kid and a lot of others. When your mother dies you do not play ball for a long time. It isn't showing the proper respect. Tar knew that. The others knew [too].

Tar stopped. The strange thing was that he played ball that day just as though it hadn't happened. Well, not quite like that. He never intended to play. What he did surprised him and the others. They all knew about the death of his mother.

The boys were playing three old cat and Bob Mann was pitching. He had a pretty good out-curve and an in-shoot and lots of speed for a twelve-year-old.

Tar climbed over the fence and walked across the field and right up to the batter and took the bat right out of his hand. At any other time there would have been a row. When you play three old cat you have to field first, then hold base, then pitch and catch before you can bat.

Tar didn't care. He took the bat out of Clark Wilder's hands and stood up at the plate. He began to taunt Bob Mann. "Let's see you put her over. Let's see what you got. Go on. Whiz 'em in."

Bob threw one and then another and Tar soaked the second one. It was a home run and when he got around the bases he took the bat right up and soaked another, although it wasn't his turn. The others let him. They never said a word.

Tar yelled, he taunted the others, he acted crazy but nobody cared. When he had kept it up for maybe five minutes he left just as suddenly as he had come.

He went, after he had acted like that, on the very day after his mother's funeral, down to the railroad station. Well, the train wasn't in.

There were some empty box cars on a railroad siding over by Sid Grey's elevator near the station and Tar crawled into one of the cars.

At first he thought he would like to be a car like that and be carried away, he didn't care where. Then he thought of something else. The cars were to [*be loaded with grain]. They stood right near the elevator and near a shed in which there was an old blind horse that went round and round in a circle, to keep the machinery going that lifted the grain up to the top of the building.

The grain was lifted up and then ran down into the cars through a chute. They could fill a car in no time. All they had to do was to pull a lever and down the grain came.

It would be nice, Tar thought, to lie still in the car and be buried under the grain. It wouldn't be like being buried under the cold ground. Grain was nice stuff, it felt nice in the hand. It was golden yellow stuff and would run down like rain and would bury you deep down where you could not breathe and you would die.

For what seemed to him a long time Tar lay on the floor of the car thinking of such a death for himself and then, rolling over on his side, he saw the old horse in his shed. The horse was looking out at him with blind eyes.

Tar looked at the horse and the horse looked at him. He heard the train that had brought his papers come in, but he did not stir. Now he was crying so that he was himself almost blind. It was as well, he thought, to do his crying where none of the other Moorehead children or none of the boys around town could see. The Moorehead children all felt something like [*that]. At such a time you can't go making a show of yourself.

Tar lay in the car until the train came and went and then drying his eyes crawled out.

The people who had been down to meet the train were walking away up the street. Now, in the Moorehead house, Margaret would be home from school and would be doing the house work. John was at the factory. It was no special fun for John, but he stuck to his job just the same. Things had to go on.

Sometimes you just had to go on, not knowing why, like the blind old horse lifting the grain [up] into the building.

As for the people walking away up the street—it might be that some of them would be wanting a paper.

A boy if he is any good has to be tending up to his job. He has to get up and hustle. When they were waiting for the funeral Margaret didn't want to make a show of herself so she closed her lips tight and worked. It was a good thing Tar couldn't be blubbering away his time lying in an empty box car. What he had to do was to bring into the family all the money he could. Heaven knows they would need it all. He had got to tend up to his job.

These the thoughts in Tar Moorehead's head as he grabbed his bundle of newspapers and wiping his eyes on the back of his hand raced away up the street.

Although he did not know it Tar was, at that very moment perhaps, racing away out of his childhood.

THE END

APPENDIXES, BIBLIOGRAPHY, AND INDEX

THE DIARIES OF SHERWOOD ANDERSON'S PARENTS[1]

By William Alfred Sutton

I. EMMA

In referring to the fictionalized Camden of *Tar* as "something special" in his life, Anderson also commented, "The men who make a romance are perhaps right after all. The reality is too terrible."

The attitude of Anderson's mother, Emma Smith Anderson, aged 18/19, as displayed in her diary for the year 1872, when she lived in Morning Sun, a town of 135 people in Southwestern Ohio, is not in agreement with that of her son. The basically literate person who wrote the following four entries, given as typical of the 266 entries made, was quite satisfied with the very limited and busy existence she led:

> *Sunday, January 7*
> cold and snowish today went
> to Somerville to church Dr.
> Scott preached we broke down
> coming home walked two
> miles got Sellors wagon. Come
> home Preaching evening
> at Acedemy
>
> *Tuesday, January 30*
> Cold went to school
> studied this afternoon
> the dog hid my muff I
> could not find it. George
> was here in the evening.
>
> *Wednesday, January 31*
> Cold today went to school
> this morning washed this
> afternoon went to prayer
> this evening they have got new
> lamps.

[1] See Part IV, below, for information relating to the diaries as documents.

Monday, July 29
Clear washed today
churned after supper
went up town to stay
all night Jack Douglas
and Tom McGrary were at
Alas had a nice time
only chickens made a good
deal of fuss

As can be seen, there is a rather routine concern for recording household duties, church and school activities, weather, visits, amusements, to which was added a regular chronicle of births and deaths. References are usually completely cryptic, and detail is almost never supplied. Religion seems to have been completely accepted. There is no discussion of any ideas relevant to religion, but there are no ideas recorded on any other subject either. School seems to have been acceptable enough. One memorandum lists other pupils in her grade, and one note gives a partial reference to grades "at the close of school term of winter." Though studying is mentioned frequently, not one book is mentioned in all the notations for the year.

At the same time she was going to school, Emma was living and working in the home of James Faris, where she earned her keep. Under a heading "Receivable" she has made fifteen notations using the name "J. Faris" and listing various amounts of money from twenty-five cents to five dollars. The likeliest assumption is that these were amounts of payment to her from time to time. In return, she performed and recorded daily a variety of different activities, clustered around washing, ironing, cleaning, and baking. There is not anywhere in the record a complaint about her duties.

Her physical self seems to have caused her little concern or trouble. She never mentioned such things as bodily functions and mentioned only briefly a few minor illnesses. But the account is liberally sprinkled with references to visits of all kinds, including one over-night to an exposition at Cincinnati, a trip to the commencement at Miami University at nearby Oxford ("had a nice time"), and participation in many Sabbath school "celebrations." Attendance at dances, picnics, croquet and card parties was carefully chronicled. Buggy and sleigh riding were enjoyed, as was blackberrying.

Emma seems to have had a good sense of fun and ready capacity for simple enjoyment. One night she went to a reading: "it was good I laghed till/I could hardly see." On one April day, "Mary Linda Ella/Rene and Ellas were here we/had a good time went/to the barn and had a big/time I wrote in Lin's/Aughagraph."

She reported "a grand time at school this morning," having had her face washed half a dozen times that February day. Another day a boy broke an earring in the same procedure. Another of the enjoyable encounters is mentioned as a "big time at school," the occasion when the boys "hid our things." She countered by hiding George Harper's top in the water pot. Another time four girls, including Emma, hid several boys' hats and coats. Resultingly, Emma was one of several girls locked in one of the rooms.

She seems to have been able to enjoy such foolery as that, seems to have been perfectly willing to do her work, could savor the excitement of a ride to nearby College Corner when it was feared a March wind would blow off the top of the buggy.

She found it interesting and worthy of note when "Uncle Sam and the girls started to California" or when someone gave her a lead pencil. When she went to an examination she had "a good time and laughed so hard" that a friend "put a rose down my back." Occasionally she noted that she and Ella and Ellas had "laughed like some silly dounces" on the way in to Sabbath school and then had "felt wrong in the business."

The Emma Smith who presents herself through the cryptic and flawed lines of this diary was just what her psychologically maimed fiction-writer son could least have afforded her to be: a healthy, rather immature older girl who was busily engaged in enjoying the surface realities of a rather routine country life.

II. IRWIN

Just as Sherwood Anderson was to write that "It is wonderfully comforting to think of one's mother as a dark, beautiful and somewhat mysterious woman," so was the deviation from the reality of his father's own portrait also caused by his own needs. Possibly seeking unconscious approval of his own irresponsibility, it would not have suited his condemnation of his father to find that his ancestor had been, at 26/27, a hard-working, pious business man.

Many entries were basically like the one for Wednesday, February 14:

> Worked in the shop
> weather very cold
> nothing worth knowing
> occured today
> Business dull
> Receipts 20.

It is a rare entry, except Sundays, which does not give, in addition to the weather, a report of having worked, sometimes till late at night, and of receipts and disbursements; usually some extra item of business, such as a list of harness and saddlery items made or sold or ordered or received, or something a little unusual, such as signing an "article of agreement" between him and Ed, the helper whose name is never otherwise given. Or he might fix the minister's wife's trunk and have her present him with "a splendid set of jewelry studs and sleeve buttons!" Though most of the entries were in clipped business-like terms, occasionally the writer would talk to himself: "That's all I guess/Oh yes Bought a Blank Book......" or "Nothing worth recording/occured not even a dog/fight."

Three subjects outstanding in his background were his Civil War experience (1863–5), his travels in the Southwest (1866–1870), and his year or more in school at Xenia, Ohio. In spite of his eventual devoted interest in the G. A. R., traces of only the latter interest can be found in this diary. There were, in the 1865–6 year, 50 gentlemen attendant at the Xenia Female College, a Christian Home for students, designed to cultivate in them Health, Energy, Industry, Promptness and constant and systematic application of Christian virtues in the interest of success in school and life.

The Irwin of the diary wrote large in it the Latin motto *Praestare Fidem Morti* (to do one's duty faithfully till death) and shows every sign of extreme faithfulness to his church as well. His entry for Sunday, May 12, in which he records that he went to church twice and to Sabbath school twice, is typical rather than otherwise. The evidence is that he at times led prayer meeting, taught Sunday school, and was helpfully in attendance on all occasions of the Hopewell United Presbyterian Church, which he had joined on November 14, 1871. Evidence of his benevolent spirit is found in his notes on watching or sitting up with one Jerome Hill in the period between November 25 and December 23.

Some evidences of literary interest may reflect the Xenia influence. On January 2 he reported that he had subscribed to the *Youth's Companion*. In March he had "raised a club" (gathered a group of subscribers) for *Our Fireside*. On May 11 he had "borrowed Reads Poems from/Irene B." It was on Friday, March 1, that he "wrought in my shop" before going to the Philomathean Society in the afternoon.

His piety, relative studiousness, and industry seem to have caused a steady flow of business. Though he jotted down many figures in the diary, they do not seem to be clear enough in their import to warrant any definite conclusions concerning money. He was able, however, to report in July that he had taken out $1,000 worth of insurance on his life and in August a policy to cover his stock. Additionally, he moved into a new shop on July 11 and pronounced himself "Delighted."

Linked to both his religion and his work, it may be surmised, was his music, which he mentions definitely but only occasionally. A man who worked for him a few years later in Camden said Irwin would spend spare moments in his shop in practice on the alto horn, which he played in the village band. In addition to two memoranda of music, evidently for school or church, he has a note on December 5 to practice music at the home of one Marshall. Even more telling is the notation on the fly leaf of the diary: "Em G. Richards/Band Teacher/Lexington/O. Richland Co."

Irwin remained in good health for the most part during this year. He had a tooth filled in June and various indispositions during related days in July, September (when he worked and "attended singing in spite of a headache"), November, December 1 ("Indisposed remain at home") and December 14 ("Done do much/not very well"). Doubtless his worst problem occurred when a horse ran away and "hurt me some." The next day he reported, "Head sore from the run/off."

He noted two major anniversaries. One was on Wednesday, August 7, when he wrote: "This is my birth day am 27/worked hard all day/attend prayer meeting/write to Sue and Mattie." Perhaps the simplicity of this observance makes it easier to understand why Emma had no mention of her birthday in her account. On Saturday, September 21, he noted that he worked in the morning and went to singing class in the afternoon as well as observing: "this is the second anniversary/of my arrival in this town."

Before this statement was found, his reception into the church in November, 1871, was the only evidence concerning his residence in Morning Sun. Further, the will of his father, James, mentioned a note for $150 loaned to Irwin and dated September 17, 1870, just a few days before. The note was still unpaid when James died in 1886, which fact may be the most eloquent over-all comment on Irwin's business career.

Irwin wrote his own epitaph for the year:

> This is the last day of 72
> Have known great joys and
> great sorrows but I feel the
> Lord has been with me through
> all nuntheless I would not
> like to live it over
> May the next year be happy.
> "Praestare Fidem Morti"

He was thinking not only of events which have been mentioned but also of a pattern of events, probably with the possible exception of his business, of most interest to him. Irwin Anderson was actually engaged in the trials of finding a wife, and an examination may now be made of the joys and sorrows which the Lord had seen him through.

III. EMMA AND IRWIN

It has been seen that her diary shows that Emma Smith, having survived her turbulent childhood, had become an attractive, healthy, industrious, pleasant, unsophisticated quasi-adult. Her diary shows that she was interested in many young men and had rather casual contacts and dates with various ones. Probably there were other sequences such as that concerning Rob McClerken. On May 21 he was mentioned as being at the Faris home all day. On the afternoon of Tuesday, June 18, Emma got a note saying that Rob wanted to call on her the coming Thursday. When she went to prayer meeting the next evening, she took a note for Rob, saw him, and gave him what was apparently an affirmative message. The last time he is mentioned in the diary is in the entry for the next day: "Rob/McClerken was here this/evening. had a good/time. he went home at/ twelve o'clock." He got more attention than Dave Kirk, of whom she simply wrote: "Dave Kirk/asked me to go./Did not go."

Her first mention of Irwin was on January 9, when she recorded that she had not gone to prayer meeting that evening but noted that "Anderson was Chairman." A week later, when she went to prayer meeting, "Irving lead." On March 20 she again observed that Anderson led at prayer. There is no evidence of what may have happened in her mind in the intervening period, but on Thursday, September 19, she, possibly with muted triumph, wrote: "Anderson was/to come and play/croquoa, but called/on me." Anderson, who evidently liked to play croquet in the daylight, moonlight, or torchlight, merely recorded: "called on Miss Smith in/the evening." Irving was recorded as having been "here this evening" on November 19 and having fixed a broken harness on November 22. It was on December 19 that Irving, as he is consistently called, came for the evening and "brought his picture."

There is probably no certain significance to be attached to the fact that 88 of the 99 days for which there are no diary entries come after September 19, the date of Irwin's first official call on Emma. But it at least gives us reason for no fuller record of the progress of the relationship. And there can be no doubt that Emma Smith had numerous thoughts of courtship and marriage. It seems a fair indication of her cast of mind to find it expressed in three pieces of doggerel found in the diary.

The first, written on the inside of the back cover, is a terse request:

> Bless me and my man
> Alice and her man
> Us four and no more.

Signed "E. Smith," it is not dated.

The first of two items written in the Memoranda space is as follows:

> One I love two I love three
> I love I say four I love with
> all my heart. Five I cast away
> six she love seven he loves
> eight both love nine he
> comes ten tarries eleven
> he courts twelve marries
> thirteen rocks cradle

The last of the items is the most elaborate:

> Sparking Sunday night setting in the
> corner ready on a Sunday eve, with a [?]
> finger resting on your sleeve; starlight eyes
> are resting on your face, their lights. Bless me.
> This is pleasure, sparking Sunday night.
> How your heart is thumping. Gainst your
> Sunday vest how wickedly tis working
> on this day of rest. Hours seem but minutes
> as they take their flight. Bless my heart
> its pleasant sparking Sunday night.
> Dreaming of the good things
> the folks in meeting said
> Love ye one another Minister recited
> Bother me, don't we do it.
> Sparking Sunday night.
> One arm with gentle pressure lingers around
> her waist. You squeeze her dimpled hand
> Her pouting lips you taste. She freely
> slaps your face. But more in love than
> spite. Oh, thunder ain't it pleasant
> Sparking Sunday night.

The realizations which lay behind her interest in such lines as these caused her to be aware of what was happening to

others. In a memorandum dated February 11, she recorded the
following:

> I bet that Linda
> would Mary Anderson I am
> to give her ten cents if he
> does not. Alice bet she would
> not and is to give me
> 10 cents if she does.

This reference precedes by a month Irwin's first mention of
going to see Lin, as she is usually known, after prayer meeting
on March 13. On March 17 he went home with Linda after
church and went with her to "The Exabition," having a "good
time." On Wednesday, March 27, he "Put a ring on L. B.'s left
hand fore finger." On March 29 he went to a lecture with her.
On Wednesday, April 10, he went to prayer meeting and sub-
sequently "spent a little hour with/ Lin very pleasantly." On
Saturday, April 20, he "called on Lin B."

On Monday, April 15, storm clouds began to gather. He "Got
a letter from/Dick with/proposal to move west/which I
accepted." He obviously did not maintain his acceptance, but
others were going west, for he reported on Wednesday, April
24:

> Called on Lin after prayer
> meeting perhaps for
> the last time she is going
> to Calafornia in a few days
> evrything looks dark. "They that are
> against me are more than
> They that are for me."

On Sunday, April 28, he recorded further reaction:

> Attended Mr. Coopers church
> This is Lins last evning at home
> At times I am disposed to murmer
> but I remember that "The Lord does
> all things well and am comforted
> I have spent the evning in prayer
> and tears looking unto God for
> strength in this my time of sorrow
> The Lord is my shepherd I shal not want"
> Precious words.

The mood continued the next day:

> Lin started of Calafornia
> this morning they say I am
> a widower dont know
> do know I am lonely spent
> the day running around not
> pooring heart to work
> am tired and so must lay down

Then it became a matter of correspondence. He mentioned writing to Lin on May 10 and May 26 and was, on May 29, impatiently waiting for a reply:

> I have been looking for
> a letter from Lin so long
> and have not as yet got
> any evrything seems to be
> against me
> The world is lonely to me so lonely
> Oh Lin why don't you write.

His lovesickness reached its depth on May 31:

> Attended an entertainment
> given by Rob Curran
> did not enjoy it as much as
> I did the previous one Lin
> was not with me
> no letter yet my god what is the
> matter I am so weary waiting
> Oh what misery
> come Ruin come death come forgetfulness
> come anything

Perhaps needless to say, the next day:

> All is bright now
> got a letter from Lin This eve
> I am the happiest man living
> I shall write to her tonight

And he used the wet weather as an excuse to stay home from church and finish her letter the next evening. On June 6 he went to a reunion and had quite a pleasant time but did not fail to stipulate that he did not have as good company as "I did 1 year agoe though." When he got a letter on June 13, he answered it and sent her an *Oxford Citizen*. Her letter of June 28 he answered on June 30. He wrote again on July 4. On August 9 the status of the relationship was such that he referred to the fact his friends "will without knowing/it tear open the old wounds." He was sufficiently healed by December 28 to go home with Emma from "the academy" and write that he had "talked awhile with Lin."

In the meantime, a marriage had begun. On September 12, Irwin went to a croquet party at the James Faris home. It was just a week later that Emma, who must have been watching the adventures of Lin and "Irving" with avid interest, was able to state that a general croquet date had turned into a call on her. Irwin's record makes it that he "called on Miss Smith." In the next month calls on Emma are recorded for October 1, 8, 22, 27, and 31, not to mention a party at the Faris home on October 17. Further calls are recorded for November 12, 15, 19, and 28 and on December 10, 15, 19, and on December 24 "went to own/Christmas Tree with Emma."

A possible reason for the fact that neither kept a diary for 1873 was the marriage of Emma Jane Smith and Irwin McLain Anderson, which took place on March 11, 1873, at the Hopewell Church, license having been granted by the Probate Judge of Preble County on February 26.

IV. THE MANUSCRIPTS

The two diaries are in booklets, commercially printed for the purpose. They are in the same format, having the same blue-green imitation-leather binding in rubbed condition. It would appear they were made by the same company, Irwin's being a little larger (3.4 inches by 5.8 inches) than Emma's (2.8 by 4.7).

Neither manuscript is easy to read, though Emma's has whole pages which are badly faded and virtually unreadable. Practically all of Irwin's could be made out, even if with great effort. Neither had good penmanship. As has been noted earlier, Emma missed entries on 99 days, but Irwin missed only two, though some items were only a word or two. Both diaries contain various jottings and memoranda in addition to actual diary entries.

The diaries were secured through the interest and thoughtfulness of Mr. James Anderson of New York, the son of Karl Anderson, Sherwood's brother. The writer had first understood there was a diary which had been kept by Emma. He attempted to secure it through a former secretary of the late Karl. She thought she had seen it but said it would probably be among effects in the Karl Anderson home in Westport, Conn., then belonging to James Anderson, then a resident of Tokyo, Japan.

Permission was obtained for the secretary to go into the attic of the rented house and make a search. She was unsuccessful. There the matter rested until the return of James Anderson to the United States in 1966. When he discovered not only the diary of Emma but also that of Irwin in his effects, he notified the writer, who had been in correspondence with him. No previous word had been heard of the diary of Irwin.

There is no information as to how the diaries came into the possession of Karl. His son did not seem to know anything about them before finding them. One is tempted to think the various markings of passages relating to the mating of Irwin and Emma were made by Karl. The word "Mother" written on Irwin's entry for September 19 that he called on Miss Smith does not look convincingly like Karl's writing. It might have been Stella's. It is also unknown who wrote in Emma's diary under Bills Payable November the facts of the marriage and the births of the five children, Carl (original spelling), Stella, Sherwood, Irwin, Jr., and Ray, excluding Earl and Fern. A usable theory might be that this list was put in after the death of Earl in 1926, listing only those living.

It seems probably that none of the people who examined the diaries was Sherwood. He wrote a biographer in 1925, "My father, Irwin Anderson, was, I have heard him say, a North Carolina man—the son of a planter. Have never looked up his people." Probably it will never be known how successful he was in closing out the reality of his parents. It seems more than likely that he must have known at least some of the facts but buried them and turned away from knowledge of the rest under compulsion of psychological pressures he seems never to have wanted to understand.

THE DEATH IN THE FOREST
Edited by William V. Miller

A NOTE ON THE MANUSCRIPT

This twenty-two-page holograph is located in the Newberry Library Anderson collection. It is accompanied with a note in Mrs. Anderson's handwriting: "Early version of short story Death in the Woods." Probably not a first draft since there are very few important revisions, the manuscript is written in black ink on one side of unlined, inexpensive paper.

Twelve times Anderson crossed out common handwriting errors (usually because of one or two misformed letters). Included in this count are three minor word changes.

There are four, more significant revisions that he apparently made as he was writing the draft. On page ten he added the word *fresh* in describing the snow. He crossed out "through forest" on page twelve and added "under black bare trees." In describing the coat on page nineteen he substituted "was of" for "had." On page twenty-two he added the word *actual* to modify "story."

In my editing I have corrected three misspelled words and thirteen obvious errors. Of the thirteen errors five are failures to use the question mark, and most of the others are the omitting of *s*'s to form the plural. Perhaps because of haste, Anderson omitted a word on page twenty-one. For "one was a newspaper," I have written "one was on a newspaper."

Although I have added punctuation in eighteen instances, most of these additions have been apostrophes in forming possessives and commas to separate dependent clauses. Most of the compound sentences which strictly require commas before coordinating conjunctions have been left without those commas. I have sought to tamper as little as possible with the colloquial flow of Anderson's prose.

One liberty needs to be noted. On page seven where Anderson ends one clause describing a stove with *there* and without any punctuation begins a new clause about odors with *there*, I have elected to delete one *there* and add a dash.

THE DEATH IN THE FOREST

It was December and snowing when Mrs. Ike Marvin—we knew her as Ma Marvin—died in the little hollow in the center of Grimes' woods, about two miles south of our Ohio town. I was a boy then and had a job in Will Hunt's general store. Well, you see, Christmas time was approaching and there was a merry tinkling thing in the air. On Friday the snow that had been falling heavily since Tuesday had let up. Everyone said the sleighing would be good over the holiday time and even though we did not own a horse and sleigh, there was a kind of gladness in the air one felt. For one thing farmers began to drive into town in bobsleds and boys, more fortunate than myself in not being tied up with a job indoors, could catch rides. Crowds of boys ran along in the deep snow in Main Street, flipping on the runners of bobs, being thrown into the deep snow, shouting and laughing.

Even at that time there were two or three young women of our place whose fathers were up far enough in the world to send their daughters away to the city to school and they had now come home. They walked past on the sidewalk outside our general store, young women with a kind of air our own girls hadn't picked up yet. It had a kind of effect I can't explain. One felt one's town putting its nose up in the air like a fine pointer dog or something like that. You know what I mean. "Well we belong to the world. We aren't just a town stuck off here on a branch railroad," one whispered to oneself.

And there was young Ben Lewis home too. He was the son of our principal lawyer and five years ago had gone off to Chicago where he had worked himself up to be reporter on the Chicago Daily News. It was said he got twenty-five dollars a week, but Will Hunt declared he would never believe any such nonsense. Anyway there was the day just as I have described, and the sun breaking through masses of white clouds now and then, and sleighs covered with the dust from haylofts dragged out, boys laughing, girls and young women walking on newly swept sidewalks, Ben Lewis with such a grand overcoat on as I had never seen before (all silk lined and everything) standing in front of Huntley's Jewelry and telling how he discovered a clue to a murder in a hammer found back of an ice chest in a Chicago house and got a scoop for the Daily News, and men and boys listening and admiring and filled with envy and at the same time with gladness that such a fellow as Ben had come from our town.

It was, right enough, a day to remember and feel right about afterward, when, along about three o'clock news came into town of how Ma Marvin had died.

Things went bang then, like putting a light out in a room where a man sits looking at a book and a woman is playing a piano and children are cutting pictures out of newspapers on the floor. There you are and then "bang" there you aren't. What I mean is everyone is fumbling around in a queer sort of way.

I remember that, at the very moment the news came, Will Hunt was counting eggs out of Mrs. John Graham's basket into a bushel basket under the counter. The big iron stove at the back of the store was just booming—there was all the smells a boy loves to smell in the winter time when he is always hungry—cheese and coffee and brown sugar in barrels and dried herring and the smell of bolts of calico over on the other side of the store too.

Mrs. Graham was going to trade the eggs she had brought for goods. Will counted them, three eggs in each hand making a half dozen every time his two hands dropped to the bushel basket. What big fat red hands.

"Five, six, seven dozen and eight Mrs. Graham. Yes mam. Eggs is nineteen cents today. They are holding up pretty well. I guess it's the Christmas coming on. There'll be a lot of cakes and pies baked these next few days. Is John going to haul his corn in or will he hold? Ed Pearson said he was going to hold until March. Sometimes it pays. Sometimes it don't. Yes 'em the sledding is bound to be pretty good. There's a good bottom to the roads. That's the best part."

That's the way it was. That's the feel of how things were when the news of Ma Marvin's death came.

Two young fellows, the Passley boys, who had been out hunting rabbits brought the news into town. They had stumbled upon the poor woman's body, all covered with snow as they tramped through Grimes' woods, or perhaps their dog had found it. Anyway they ran nearly all the way to town and it was amazing how the news spread. Now that I think back on it all—the two young men, with the shot guns over their shoulders, half running, half walking over snow covered fields, climbing fences into the road, hurrying hurrying through the deep white fresh snow, shouting to drivers of passing bobsleds, shouting to farm women who came to front doors, to farm men too, standing in barnyards, getting to the scattered houses at the edge of town, running into Main Street, shouting and telling the news, well now, after all these years their two figures become in my imagination not quite human. They are more like Gods that run pushing before them dark clouds that shut out the sun on the snow and make the light in the houses dim.

Because, with their coming, and right away, everything in town changed. Boys quit laughing and flipping on and off bobs, Mrs. John Graham forgot what she wanted in goods in exchange for the eggs she had brought in, Ben Lewis stopped telling his wonder tale of the Chicago murder, done with the hammer he had found back of an ice box. Even the day changed. White clouds became a smokey grey. The sun went away. And we all closed up the stores and went out to Grimes' woods. Even women who had no babies to look after went. Right away there was the whole town tramping, strange little silent black massed dots moving over the white snow, climbing fences, tearing rail fences down, going across white fields and under black bare trees to the little white open space in Grimes' wood.

It was a simple poor little story after all. Everyone had known for a long time that Ma Marvin, although she couldn't have been more than thirty-five or six, was about worn out. That with cooking and slaving for that big lazy brute of an Ike Marvin and her three equally big lazy brutes of sons, all of them always getting drunk and raising the devil, that with the work and worry poor Ma Marvin had lived through, what was one to expect?

The whole story was just as plain as though there had been an eye witness to her death there to tell the tale.

Ma Marvin had been into town for supplies. That must have been on Tuesday, the day when the snow storm began. It was just like the Marvin men to let her come afoot. There were two or three old bony horses still left about the Marvin place, but no doubt the men had wanted them to drive off to some other nearby town and sell a load of stove wood to get money with which to get drunk and raise the devil.

So Ma Marvin, poor little old thing, had come just as you could see, by the path through the wood to our town, and she had got a sack of flour, potatoes, a chunk of salt pork, coffee, a small sack of sugar and other things. I remember there was a small cloth bag of salt.

And of course a pack of the big ugly dogs one always saw lying in the shadow over about Ike Marvin's ruined saw mill on Sugar Creek had come with her.

She had put all of the supplies into an old grain bag and had tried to carry it over her shoulder. "Lord Amighty," Will Hunt said, "I never sold her them things. Look at that bag of things. It is almost as big as she is, poor little old thing. Tom Friend must have sold her them things. He never ought to have let her set out with no such load."

It is odd what one remembers and doesn't remember. There was the white, half frozen little old figure, pitched a little forward (she had stopped to rest, sitting on the ground by a little pile of stones) and the Marvin dogs had grown bold after she was dead and had torn the grain bag and got at the hunk of salt pork within.

She must have come over to town on Tuesday and when she started home the storm began—the wind howling, the blinding snow, the woman, old before her time, putting down her load to rest a moment.

Then the stillness of death coming softly, night and the cold. My boy's mind couldn't grasp it then. We all stood about for a long time before some men, directed by Ben Lewis, got a barn door from a nearby barn, put the dead woman's body upon it and tramped off to the Marvin place, two more miles away.

It was said later about town that they found but two of the Marvin men at home and they both drunk and quarreling. There was even talk of lynching on our Main Street later but nothing came of it.

What I am myself trying to say is that as we stood about the dead figure in the snow, Ben Lewis seemed suddenly to feel that it was his part, as a city man among us, to do something. I happened to stand near him and he jerked off his overcoat and gave it to me to hold. Then he grew excited and went off with the others to carry the body home and there was I with that precious garment in my charge and night coming on. There was nothing to do of course but to carry it home with me and keep it safe for him until the next morning.

That I did and the charge lay upon me with a delicious weight. Could men, actual flesh and blood men, who had been raised in our town wear such gorgeous garments? Did such unbelievable things happen to young fellows who left our town and become reporters on city newspapers?

The coat was of broad yellow and green plaid and to my fingers the touch of it was delicious. How I wanted to put my hands into the pockets.

And it was lined with silk. How reverently I carried it home to our house and how good and kind I thought my mother when she laughingly permitted me to have the coat hanging in my own room over night.

I slept but little that night and often crept out of bed to touch the coat again. How deliciously soft the fabric. I thought it like touching the soft fur of a cat in the darkness and all night I remembered that in the afternoon in the woods when Ben Lewis had unbuttoned his coat and when it was still light enough to see, the lining was a reddish running color that changed in the light. The death of Ma Marvin in the snow in the wood was forgotten. Ben Lewis had gone from our town to the city and now wore a coat such as a king might wear. Would I, could I, sometime, grow up, go away to a city, get a job on a newspaper and like Ben Lewis wear a coat like a king? The thought thrilled me beyond words and so, as the dead frozen body of Ma Marvin lay in the tumble down house five miles away, I lay awake dreaming of a triumphant life wherein one was on a newspaper and wore plaid overcoats lined with silk such as only nobles and kings might wear.

As to the actual story of Ma Marvin's death—I found all about it in a rather queer way nearly twenty years later. Now I will tell you of that.

DELETIONS FROM THE TYPESCRIPT AND UNINCORPORATED TYPESCRIPT READINGS

6.17 or heroes any of us.

14.10 Automobile tourists

17.32 thing too bad for

21.25 A lot of New Englanders had

23.25 all the Mooreheads listening

24.6 where New Englanders have come in

34.22 solid citizen. The Mooreheads were always strangers in the towns, people on the move.

35.3 grows slowly. I must know you and you must learn to know me. You must learn to forgive. I must learn to forgive. Once when Tar had become a grown man and when his name was a little up in the world the editor of a newspaper wrote him a letter from the town of Camden, Ohio, that strange place of his family. It was the town in which he was born but the editor had difficulty finding traces of Mooreheads there. There were a few signs, some unpaid debts perhaps. Such and such a family, bearing that name, had lived there a short time. An old woman remembered but she had gone deaf and blind. There was a hint that the family in question were not very respectable, rather a gypsy tribe. The man at the head of the family did not always keep his word. Something like that.

"You have us. There are our marks," Tar had to write to the man.

37.30 sister—two years

39.2 something huge

42.22– .23	time terrible place
42.33	great yearning doors
43.6	of Tar for the time being
49.8	had achieved a mouthful
52.19	babe who wanted his place
53.23	trunk that had belonged to his father
57.31– .32	would not be permitted to go.
58.22	abroad. It was like an experience once Tar had later, all his life, the experience in fact that made him a writer. If the child could only grow up and be a man and at the same time remain always a child, his hand in his mother's hand, walking in darkness.
60.10	but no one need care.
61.22	He thrust them
62.32	children. And the farmers laughed. "They like nothing better than to get down town among the stores. I guess you fellows all know," Dick said. He paid little or no attention to the woman and the child. It was Saturday night. He was a man of business.
62.34	never hurt much. He never meant
63.11	say. This man had not banged him roughly. One knew at once by looking at him that he would never bang anyone. "Thank you," he said. The old work man's being shy made him feel shy himself.
65.27	sound. Tar could also hear sometimes at night when he did not sleep and when his father and mother talked.
66.19	names. What a man his father was. Tar remembered the days in the country, the evenings in the bed in the farm house, that other evening by the fire in the woods when his father kept all the other people laughing. What a change had come over Dick. Nowdays he was often sad and grim and Tar's mother was more silent than ever. A year or two before, when

Tar was as yet almost a baby, his father stayed at home at night. He or Tar's mother read aloud, stories from the Bible or from some other book or a neighbor came in and Dick talked of the war. When he had been talking of the war he spoke sometimes, quite casually, of men mentioned in books as though they had been his personal friends. He spoke of Grant, who had since been president, and of General Sherman as the man who carried the beard on his head, had spoken to him. "Well," he explained, "I was talking to Grant. 'Ulysses,' I said." It was evident that men who had their names in books, who were presidents and generals, had known his father intimately. How wonderful to be a man.

68.10   special. Tar had seen his father drink wine, had already tasted wine himself, had seen his father gay with wine but now his father was drunk.

70.15   one. What had happened in the house was that age was declaring its impotence in the presence of youth. Although Dick was as yet a young man he felt himself defeated in life. Fall had come and he could no longer go riding about through the county. Now he had to stay in town, had to work all day in a shop. [One page missing.]

All of them had to go home now and face their wives. After all how much can a wife understand?

The men had separated as soon as they came out the front door of the saloon and Dick had been compelled to walk home alone. He was cold. Winter was coming fast now and because he was hard up he had no overcoat. He had to walk a long way first on the sidewalks of the town and then in a road. Plenty of time to think. This was not the first time he had taken so much to drink that his legs were unsteady but he had never before gone home to his wife when he was in such a condition.

Dick had thought about his situation in life during the walk to his house and when he got inside he was angry. Well, now he was not angry at the government. He had formerly owned a harness shop of his own and had been too liberal about giving credit. His very goodness had been the cause of his fall.

71.12–
.13   on his head

71.27   was there. He sat so near her that by putting out his hand he could touch her dress. Did the others see what he saw? That was a question Tar did not ask, then or later. During all his after life he was uncertain about others seeing what he sometimes saw, in the face of a man or woman passing him in the street, in a room of a house into which he had gone.

72.9   silent. Was he growing too much like his mother? Sometimes when his father came home from the shop he looked at the sick boy with the same queer self-conscious look that came on his face when he was in the presence of his wife.

72.33   afraid. Sometimes he remembered the words of the man of the hillside, words about Heaven and Hell. Already he knew vaguely what Hell was. In Hell everything is distorted, out of place.

73.11   again. Well, things had got out of gear. The world is a machine. If you cannot adjust yourself to it, cannot live in the world as it is not one thing alone is wrong. All things are wrong.

73.13   sure. The battle of Verdun may be fought in a human soul as well as in front of a famous French fort, it may be fought in the soul of a child.

73.19   white. Being absorbed in each other neither the child's father or mother saw what was going on. All the time of his childhood illness had been for him a strange time and now everything in the Moorehead house had become strange. Even his mother could not help now.

There was the room, the poor little table set in the kitchen that the heat used for cooking the food might be utilized for warming the bodies of the people who ate it. The other children were trying to eat and staring at Dick, angry words kept coming from his lips, the room outside the two little circles of light made by the lamp and the kitchen stove was dark, the world outside the Moorehead house was dark.

75.18   Tar had seen things, heard things.

75.20   more sensitive

77.15   to Tar and his brother Robert

78.30   Weeks later the new

79.24   At a time like that a child lies listening

79.28   expression of impulses, all such things

80.10   cold dark place

80.28   be reassured.

80.30   see, what he had heard was just a thing of the fancy, just another distorted dream.

81.7   sounds? When he grew to be a man other and wiser men told him what such an action on the part of a child meant. They tell you what such things mean but what good does it do? Can you tell another child? Can you go back into your own childhood and bring light into dark dreary moments?

Well, you are running away from life, from actuality. You come out of the dark warm flesh—that is your mother—and you want to return into the warmth and darkness. You have the Oedipus complex—what ho! Without it what a little monster you would be.

81.28   illusion. What is life without illusions? You have to learn to bear things in life.

81.32   there. His illness had taught him something.

83.9   would be all right.

83.16   something dreadful to have to be thinking about.

87.2   Tar. He was not in Tar's room in school but for a long time was much in Tar's thoughts.

101.34 had to run.

106.24 whole house

107.14 little. Still she must have. It stands to reason.

107.31   Lincoln and was something like him too.
107.33   glad. He never liked funerals.
109.15   boy but his cheating when he takes advantage of it.
111.2   friend who was better to be with than any boy he
          knew.
114.18   man, like Alfred Stieglitz or Theodore Dreiser or
          Clarence Darrow.
115.35   horseman. One day when he was nine something
          happened.
122.11   Tar didn't feel a bit guilty. Sunday was
124.22   It may be just gladness. There is
132.28   woman a cuff
134.12   he'd see them
141.10   understood. It is that many lives have little or no
          variation. Men and women are born live and die
          and remain nameless, forgotten. They, in their
          conscious selves, have little or nothing to contribute
          to the life about them but the lives seem whole to
          contribute.
141.11   who feed animal life
141.24   heels.
              It was to Tar, later, just a story picked up in
          childhood. Most of the stories he told all during
          the rest of his life had been picked up in childhood.
          There was an impression made on his mind. Some-
          thing got fixed. The seeds of a story had lodged
          in his mind and had to lie there until they were
          fertilized by the experiences of his own life. Then
          some of them got told. Others never got told. It all
          depends upon what happens after a man has got
          through with his childhood.
              But at any rate here is the story of the death in
          the woods.
142.4–   better. Tar had his papers to sell, but
  .5
148.33   only the paper boy
154.31   he brought her off himself
154.34   my niece
158.1   roots. In just such a place as Tar was in now.

158.23   young birch
158.25   one—why does a boy single out some one girl to
          think and dream about when you come to that—
          a boy in a town sees plenty of young girls—there
          was one young bare tree—
158.35   not miss him.
159.26   It might be that did happen. It might
161.22   but the McNutts.
162.6–   but there were plenty like that.
.7
162.8   since Ester Grey had
164.37   for Roy Walsh and Herman Hurd
166.3   like that.
               If you can think what a person feels when they
          are dead, have gone to Heaven and are admitted
          into the presence of God you will know how he
          felt at that moment. Christians are always talking
          about Heaven and God and school boys are always
          talking about women and girls. Christians are al-
          ways saying they are going to die and be taken to
          Abraham's bosom. Huh!
167.9   Something startling
194.1   but loneliness
194.31   woke up.
               Tar was sorry for Margaret who had to sleep
          alone because she was a girl. He was sorry for Hog
          Shovers.
               Such a man, all alone like that, hating everyone,
          trying to save pennies, living in a house with no
          one about but the hogs in the yard and in the
          tumble down pens in the yard.
195.22   about to see. He didn't want the baggage man, the
          express man or the train men to know and most
          of all he didn't want John to know.
               He felt a little disloyal to the Mooreheads, stand-
          ing like that and seeing the old hog buyer as he
          went chuckling off along the street holding tight
          to the paper for which he hadn't paid a cent.
198.6   a boy than

198.12   the young man got
207.10   Robert and Jacob.
208.29   figure good.
215.17   childhood.
          Who knows when one thing ends and another
          begins?

A SELECTED
BIBLIOGRAPHY

I. Books by Sherwood Anderson

Windy McPherson's Son. New York: John Lane Company, 1916; New York: B. W. Huebsch, 1922 (revised); Chicago: University of Chicago Press, 1965, Introduction by Wright Morris.

Marching Men. New York: John Lane Company, 1917; New York: B. W. Huebsch, [1921].

Mid-American Chants. New York: John Lane Company, 1918; New York: B. W. Huebsch, [1921].

Winesburg, Ohio. New York: B. W. Huebsch, 1919; New York: Viking Press, 1960, Introduction by Malcolm Cowley [with critical essays, edited by John Ferres, 1966].

Poor White. New York: B. W. Huebsch, 1920; New York: Viking Press, [1966], Introduction by Walter B. Rideout.

The Triumph of the Egg. New York: B. W. Huebsch, 1921.

Horses and Men. New York: B. W. Huebsch, 1923; New York: Peter Smith, [1933].

Many Marriages. New York: B. W. Huebsch, 1923; New York: Grosset and Dunlap, [1929].

A Story Teller's Story. New York: B. W. Huebsch, 1924; New York: Grove Press, [1958].

Dark Laughter. New York: Boni and Liveright, 1925; New York: Liveright Publishing Corporation, [1960], Introduction by Howard Mumford Jones.

The Modern Writer. San Francisco: Lantern Press, 1925.

Sherwood Anderson's Notebook. New York: Boni and Liveright, 1926.

Tar: A Midwest Childhood. New York: Boni and Liveright, 1926, [1931].

A New Testament. New York: Boni and Liveright, 1927.

Alice and the Lost Novel. London: Elkin Mathews and Marrot, 1929.

Hello Towns! New York: Horace Liveright, 1929.

Nearer the Grass Roots. San Francisco: Westgate Press, 1929.

The American County Fair. New York: Random House, 1930.

Perhaps Women. New York: Horace Liveright, 1931.

Beyond Desire. New York: Liveright, Inc., 1932; New York: Liveright Publishing Corporation, [1961], Introduction by Walter B. Rideout.

Death in the Woods. New York: Liveright, Inc., 1933.

No Swank. Philadelphia: Centaur Press, 1934.

Puzzled America. New York: Charles Scribner's Sons, 1935.

Kit Brandon. New York: Charles Scribner's Sons, 1936.

Plays, Winesburg and Others. New York: Charles Scribner's Sons, 1937.

Five Poems. San Mateo, California: Quercus Press, 1939.

A Writer's Conception of Realism. Olivet, Michigan: Olivet College, 1939.

Home Town. New York: Alliance Book Corporation, 1940.

Sherwood Anderson's Memoirs. New York: Harcourt, Brace and Company, 1942.

The Sherwood Anderson Reader, edited by Paul Rosenfeld. Boston: Houghton Mifflin Company, 1947.

The Portable Sherwood Anderson, edited by Horace Gregory. New York: Viking Press, 1949.

Letters of Sherwood Anderson, edited by Howard Mumford Jones and Walter B. Rideout. Boston: Little, Brown and Company, 1953.

Sherwood Anderson: Short Stories, edited by Maxwell Geismar. New York: Hill and Wang, 1962.

Mid-American Chants, 6 Mid-American Chants by Sherwood Anderson/11 Midwest Photographs by Art Sinsabaugh. Highlands, N. C.: Nantahala Foundation, 1964, Introduction by Edward Dahlberg.

Return to Winesburg: Selections from Four Years of Writing for a Country Newspaper, edited by Ray Lewis

White. Chapel Hill: University of North Carolina Press, 1967.

A Story Teller's Story: A Critical Text, edited by Ray Lewis White. Cleveland: Press of Case Western Reserve University, 1968.

Sherwood Anderson's Memoirs: A Critical Edition by Ray Lewis White. Chapel Hill: University of North Carolina Press, 1969.

II. Books about Sherwood Anderson

Anderson, David D. *Sherwood Anderson*. New York: Holt, Rinehart and Winston, 1967.

Burbank, Rex. *Sherwood Anderson*. New York: Twayne Publishers, 1964.

Chase, Cleveland B. *Sherwood Anderson*. New York: R. M. McBride, 1927.

Fagin, Nathan Bryllion. *The Phenomenon of Sherwood Anderson: A Study in American Life and Letters*. Baltimore: Rossi-Bryn, 1927.

Howe, Irving. *Sherwood Anderson*. New York: William Sloane, 1951; Stanford: Stanford University Press, [1966].

The Newberry Library Bulletin, 2d Ser., No. 2 (December, 1948). The Sherwood Anderson Memorial Number.

La Revue des Lettres Modernes, Nos. 78–80 (1963). *Configuration Critique de Sherwood Anderson*, edited by Roger Asselineau.

Schevill, James. *Sherwood Anderson: His Life and Work*. Denver: University of Denver Press, 1951.

Sheehy, Eugene P. and Kenneth A. Lohf. *Sherwood Anderson: A Bibliography*. Los Gatos, California: Talisman Press, 1960; New York: Kraus Reprint Corporation, [1967].

Shenandoah, XIII (Spring, 1962). The Sherwood Anderson Number.

Story, XIX (September–October, 1941). The Sherwood Anderson Memorial Number.

Sutton, William A. *Exit to Elsinore*. Muncie, Indiana: Ball
State University, 1967.

Weber, Brom. *Sherwood Anderson*. Minneapolis: University of Minnesota Press, 1964.

White, Ray Lewis, editor. *The Achievement of Sherwood
Anderson: Essays in Criticism*. Chapel Hill: University
of North Carolina Press, 1966.

III. MAJOR AREA STUDIES

Aaron, Daniel. *Writers on the Left: Episodes in American
Literary Communism*. New York: Harcourt, Brace and
World, 1961.

Åhnebrink, Lars. *The Beginnings of Naturalism in American Fiction.* . . . Upsala, Sweden: American Institute in
the University of Upsala, 1950.

Berthoff, Warner. *The Ferment of Realism: American
Literature, 1884–1919*. New York: Free Press, 1965.

Bridgman, Richard. *The Colloquial Style in America*. New
York: Oxford University Press, 1966.

Brooks, Van Wyck. *America's Coming of Age*. New York:
B. W. Huebsch, 1915.

———. *The Confident Years: 1885–1915*. New York: Dutton, 1952.

Cargill, Oscar. *Intellectual America: Ideas on the March*.
New York: Macmillan Company, 1941.

Curti, Merle. *The Growth of American Thought*, revised
edition. New York: Harper's, 1951.

Duffey, Bernard. *The Chicago Renaissance in American
Letters: A Critical History*. Lansing: Michigan State
University Press, 1954.

Geismar, Maxwell. *The Last of the Provincials: The American Novel, 1915–1925*. Boston: Houghton Mifflin Company, 1947.

———. *Rebels and Ancestors: The American Novel, 1890–
1915*. Boston: Houghton Mifflin Company, 1953.

———. *Writers in Crisis: The American Novel Between
Two Wars*. Boston: Houghton Mifflin Company, 1942.

Herron, Ima Honaker. *The Small Town in American Literature*. Durham: Duke University Press, 1939.

Hoffman, Frederick J. *Freudianism and the Literary Mind*, revised edition. Baton Rouge: Louisiana State University Press, 1957.

——. *The Twenties: American Writing in the Post-War Decade*, revised edition. New York: Free Press, 1962.

——, Charles Allen, and Carolyn Farquhar Ulrich. *The Little Magazine: A History and a Bibliography*. Princeton: Princeton University Press, 1947.

Hofstadter, Richard. *Social Darwinism in American Thought, 1860–1915*. Philadelphia: University of Pennsylvania Press, 1944.

Jones, Howard Mumford. *The Bright Medusa*. Urbana: University of Illinois Press, 1952.

Kazin, Alfred. *On Native Grounds: An Interpretation of Modern American Prose Literature*. New York: Reynal and Hitchcock, 1942.

Kramer, Dale. *Chicago Renaissance: The Literary Life in the Midwest*. New York: Appleton-Century, 1966.

Lillard, Richard Gordon. *American Life in Autobiography: A Descriptive Guide*. Stanford: Stanford University Press, 1956.

Martin, Jay. *Harvests of Change: American Literature, 1865–1914*. Englewood Cliffs, New Jersey: Prentice-Hall, 1967.

Marx, Leo. *The Machine in the Garden: Technology and the Pastoral Ideal in America*. New York: Oxford University Press, 1964.

May, Henry F. *The End of American Innocence: A Study of the First Years of Our Own Time, 1912–1917*. New York: Knopf, 1959.

Rideout, Walter B. *The Radical Novel in the United States, 1900–1954: Some Interrelations of Literature and Society*. Cambridge: Harvard University Press, 1956.

Walcutt, Charles Child. *American Literary Naturalism: A Divided Stream*. Minneapolis: University of Minnesota Press, 1956.

Wector, Dixon. *The Age of the Great Depression, 1929–1941.* New York: Macmillan Company, 1948.

West, Ray B. *The Short Story in America.* Chicago: Regnery, 1956.

West, Thomas Reed. *Flesh of Steel: Literature and the Machine in American Culture.* Nashville: Vanderbilt University Press, 1967.

IV. COMPARABLE AMERICAN AUTOBIOGRAPHIES

Austin, Mary. *Earth Horizon: Autobiography.* Boston: Houghton, 1932.

Benton, Thomas Hart. *An Artist in America.* New York: Twayne, 1951.

Calkins, Earnest Elmo. *"And Hearing Not—": Annals of an Adman.* New York: Scribner's, 1946.

Clemens, Samuel L. *Mark Twain's Autobiography,* edited by Charles Neider. New York: Harper's, 1959.

Coolidge, Calvin. *The Autobiography of Calvin Coolidge.* New York: Cosmopolitan, 1929.

Croy, Homer. *Country Cured.* New York: Harper's, 1943.

Darrow, Clarence. *The Story of My Life.* New York: Scribner's, 1932.

Douglas, Lloyd C. *Time to Remember.* Boston: Houghton, 1951.

Dreiser, Theodore. *A History of Myself: Dawn.* New York: Liveright, 1931.

———. *A Hoosier Holiday.* New York: John Lane Company, 1916.

Eleazer, James Malcolm. *A Dutch Fork Farm Boy.* Columbia: University of South Carolina Press, 1952.

Feller, Robert W. A. *Strikeout Story.* New York: Barnes, 1947.

Ferber, Edna. *A Peculiar Treasure.* New York: Doubleday, 1939.

Garland, Hamlin. *A Daughter of the Middle Border.* New York: Macmillan, 1921.

———. *A Son of the Middle Border.* New York: Macmillan, 1917.

Hapgood, Hutchins. *A Victorian in the Modern World*. New York: Harcourt, 1939.

Hecht, Ben. *A Child of the Century*. New York: Simon, 1954.

Hertzler, Arthur E. *The Horse and Buggy Doctor*. New York: Harper's, 1938.

Howells, William Dean. *Years of My Youth*. New York: Harper's, 1916.

Hunt, Frazier. *One American and His Attempt at Education*. New York: Simon, 1938.

Hughes, Langston. *The Big Sea: An Autobiography*. New York: Knopf, 1940.

Lamont, Thomas W. *My Boyhood in a Parsonage*. . . . New York: Harper's, 1946.

Lutes, Della Thompson. *The Country Kitchen*. Boston: Little, 1938.

———. *Country Schoolma'am*. Boston: Little, 1941.

———. *Home Grown*. Boston: Little, 1937.

Masters, Edgar Lee. *Across Spoon River*. New York: Farrar and Rinehart, 1936.

Monroe, Harriet. *A Poet's Life: Seventy Years in a Changing World*. New York: Macmillan, 1938.

Moody, Ralph. *Little Britches: Father and I Were Ranchers*. New York: Norton, 1950.

Moses, Anna Mary Robertson. *Grandma Moses: My Life History*, edited by Otto Kallir. New York: Harper's, 1952.

Muir, John. *The Story of My Boyhood and Youth*. Boston: Houghton, 1913.

Nock, Albert Jay. *Memoirs of a Superfluous Man*. New York: Harper's, 1943.

Norris, George W. *Fighting Liberal: The Autobiography of George W. Norris*. New York: Macmillan, 1945.

Orchard, Hugh Anderson. *Old Orchard Farm*, edited by Paul F. Sharp. Ames: Iowa State College Press, 1952.

Quick, Herbert. *One Man's Life: An Autobiography*. Indianapolis: Bobbs-Merrill, 1925.

Roberts, Isaac. *Autobiography of a Farm Boy*. Ithaca: Cornell University Press, 1946.

Ross, Edward Alsworth. *Seventy Years of It: An Auto-biography.* New York: Appleton, 1936.

Stuart, Jesse. *Beyond Dark Hills: A Personal Story.* New York: Dutton, 1938.

Sullivan, Mark. *The Education of an American.* New York: Doubleday, 1938.

Tarbell, Ida Minerva. *All in a Day's Work: An Autobiography.* New York: Macmillan, 1939.

Thompson, Era Bell. *American Daughter.* Chicago: University of Chicago Press, 1946.

Trowbridge, John T. *My Own Story, with Recollections of Noted Persons.* Boston: Houghton, 1903.

Van Doren, Carl. *Three Worlds.* New York: Harper's, 1936.

Vanderlip, Frank A. (with Boyden Sparkes). *From Boy to Financier.* New York: Appleton, 1935.

White, William Allen. *The Autobiography of William Allen White.* New York: Macmillan, 1946.

Wilkinson, Herbert E. *Sun Over Cerro Gordo.* Ames: Iowa State College Press, 1952.

Wilson, Jock. *The Dark and the Damp: An Autobiography of Jock Wilson.* New York: Dutton, 1951.

V. TRANSLATIONS OF *Tar: A Midwest Childhood*

Tar. Paris: Stock, Delamain and Boutelleau, 1931. Tr. Marguerite Gay and Paul Genty; preface by René Lalou.

Tar. Budapest: Athenæum, 1934. Tr. Andor Gál.

Tar. Barcelona: José Janés, 1948. Tr. Mario G. Alcántara.

VI. REVIEWS OF *Tar: A Midwest Childhood*

American Mercury, X (March, 1927), 382–83—H. L. Mencken.

Booklist, XXIII (February, 1927), 224.

Boston Transcript, December 11, 1926, p.4—Karl Schriftgiesser.

Dial, LXXXII (March, 1927), 256.

Forum, LXXVII (April, 1927), 636—Anne Cleeland.

Nation, CXXIV (February 2, 1927), 121–22—Clifton Fadiman.

New Statesman, XXX (December 17, 1927), 330, 332.

New York Evening Post Literary Review, January 22, 1927, p. 2.

New York Herald Tribune Books, November 21, 1926, p. 1—Rebecca West.

New York Times Book Review, November 21, 1926, p. 2—H. S. Gorman.

New York World, December 5, 1926, p. 2M—H. S. Gorman.

New York World, December 5, 1926, p. 11M.

Outlook, CXLV (January 12, 1927), 60.

Revue Anglo-Américaine, V (April, 1928), 400–1—C. Cestre.

Saturday Review, CXLIV (November 19, 1927), 709—L. P. Hartley.

Saturday Review of Literature, III (December 18, 1926), 451.

Saturday Review of Literature, III (February 19, 1927), 593—Arthur Colton.

Springfield Republican, December 20, 1926, p. 6.

Times Literary Supplement, October 13, 1927, p. 712.

Wisconsin Library Bulletin, XXIII (January, 1927), 24.

World Tomorrow, X (February, 1927), 89.

INDEX

This book was set in eleven-point Caledonia.
It was composed, printed, and bound by
Kingsport Press, Inc., Kingsport, Tennessee.
The paper is Warren's Olde Style,
manufactured by the S. D. Warren Company, Boston.
The design is by Edgar J. Frank.